UNDERSTANDING ISLAM

UNDERSTANDING ISLAM

A Guide for Teachers

IMRAN MOGRA

SAGE

Los Angeles | London | New Delhi
Singapore | Washington DC | Melbourne

SAGE

Los Angeles | London | New Delhi
Singapore | Washington DC | Melbourne

SAGE Publications Ltd
1 Oliver's Yard
55 City Road
London EC1Y 1SP

SAGE Publications Inc.
2455 Teller Road
Thousand Oaks, California 91320

SAGE Publications India Pvt Ltd
B 1/I 1 Mohan Cooperative Industrial Area
Mathura Road
New Delhi 110 044

SAGE Publications Asia-Pacific Pte Ltd
3 Church Street
#10-04 Samsung Hub
Singapore 049483

Editor: James Clark
Assistant editor: Diana Alves
Production editor: Nicola Carrier
Copyeditor: Christine Bitten
Proofreader: Aud Scriven
Marketing manager: Lorna Patkai
Cover design: Naomi Robinson
Typeset by: C&M Digitals (P) Ltd, Chennai, India
Printed in the UK

First published 2020

Library of Congress Control Number: 2019947354

British Library Cataloguing in Publication data

A catalogue record for this book is available from the British Library

ISBN 978-1-5264-3858-4
ISBN 978-1-5264-3859-1 (pbk)

I write in the name of Allah, the Most Gracious, the Most Merciful.

Whoever travels a path searching knowledge, Allah makes easy the path to Paradise for them. Prophet Muḥammad (ﷺ)

To Rehana for her dedication and services to education.

TABLE OF CONTENTS

FIGURES AND TABLES

Tables

Figure

ABOUT THE AUTHOR

Imran Mogra is a senior lecturer in professional studies and religious education at Birmingham City University, United Kingdom. He teaches on the undergraduate and postgraduate courses. Imran is the author of *Jumpstart! RE* (Routledge, 2018). He has published numerous academic and professional articles.

ACKNOWLEDGEMENTS

I would like to first offer my sincere heartfelt gratitude to Allah, Knower of known and unknown, whose blessings have materialised in the time, effort, resources and ability which have enabled me to accomplish a long awaited service to teachers and educators.

I also owe a special debt of appreciation to my supportive family for their understanding and for patiently giving me their space from conception, development to completion. Jazāk Allahu Khayran. Their constant inquiry about its completion kept me focussed, otherwise the book may not have seen the light of day!

Likewise, I wish to thank my students and to the 'Ulamā' and an 'Ālimah who kindly read the chapters. Thanks must also be extended to the staff at SAGE Publishers: James Clark for warming to the initial idea and for believing in the importance of the book and a special thanks to Diana Alves for being supportive.

Thank you to those who have contributed with their voices to the chapters.

INTRODUCTION

Why a book about understanding Islam?

This book has been written to help you to develop your knowledge and understanding of Islam which you will need for your own professional development as a teacher for the pupils under your care. This introduction sets the scene for the book and introduces the chapters that follow.

The overarching aim of the book is to position Islam as part of the excellent primary education on offer to pupils. The book conveys a positive perspective on Islam and Muslims and their engagement in diverse spheres of life. It also seeks to extend the knowledge-base of existing and future teachers in contemporary schools.

The twenty-first century has experienced a surge in recognising the significance of religions and beliefs at a global scale. Out of this has emerged a challenge in regard to the presentation of information regarding religious traditions from individuals and organisations. Undeniably, Islam has suffered considerable 'bad' publicity in recent times. However, this is not a new phenomenon, albeit the nature is different. The portrayal of Islam by orientalists and the 'West' has a long history. This book will attempt to present the discourse of Islam in such a way that it veers away from being defensive and apologetic in its stance, and focusses on education rather than being polemical. In this broader context, it is observed that interest in Islam is not necessarily matched with knowledge about Islam and Muslims, and so, an insider perspective will further enrich the material available for subject knowledge development among teachers providing them with well-sourced and accessible knowledge and perspectives.

The book also raises issues and challenges some misconceptions. Misconceptions and misunderstandings are currently, as they have done in the past, contributing to what has now become hate crime and Islamophobia, and present a deficit viewpoint of the Muslim community, part of which involves constructing them as 'the other' and 'a problem' that needs to be sorted. Encouragingly, however, there appears to be a strong desire among teachers in particular for the need of knowledge that they can use to counter these and conduct a dialogue with their pupils on some of the topics significant to them and the community at large, as schools are expected to prepare young people for future life.

Religious education subject leaders, trainers and continued professional development providers will be able to use this text to enhance and strengthen the knowledge and understanding of Islam. This text is designed to enable primary and lower secondary teachers in particular to become better equipped with the core knowledge of Islam so that their confidence is further enhanced and their effectiveness in meeting the curricular needs of the subject, as teachers in contemporary Britain, is further strengthened. The context for the presentation of this content is mainly Religious Education and Islam, although it could equally be used in other areas. This text introduces readers to the most important and relevant aspects of Islam and presents Muslims as a heterogeneous and multicultural phenomenon. Thus, it is a timely text. Society in many parts of the world is becoming complex, yet with this sophisticated awareness, the continued echoes of depicting Islam as monochrome and of positioning it as 'the other', warrant an appropriate presentation of Islam. This book presents the essential core beliefs, institutions and values in such a way that its diversity is recognised.

Importance of the content

The content of this book is important as it will attempt to demonstrate that for some minorities, religion is a source for social mobility and informs their ideas of spirituality, fairness and justice. Religion, rather than being a personal belief, concerns identity and community membership at various levels. In a climate of change, there is an increased demand for alternative ways of interpreting the past and present, and of looking to the future. International processes like migration and pluralism challenge the conception of cultures, religions, nationalities and ethnicities. In recent years religion has become more relevant and an important player in the public space and discourses of religion, and Islam, in particular, is at the heart of these debates – as such, it makes the content important.

Anyone interested in understanding the contemporary world, or in the developments in some parts of the world and what shapes them, would need to understand something about Islam, which is the second largest religion in the world. To understand the modern world, it is important to recognise why Islam continues to have such a prominent presence in many parts of the world. A basic understanding of Islam is essential to gain a basic education for all, especially in Europe and Britain, where there is a growing Muslim community, so that better relationships can be fostered. Globally, nearly a quarter of the population is Muslim, the name given to the followers of the faith of Islam. Along with Judaism and Christianity, Islam is seen as one of the three Abrahamic religions so it is important for you to know that when reference is made to the community of Muḥammad (ﷺ) it means all of humanity after him. This community is distinguished by some Muslims as those who have accepted (*ijābah*) his message and those who are to be invited (*da'wah*).

Muslims are a diverse community, representing different strands from across the globe. In the United Kingdom, it is thought that there are approximately three million, of which approximately 70 per cent are associated with South Asian heritages (Hamid, 2016). The Islamic community has a core normative set of beliefs and practices. At the same time, it has a colourful internal diversity of different theological strands, schools of jurisprudence, philosophical perspectives and spiritual tastes. This diversity is further complicated by visible factors such as their nationality, migration history, geography, settlement pattern, ethnicity, kinship, tribal network, duration of residence, socio-economic class, education, political affiliation and religious observance.

Who would find this book relevant?

It is the hope of this book that it will be relevant to people who have chosen to become primary teachers regardless of the route that they are taking, from well-established university and college-based PGCE and degree courses to the vast array of school-based training programmes that have developed in the country over the years. It is also relevant for tutors in initial teacher education and those engaged in continued professional development.

The approach

The approach taken is an educational one. The book aims to raise awareness, create sensitivity and promote mutual understanding, and although it will not provide all the answers, attention has been paid to the common, essential and indispensable aspects of Islam. The approach has been primarily driven by the needs of educators, especially those in training in primary and Key Stage 3 phases. Thus, the content has been guided by the needs of the curriculum of the subject in the context of Religious Education. Nevertheless, to maintain relevance and readability, excessive sophistication of the content and undue detail have been minimised.

Organisation and structure of chapters

The book is presented in two parts. The first part – about key concepts in Islam – comprises Chapters 1–7, and the second part – about contemporary issues – comprises Chapters 8–12.

The chapters in the first part of the book provide the theological and contextual information as a framework for knowing and understanding the foundations of belief and practice as taught by Islam and practised by Muslims.

Chapter 1: Allah summarises the theological basis of Islam by positioning *tawḥīd* as a central concept to demonstrate its pure monotheistic beliefs. It illuminates an overview of God according to Islam and God's attributes as evident from the Qur'ān so that God being Greater than everything is shown and making God incomprehensible yet very close to humans. To enable teachers to transfer some of these beliefs into the classroom, an appreciation of *tawḥīd* is facilitated through the consideration of certain *Suwar* (chapters) and verses. The chapter also demonstrates the common fundamental beliefs among Muslims which have been sources of unity and diversity.

Chapter 2: The Word of God shows the Qur'ān as a continuous link between God and people. Some structural and organisational information is presented to enable you to appreciate how some Muslims use it in their daily life and to impress the particular features of the Qur'ān. Thereafter, some key beliefs held by Muslims about the Qur'ān and how it is understood and interpreted are discussed. An exemplification of some of the rules, teachings and messages features in many parts of the book so that you become familiar with its content in addition to the historical and structural information. Part of the chapter shows the manner in which the Qur'ān is treated by some Muslims and how it is embodied by them. As teachers you will appreciate the Qur'ān not just as a sacred book but as one which is a guide and central to Muslim lives and which gives meaning to those lives. A relatively untapped section on the science of recitation has been incorporated.

Chapter 3: The Prophet of God develops your knowledge and understanding of the concept of prophethood. It analyses some well-known significant events in the life of the Prophet (ﷺ). However, it goes beyond this conventional approach to include personal encounters and dispositions of the Messenger (ﷺ) through vignettes from his life. Some of his profound sayings appear revealing how and why he is considered by Muslims to be their model and how this impacts on their devotion and everyday situations. This presentation captures an understanding of the Prophet (ﷺ) beyond that of a 'founder' of Islam, often a generalised term. In essence, it is concerned with presenting the biography (*sīrah*) and life of the Prophet (Sunnah). It introduces, in relation to him, two less familiar ideas of obedience (*Iṭā'a*) and following (*Ittibā'*).

Chapter 4: The Stories of Prophets offers several stories all featuring in the Qur'ān revealing some of the important live events and miracles performed at their hands.

Due to limitations of space only some of the prominent ones have been included. However, to extend your familiarity and introduce fresh material some hitherto less-used narratives have been expounded. A brief section on the use and purposes of stories from the viewpoint of the Qur'ān demonstrates the theological and moral significance of these critical incidents in the lives of these prophets. To this end, a synthesis of their main characteristics as reflected in the Qur'ān has been created.

Chapter 5: Foundations of Faith discusses 'Īmān, Islam and Iḥsān drawing on the verses of the Qur'ān, traditions of the Prophet (ﷺ) and scholarly works to offer explanations and implications of these facets. Thereafter, the articles of faith are addressed to emphasise Muslim ideas about belief and faith which are central for understanding Muslim life and theology. This covers beliefs about angels, their nature, types and their roles, Satan and the jinn. It also considers Torah, the Scrolls of Moses and Abraham, and analyses eschatological matters of Afterlife, Judgement Day and predestination.

Chapter 6: Obligations of Faith revisits the well-known five pillars as a framework for Muslim worship which has tended to adopt a ritualistic presentation. However in this book each term is explained and their implications and evidence from the sources of Islam are described. Moreover, a different approach is taken in that the spiritual, philosophical, social, moral and personal dimensions are taken account of, in addition to the ritualistic and religious perspectives. Moreover, an attempt has been made to show how these five pillars affect Muslims in various parts of the world, using the UK as the main focus.

Chapter 7: Expressions of Practice recognises that the Muslim is an individual unit connected to many other Muslims in different ways. This relationship is important for you to understand as Muslims are located within global Muslim communities. This chapter will focus on ideas such as identity, belonging, community, culture and citizenship. The teachings of Islam and the model of the Prophet (ﷺ) provide meaning for existence and so these rituals and rites are seen as significant milestones along the journey of life. The various sections incorporate birth, adulthood, marriage, death as life cycle rituals to provide an awareness of how Islam and Muslims celebrate and interpret the beginning and end of human life. A calendar approach is used to explain the main festivals and symbols which provide transcendent meaning through symbolic practices.

The chapters in the second part of the book about contemporary issues are in a way informed and an outcome of the first part. It encompasses explicit teachings which have direct relevance to the lived realities of Muslims. It makes links between the historical legacy and contemporary matters.

Chapter 8: The Ethical Dimension focusses on the obligations placed upon Muslims to observe the lawful and abstain from the unlawful. In general, this subject matter usually features in the context of dietary laws. However, this chapter presents you with a richer and wider conception, and application of these two major ethical principles. In addition, some main concepts related to character education have been expounded and emphasis is placed on individual responsibility as envisioned by the teachings of Islam.

Chapter 9: Education in Muslim Communities sheds light on the multifaceted institutions nurturing and developing Muslim personality. Some of this first-hand material includes the innovative and creative ways in which curricula and pedagogy have evolved and challenge some stereotypes regarding how and what some Muslim children are taught. An example of a mosque reveals a holistic approach to communal learning. In addition to the higher institutes of learning which train Imāms, a programme for 14–19 years old has been delineated. A section is devoted to Muslim educational thought and practice to demonstrate how Muslim scholarship problematised theoretical and pedagogical issues of education. A brief section recognises the contribution of Muslim scholars, scientists and philosophers.

Chapter 10: The Shīʿa Traditions covers Shīʿism through its historical development with an elaboration of its key principles. It details the major variants of Shīʿism showing their spectrum. The role of the Imām, the status of Karbalā and other key doctrines have been elucidated to establish their theology. A section has been dedicated to cover the ten pillars and five foundations of Shīʿism.

Chapter 11: Muslim Heritage and Intellectual Contributions engages with the various legal, theological and spiritual schools among Muslims. In terms of the legal schools, you will learn about the main canonical schools of thought of jurisprudence followed by most Muslims. In addition, a brief section covers the key issues raised within the prominent theological schools. The philosophical part highlights some key persons and their ideas. In regard to spirituality, the chapter presents it as an essential dimension of Islam by emphasising the interdependence between the law and the 'path'. A notable inclusion is that of the science of ḥadīth.

Chapter 12: Islam and Contemporary Britain identifies some current issues facing the community. It begins with the history of Muslims in Europe and their contributions in the world wars and describes the impact of the controversial Prevent strategy. It draws attention to some of the challenges faced by the communities having established themselves as Muslims in Britain. Brief accounts of some of the main reformist movements of Muslims are included to illustrate Muslims' religious activism.

Chapter features

The book contains a number of structural and study support features:

- At the start of each chapter you will find a list of **chapter objectives** which provide you with the intended focus of each chapter.
- There is an **overview** to help note the broader perspective of the chapter and contextualise the content. In some cases it raises certain issues which exist but are

beyond the scope of the book and, in others, your attention is drawn to divergent perspectives.

- Some **diagrams** facilitate and enhance the presentation of the content in selected chapters.
- Each chapter has a **voice of a Muslim** or **Muslimah**, some of which are from experts to offer authenticity and an anthropological flavour in relation to their experiences. The names of those Muslims whose voices feature in the book have been anonymised and pseudonyms have been used instead.
- There are **case studies** encouraging you to think deeply on the issues raised by the case and make links to the classroom context. They demonstrate different contexts and a variety of experiences and perspectives.
- All chapters have **summaries** with a review of some key concepts and messages of the chapter.
- At the end there are **reflective tasks** to assist you to become deeply and actively engaged in the content of the chapter. Sometimes they invite you to reflect on your own reading or to think about how you could implement the material you have read in the classroom. You may find that carrying these out with your peers is more profitable.
- There are suggestions for selected **further readings** to add rigour and make you aware of sources for further detailed and specialised study.
- A **reference list** points you to the details of the sources which informed the chapters.
- There is a **glossary** to assist you in acquiring the terminology of Islam and an extended and better understanding of the concepts.

Presentational features

As you read the book you will notice that certain words have been spelt in a way that you may be unfamiliar with. The use of Qur'ān has been made rather than Koran to shift away from the previous conventions and also to reflect proximity to the initial Arabic letter ق with its corresponding letter Q in English. Similarly, Makkah has been preferred rather than Mecca for being the official spelling adopted by the Kingdom of Saudi Arabia. The modern usage of Khalīfah rather than Caliph has been used in an attempt to move away from its negative and historical connotations. In so doing, these become better aligned with the main accepted forms of transliteration and modern usage.

In most cases, a full translation of a verse has been provided. One of the reasons for presenting them as such is to show the completeness of the verse.

Some Muslims and non-Muslims, for a variety of positive and negative reasons, present incomplete verses. In many cases, this practice is unproblematic. However, there are some verses which, if not presented in their totality, not only misrepresent the Qur'ān but may sometimes also omit the historical and contextual information. A case in point may be the verse 'when you meet disbelievers, smite their necks'; this would suggest 'be in pursuit of disbelievers with a view to killing them'. However, the rest of the verse states 'until the way lays down its burden' (47:4). Thus, exegetes have noted that this is referring to reciprocal combat between fighters and the application was confined to the battlefield.

In presenting the references of the six canonical collections of ḥadīth literature, first names have not been used and popular terms have been given instead. For example, Abū Dāwūd is used for citations in text for the compiler of the collection *Sunan Abū Dāwūd* or al-Tirmidhī for the compiler of *Jāmi' al-Tirmidhī*. Most of the interpretations and meanings of these texts have been adapted from sunnah.com unless otherwise stated. The references of printed sources are given. In making reference to the Qur'ān the format sūrah number and ayat number is applied. It would have been ideal to provide the name of a sūrah. However, in this book, it has been omitted for ease and brevity. The stories have been crafted from the verses of the Qur'ān. The specific references have been removed to enhance accessibility and readability. In some cases modification has taken place for clarity and an interpretive style has been adopted to facilitate their transference to the classroom. Dates have been cited in the Hijrī/Gregorian styles unless otherwise indicated. In an attempt to minimise the distance between the reader and the text of subsequent chapters, the references and glossary have been consolidated into a single list at the end of the book.

The ligature (ﷺ) has been included as the honorific phrase and prayer expected of Muslims when they mention the name of Prophet Muḥammad (ﷺ). It states (صلى الله عليه وسلم) meaning 'May God's peace and blessings be upon him'. For other prophets the phrase عليه السلام is used. The phrase is known as *ṣalāh* and *salām*. Similarly, for other messengers, prophets and prominent angels and among the Shī'a for the Imāms, the phrase (*'alayhi al-salām* عليه السلام), meaning 'peace be upon him' is used. At the mention of a name of a Companion of the Messenger, the phrase (رضي الله عنها) *raḍiya 'llāhu 'anha* (for women) and for males رضي الله عنه is uttered by Sunnīs which translates as 'May God be pleased with her/him'. At times the abbreviation RA is used and gender appropriate pronouns are altered.

PART 1

KEY CONCEPTS IN ISLAM

1

ALLAH

In this chapter you will:

- know and understand the meaning of *Tawḥīd* and its implications for Muslims
- consider the central beliefs held about God in Islam
- reflect on the names of God and three important chapters of the Qur'ān
- know and understand the concepts of *Shirk* and *Kufr*.

Overview

The teachings of Islam unapologetically accentuate the cardinal belief in the unity of God. This is because Islam in its current form maintains that belief in the Oneness of God has been a message always transmitted from God and it is His Will. According to Muslims, the knowledge, understanding and gnosis of God have been relayed to humans through chosen prophets and messengers of God, who received Divine revelations from God during their lifetime. One of their beliefs is that, without exception, all these messengers conveyed the fundamental message of the doctrine of absolute monotheism. Thus, belief in the existence of God and in His Unity is a necessary principle of Islam. To know and understand Islam, it is important for you to engage with the concept of *Tawḥīd*, upon which the entire Muslim belief system rests.

Tawḥīd is an Arabic noun derived from a transitive verb, *waḥḥada* ('to make one') denoting the Oneness of Allah. According to the Qur'ān, human beings had testified to *Tawḥīd* prior to the creation of the universe in the realm of souls and had taken an oath acknowledging God as their Lord (7:172). All prophets from Adam to Muḥammad (ﷺ) taught this same belief and were simultaneously opposed to anything which contradicted it (16:36). Similarly, the foundation of the theology of the Qur'ān is precisely monotheism. For Muslims, never once did any one of these prophets compromise on this fundamental principle, for which they had to endure great sacrifices.

Tawḥīd is one of the three fundamental themes recurring throughout the Qur'ān, the other two being ***Risālah*** (prophethood) and ***Ākhirah*** (afterlife). You will learn about the latter two in Chapters 3 and 5 respectively. The following verse illustrates the emphasis placed on monotheism and demonstrates the continuity of this one eternal true message. The first is a statement made by Yūsuf (Joseph) as he talks about his faith to his fellow prisoners when Pharaoh had imprisoned him. He declared to them, 'I have followed the religion of my fathers, Abraham, Isaac and Jacob. And it was not for us to associate anything with Allah. That is from the favour of Allah upon us and upon the people, but most of the people are not grateful' (12:38).

This uncompromising stance taken by Islam regarding *Tawḥīd* distinguishes its belief in God from the conception of God in other religions. Such was the importance of *Tawḥīd* that since the revelation of the Qur'ān in Makkah, in the early years immediately after 610AH (571CE), its significance, meanings and implications were expounded in various ways. The Qur'ān presented arguments against those who held beliefs contrary to *Tawḥīd* based on their own personal beliefs (17:46; 39:45). The Qur'ān presented the doctrine of *Tawḥīd* in simple and clear terms and in a way that people could easily understand and relate to God (6:101; 56:85). Prophet Muḥammad (ﷺ) offered people a pure and lofty concept of *Tawḥīd*. He also presented irrefutable arguments in support of *Tawḥīd* and invited them to consider the historical fact that all prophets before him had taught the same message (6:74–80). He reminded the people of Makkah that when they faced disasters or calamities they returned and sought assistance from the One True God (30:33). Moreover, the Qur'ān presents examples from diverse aspects of the physical world so that humans can reflect and ponder over their own creation and the many signs of God's work in the cosmos (2:22; 30:20–25). Finally, the Qur'ān addresses people, sometimes in strong terms, with convincing arguments and an invitation for an honest appraisal of their own claims (10:66; 31:21–22).

The second distinguishing feature of Islam's belief in the Oneness of God is that it forms the foundation of their remaining beliefs, practices, attitudes, customs, rites and rules. Thus, this belief in God finds expression in every religious, intellectual, social, moral and spiritual dimension of Muslim life.

The implications of a belief in *Tawḥīd* are many for Muslims. Once it is recognised that *Tawḥīd* is Truth and God rejects polytheism and infidelity, it becomes incumbent upon a Muslim to worship none other than God. Simultaneously, a Muslim becomes duty bound to serve and offer devotion to God alone. In fact, it would be forbidden to invoke others (40:66). In addition, it becomes necessary to abstain from seeking help of a kind that is only God's prerogative from others (10:106). Moreover, just as the offering of sacrifices to idols had been rejected at the time of the revelation of the Qur'ān, based on *Tawḥīd*, the offering of a sacrifice to any person, saint or god other than God is shunned. It also becomes necessary that a Muslim submits to God in matters related to their social, moral, spiritual, economic, legal and political affairs.

In other words, whatever has been deemed prohibited should be abstained from and whatever has been declared permissible should be accepted as such. It also means that nobody has the authority to declare something lawful as unlawful and vice versa (5:44–47; 10:59; 42:10).

Voice of a Muslim

For me, as a businessperson, *Tawḥīd* plays a pivotal role in my daily life. From the moment I open till the end there is nothing I do without being God conscious. It influences my conduct with customers, dealings and sales. The realisation of *Tawḥīd* makes me an honest person, as I know I am answerable to my Creator for every transaction. I strongly believe that my business is ordained by God so I always put my trust in God because I believe and worship God, who is my sole Sustainer and of the creation. This gives me a lot of contentment in my business and peace. I rely on *Tawḥīd* as an organising principle for my financial activities. (Aḥsān, businessperson, British-Asian, male)

The belief in *Tawḥīd* affects Muslims in all walks of life and not only who and how they worship. In fact, even those actions, which might be considered mundane, are prefaced with a declaration of *Bismillāh* (with the name of God) such as before eating, typing or beginning a lesson, for that matter. When they intend to do something in the future, you might hear them say *In shā' Allah* (God willing) and *Allah Ḥāfiẓ* (Allah is [your] Protector) when bidding someone farewell. These simple invocations and prayers are a social manifestation of *Tawḥīd* where God is frequently mentioned. In the parlance of ***Sharī'ah***, these are terms which convey submission to God – an expression of their faith. The whole system of belief and practice in Islam is founded upon the acceptance and attestation of the truth in the Oneness of God. This Being is Allah.

Allah

Amongst the pagans and various religious communities during the time of the revelation of the Qur'ān, belief in the existence of God was known and common in many communities in the Arabian Peninsula and around the world. However, Islam asserted that there was an absence of the correct understanding of the nature and attributes of Allah. One of the principle aims of the Qur'ān was to address this misconception about the Creator, as you will learn below.

The Qur'ān deploys a wide range of symbolic vocabulary to describe God. By considering some of these, you will gain a clearer knowledge and understanding of how and what Muslims believe about God. In using these beautiful names, the purpose seems at least twofold: conceptual clarification and comparative argumentation. These descriptions of God are significant to know the God worshipped by Muslims and the kind of relationship that exists between the Creator and the creation, according to Islam.

Some Muslims may point out that if God is the Creator, then logically there could be nothing 'higher' than God at all in any respect, otherwise God would be 'lower' than that 'something'. This is because limits would be imposed upon God and limiting God in any way would be incompatible with being the Ultimate Reality or the Primary Cause. Hence, all of God's attributes in all respects are expressed in terms of being infinite. As finite beings, humans cannot comprehend the infinite. On the other hand, God, being infinite, can comprehend His creation. Humans can know God by knowing the signs of God in creation and within themselves. When God is infinite, there can only be One God. Some Muslims will also say that it is not possible by definition to have two first causes, thus there is no god but God. This Unity of God is the foundation of Islam.

The use of He to refer to God is often questioned. According to the Qur'ān, God is neither male nor female; God is unlike any created being. There are no gender connotations in this application. God is beyond such categorisation and conceptions, and, therefore the issue is a matter of linguistics, which itself is both finite, limiting and arbitrary in talking about God. For instance, the English language does not have a word to denote the One Creator and so it resorts to the capitalisation of *God* to distinguish it from other *gods*, which is shown by a lowercase 'g' (Hewer, 2006). In the Arabic language, God is Allah. This should help you to put to rest a question which some pupils often ask, if Muslims worship God, then who is Allah? In other words, Muslims do not have a separate God called Allah.

There are hundreds of verses in which the Divine Attributes are rehearsed in the Qur'ān. For brevity, some of the more significant ones are presented hereunder. To begin with, as you have noted above, God is beyond human comprehension. This makes any human endeavour to talk about God inadequate. There is nothing like unto Him, and He is the Hearing, the Seeing (42:10–11). This means that even the language which is ultimately utilised, is incapable of capturing the reality of God. God is One and Unique. Therefore, God does not share divinity with any of His creation (112:1–4).

God is far from being the ancient Sun-god or Moon-god. The Qur'ān asserts that these are both creations and signs of God for humans to reflect and know who their Creator is. A verse addresses this misconception: 'And of His signs are the night and day and the sun and moon. Do not prostrate to the sun or to the moon, but prostate to Allah, who created them, if it should be Him that you worship' (4:37).

The Qur'ān describes God as being very close to His creation and yet beyond everything. Both qualities of immanence and transcendence become evident which has given rise to a tension between distinct, and often conflicting, understandings of God, the nature of Divinity, and God's relationship to human beings. Not only have these conceptions been historically negotiated, intellectually and spiritually, they are commonly debated among contemporary Muslims. On the one hand, His Being is not constrained by the laws of creation such as those governing space and time. Yet, the Qur'ān speaks of God in human terms in many instances. Take for example, the verses which mention God's hands (3:73), God's face (2:115), God's eyes (11:37) and that God is extremely near: 'And We have already created man and know what his soul whispers to him, and We are closer to him than [his] jugular vein' (50:16). You will find out more about these different schools of theological thinking and philosophical standpoints in Chapter 10.

The usage of the Master–servant relationship might invoke the thought that amongst Muslims the relationship between God and His people is a distant one. On the contrary, as discussed above, this relationship is close, deep and intimate. The Qur'ān invites the development of a relationship, which is full of heartfelt love with total consciousness of God at all times and in all places (Nadwī, 2017).

Another misconception in the Qur'ān's argumentation is the rejection of some of the ideas that the contemporaries of Prophet Muḥammad (ﷺ) had, for example, those they attributed to Allah as daughters (16:57–59). They regarded their goddesses and angels as intercessors and daughters of God. Some people at that time had contempt regarding daughters. This verse highlights their ignorance regarding God. On the one hand, they were happy to assign daughters to God but they themselves considered having daughters a matter of disgrace. This attitude showed that they had a very low estimation of God, which had resulted from their ways of *Shirk* (idolatry). Therefore, they felt nothing wrong in ascribing such absurd things to God who is above such things (Mawdūdī, 2016). In a similar vein, the Qur'ān is equally emphatic in rejecting the belief that God has a son (4:171). Thus, the problem it is trying to address is not gendered but that of projecting a foreign concept onto God.

In addition to denying God having a son and the concept of Trinity, there is no belief in dualism. The Qur'ān guides: 'And Allah has said, "Do not take for yourselves two deities. He is but one God, so fear only Me"' (16:51). Moreover, God has no consort either. This is reasoned in the following verse: 'How could He have a son when He does not have a companion and He created all things? And He is, of all things, Knowing' (6:101) and the Qur'ān teaches that 'exalted is the nobleness of our Lord; He has not taken a wife or a son' (72:3).

Beautiful names (*Asmāʾ al-Ḥusnā*)

One of the reasons for elucidating the names of God is to ensure that people do not fall victim to ascribing partners to God (Nomānī, 1978). As you have read, the belief and concept of *Tawḥīd* is apparently simple yet the Qur'ān profusely recounts verses consisting of the numerous names of God, which offer deeper insights into what are presented as the attributes and characteristics of God. The most often repeated ones are *Al-Raḥmān* and *Al-Raḥīm* which appear before all but one of the chapters (sūrahs/suwar) of the Qur'ān. Nevertheless, single attributes cannot holistically explain the nature of God, and therefore it is necessary to recognise all of them simultaneously (Hussain, 2016). In practice, various names are used in prayer and supplication (Saritoprak, 2018). It has been suggested that the schools of Muslim theology have focussed upon certain of God's names to explain their theological and devotional positions; they include the Mu'tazili, Muslim philosophers, Sufis and 'orthodox' Muslims represented by al-Ash'ari (Ridgeon, 2009).

Nevertheless, you will have read or met Muslims with names such as *'Abd Allah* or *'Abd al-Raḥmān*. These names have the suffix of *'Abd* (servant) to the name of Allah and His other attributes to derive personal names. Thus, *'Abd Allah* means God's servant and *'Abd al-Raḥmān* means Servant of the Merciful. Some Muslims select these names because they believe that when they are summoned on the Day of Resurrection, they will be called by their names and their father's names (Abū Dāwūd, 3:4930). Others will choose them as they express humility before God and are an expression of their love for God.

In Chapter 3 you will find out that Prophet Muḥammad (ﷺ) emigrated from Makkah to Madīnah. After ten years, he returned to Makkah and reinstated the **Ka'bah** as a centre dedicated to the worship of the One True God. In part, he physically achieved this by emptying and spiritually cleansing the Ka'bah by removing 360 idols which had been placed inside it. Thus, the principle of absolute monotheism was once again restored. After this, Muḥammad (ﷺ) did not place any tangible images, symbols, statues, idols or icons inside it. This reflected the key principle of aniconism, which necessitates that God is beyond all images (Gwynne, 2018). Since God is *Al-Khāliq*, the Creator, nothing in His creation can be His equal, and as such, He cannot be represented in any art, shape or form, since that would 'diminish' Him (Hawkins, 2004).

Al-Fātiḥah (The Opening)

Having learnt about Muslim beliefs regarding God, you will learn about three great **Suwar** (Chapters) of the Qur'ān along with some of their benefits and virtues including its use in Muslim life. A closer examination will assist you in understanding some of the beliefs and attributes of God and give you a glimpse of how Muslim life is affected by these significant Chapters.

One of the students of Prophet Muḥammad (ﷺ) tells a story about his learning of a Chapter directly from the Prophet in his mosque in Madīnah.

> Abū Sa'īd says that one day he was praying in the Mosque when the Messenger (ﷺ) called him. He did not respond to him, as he should have. Later, he excused himself saying, 'O Allah's Messenger I was praying.' To which the Prophet (ﷺ) replied, 'Didn't God say: "Give your response to God and to His Messenger when he calls you"' (8.24). The Prophet (ﷺ) then said to Abū Sa'īd, 'Before you leave the Mosque, I will teach you a Sūrah which is the greatest Sūrah in the Qur'ān.' Then the Prophet held his hand and intended to leave the Mosque. At this point Abū Sa'īd reminded him, 'Didn't you say to me, "I will teach you a Sūrah which is the greatest Sūrah in the Qur'ān?"' The Prophet (ﷺ) replied, [It is] "Al-Ḥamdu ..." (Praise be ...) which is [also known as] the seven repeatedly recited verses and the Great Qur'ān. (al-Būkhārī, 6:528)

It is from narratives of this kind that Muslims consider *Al-Fātiḥah* to be the best and most superior part of the Qur'ān. Chronologically, *Al-Fātiḥah* is the first Sūrah of the Qur'ān and it is for this reason that some commentators call it *Al-Fātiḥah* (lit. the opener) as it opens the contents of the rest of the Scripture and because it is the first portion that is recited in the daily prayers. This chapter has many other interesting names, each one highlighting a different aspect of its meaning. In other words, having many names indicates its significance.

It is called `*Umm al-Qur'ān* (Mother of the Qur'ān) by the Prophet (ﷺ) (al-Tirmidhī, 5:3124). Imām Ibn Jarīr al-Ṭabarī (224–310AH/839–923CE) explained that it was named so because the meaning of the entire Qur'ān is summarised therein (al-Ṭabarī, 1989). Others refer to it as *Al-Ḥamd* (The Praise) because it mentions praise to God, whereas some call it *Al-Ṣalāh* (The Prayer) since its recitation is a condition for the validity of the daily prayers. This Sūrah is commonly seen as having a healing effect and is therefore recognised as

Al-Shifā' (The Cure) (al-Būkhārī, 6:529). Unsurprisingly, Muslims believe that this Sūrah is a gracious gift from Allah.

The vast majority of Muslims across the world would know it by heart. From childhood, this Chapter becomes 'as familiar as breathing' to them. Since Muslims embody it, some of its main themes and concepts are discussed below. These include obedience to the will of God, praise, good and evil, and guidance. The Chapter emphasises the acknowledgement of the supremacy of God as Lord and Guide for all humanity.

The Chapter is recited at the beginning of the required five daily and other prayers. Depending on the number of prayers (**Ṣalāh**) offered, some would read it no less than 20 times daily; perhaps making it the most often recited Chapter in the world. This Sūrah, like many others, is used for contemplation and serenity. Muslims ponder over the names and attributes of Allah, the creation, and acknowledge that God Alone is worthy of worship and that assistance should be sought exclusively from none other than God. Muslims learn from this not to be over reliant on the unlimited mercy of God into thinking that God will not question their sin and wrongdoing. God is both Most Kind and Most Merciful and Just. They believe these attributes will come to fruition on the Day of Judgement when reward and punishment will be dispensed. Thus, Muslims affirm Resurrection and that guidance to prepare for it has been revealed. Therefore, they believe, everyone should follow revelation. The Sūrah is also an invitation to scrutinise the nature of their relationship with their Lord. In other words, Muslims use it to orient their beliefs, actions and thoughts around *Tawḥīd*.

Since it consists of some of God's names and attributes such as *Al-Raḥmān* (Lord of Mercy) and *Al-Raḥīm* (The Mercy Giver), Muslims use it as part of their invocations and petitions to God. They use it to express their dependence on God's guidance, assistance and sustenance, as Allah is the One who is the Provider. Spiritually, they seek protection from God's wrath and from those who have been led astray. Muslims hope that it purifies their heart and reminds them of God's justice, grace and generosity. It is also regarded as a private conversation between a person and God.

In addition to being a cure for the diseases of the heart and soul, *Al-Fātiḥah* is believed to be a cure and antidote for physical diseases. Some Muslims will recite it and blow over their body or into water and drink it. Some might wrap the text into an amulet and keep it on their body. In some cases, where the words of sorcery have affected a person, *Al-Fātiḥah* is included as part of prayer formulae and breathed into water or unto the person. Thus it is believed that there is spiritual force at work when the meanings and faith contained in *Al-Fātiḥah* are fully appreciated. In addition to the blowing that follows such a recitation, there is an intended effect of curing and removing harmful effects.

Professor Abdel Haleem (2015) has translated the meaning of *Al-Fātiḥah* into English in the following words:

> Praise belongs to God, Lord of all worlds,
>
> the Lord of Mercy, the Giver of Mercy,
>
> Master of the Day of Judgement.
>
> It is You we worship; it is You we ask for help.
>
> Guide us to the straight path:
>
> The path of those You have blessed,
>
> those who incur no anger and who have not gone astray.

Al-Ikhlās (The Sincerity)

One of the linguistic features of the Qur'ān is that it uses negative statements from which the nature of God can be pondered and known. A good example of this is *Sūrah Al-Ikhlās* (112). It is taken to be one of the core instruments for negating attributions to God, which constitute polytheistic beliefs. The Qur'ān states:

> Say: 'He is Allah, [who is] One,
>
> Allah, the Eternal Refuge;
>
> He neither begets nor, is born,
>
> Nor is there to Him any equivalent'.

The word *Ikhlās* means sincerity, purity or separation. The lessons for Muslims from this Sūrah are threefold: purification of belief, deeds and intentions.

For Muslims, this brief but extraordinary Sūrah establishes fundamental beliefs about God. God is One and not Trinity and God has not been created, nor is God in any kind of relationship of father, mother or son with anyone else in Allah's creation. Moreover, Allah is self-sufficient and has no needs of any kind. God has no imperfections and nothing resembles God at all. In other words, it encompasses the supreme expression of *Tawḥīd* within four short verses by instituting God as a unity, independent and absolutely unique.

Following the purification of belief, for Muslims, this now means that all their deeds and thoughts should be cleansed from hypocrisy and ostentations so that in executing them, only God is considered. The same applies to the motives for any words and actions, whose purpose must be to seek the pleasure of God.

This can prove challenging for many Muslims in all walks of life since the desire to name and shame others is attractive in many shapes and forms. This frequently repeated Sūrah reminds Muslims to monitor their words, deeds and thoughts because God is aware of all these. They reflect on the higher purpose, which aims to purify their heart and intentions.

Unsurprisingly, though it is one of the shortest chapters of the Qur'ān, it is highly meritorious and loved and carries a third of the reward of reciting the Qur'ān (Muslim, 2:1771). On one occasion, a **Companion (*Ṣaḥābī*)** of the Prophet Muḥammad (ﷺ) said to him that he really loved this Sūrah. Thereupon, the Prophet (ﷺ) replied: 'your love for it will enable you to enter paradise' (al-Bukhārī, 1:413). Thus, as a means of entering paradise, Muslims memorise, study and develop a love for it. This love is expressed by reciting it as frequently as possible in formal prayer and at other occasions.

Āyat al-Kursī

This is the greatest verse of the Qur'ān (Muslim, 2:1766) known as the *Verse of the Throne*. It is recited after prayer and at other occasions. To seek protection some display it in their homes and shops.

> Allah – there is no deity except Him, the Ever-Living, the Sustainer of [all] existence.
>
> Neither drowsiness overtakes Him nor sleep.
>
> To Him belongs whatever is in the heavens and whatever is on the earth.
>
> Who is it that can intercede with Him except by His permission?
>
> He knows what is [presently] before them and what will be after them, and they encompass not a thing of His knowledge except for what He wills.
>
> His Kursī [throne] extends over the heavens and the earth, and their preservation tires Him not.
>
> And He is the Most High, the Most Great. (2:255)

The various segments of this verse highlight four main themes: the attributes, the power, the sovereignty of Allah and His will. At the heart of all this is that the knowledge of Allah encompasses everything. In other words, the knowledge of Allah is being praised.

This verse is called *Āyat al-Kursī* – the term *kursī* gives the verse its name. In an attempt to understand the nature of *kursī* and thereby the nature of God, Muslim scholars of the Qur'ān have held diverse viewpoints. Some take the word to mean a material reality and object, which represents the place of the footstool of God. Others interpret the *kursī* as a metaphor of God's knowledge and dominion (Suyūtī, 2007).

Whatever the scholastic interpretation accepted by the lay person, all Muslims consider this verse to be among the most powerful and is recited by many for protection in terms of spiritual, physical and emotional well-being at various times and places including after daily prayers, before sleeping, upon leaving the house and before setting out on a journey (al-Būkhārī, 6:530).

Voice of a Muslim

Understanding our local, national and intergovernmental political institutions can help achieve Muslims' goals. It is key to know when and where we should be lobbying for or against legislation, policies and regulations. While these institutions may not be ideal we can never change them or have any influence without engaging in what currently exists. ('Uthmān, civil servant, Indian, male)

Kufr

You will now learn about ***Kufr*** to understand the seriousness of this concept as part of the foundation of Muslim beliefs.

In recent years, the use of the term *Kāfir* has been brought into controversy and, as a result, it has become a contentious word in the discourses about relations between Muslims and those who are not Muslims. Some use this term for the purpose of polarisation. This situation makes it important for you, as a teacher in schools, to develop a nuanced understanding of the word and its application so that you can appreciate the Islamic concept of '*Kufr*' and its complexity.

Epistemologically, the word is derived from the root *k-f-r*, which provides multiple meanings such as 'to cover' and 'to reject'. The word '*kāfir*' is the active participle. The noun would be *kufr*, meaning denial. These terms occur hundreds of times in the Qur'ān. To begin with, a *kāfir* refers to an individual rather than to a collective for which *kuffār* is applied. Linguistically, therefore, in Arabic, a *kāfir* is one who conceals something and not a 'disbeliever'.

The word has many derivatives in the Qur'ān, which are used to convey a wide range of different meanings depending on the context and purport of the verse. In fact, the word '*kāfir*' itself is used at different times to mean different things. Thus, when translating the term into another language, a distinction is required based on the context of the verse being interpreted.

In everyday parlance, the word *k-f-r* may be used when a farmer covers the sown seed with soil or when clouds conceal the sky. In the Qur'ān, an example of this literal application is evident in the verse:

> Know that the life of this world is but amusement and diversion and adornment and boasting to one another and competition in increase of wealth and children – like the example of a rain whose [resulting] plant growth pleases the tillers; then it dries and you see it turned yellow; then it becomes [scattered] debris. And in the Hereafter is severe punishment and forgiveness from Allah and approval. And what is the worldly life except the enjoyment of delusion. (57:20)

Here *kuffār* is used to mean tillers who sow their seeds by covering them with soil (Suyūtī, 2007).

Having established the literal meaning of *kufr*, it is also used to denote 'disbelief'. This is because when a person disbelieves in God, he or she rejects God and hides the Truth. For instance, there are three consecutive verses in the Qur'ān wherein reference is made to Jews and Christians and, in each of them, three different words have been used to refer to them. In the first, *kafara* is preferred for their disbelief:

> They have certainly disbelieved who say that Allah is Christ, the son of Mary. Say, 'Then who could prevent Allah at all if He had intended to destroy Christ, the son of Mary, or his mother or everyone on the earth?' And to Allah belongs the dominion of the heavens and the earth and whatever is between them. He creates what He wills, and Allah is over all things competent. (5:17)

In the second, their titles are chosen:

> But the Jews and the Christians say, 'We are the children of Allah and His beloved.' Say, 'Then why does He punish you for your sins?' Rather, you are human beings from among those He has created. He forgives whom He wills, and He punishes whom He wills. And to Allah belongs the dominion of the heavens and the earth and whatever is between them, and to Him is the [final] destination. (5:18)

In the third, the *Ahl al-Kitāb* appears:

> O People of the Scripture, there has come to you Our Messenger to make clear to you [the religion] after a period [of suspension] of messengers, lest you say,

'There came not to us any bringer of good tidings or a warner.' But there has come to you a bringer of good tidings and a warner. And Allah is over all things competent. (5:19)

The term *kāfir* is applied to Christians and Jews because both conceal the knowledge that Prophet Muḥammad (ﷺ) was foretold in their own Scripture and about his prophethood after Jesus. Also for claiming Jesus as Lord (Suyūtī, 2007).

The word *kāfir* does not only mean *kāfir* in the sense described above as some Muslims might think as well. Such an understanding might lead to the misinterpretation of several verses in the Qur'ān. It is for this reason that it is important to consider the other shades of meaning that it holds. In the moral and social sense, it is applied to express ingratitude (2:152; 2:243). When a person receives a favour from fellow humans or God, and is ungrateful, the person is said to be a *kāfir*. In this context, the audience for such an application would be generalised and would include Muslims as well as non-Muslims.

Theologically, this controversial and oft-repeated term, is used to designate a community or a person, with repercussions for the Hereafter. It is sometimes used, exclusively, to encompass those who reject the existence of God. Occasionally, it is used generally to include all non-believers of Islam and Prophet Muḥammad (ﷺ) including the Jews and Christians. It is also used for other purposes such as warnings to Muslims to abstain from certain actions. Moreover, *Kufr* is a form of ignorance and tyranny as it consists of rebellion and ingratitude of God, the greatest benefactor of humankind and the Nourisher of the heart, mind and soul. Consequently, this has led scholars to create two categories of *kufr*; major and minor, each with several sub-categories (Khan, 1994).

Nevertheless, in common vernacular, most Muslims would use the term for all non-Muslims and rejecters of God per se. Having said that, in the past few decades, some Muslim 'extremists' have tried to monopolise the term and used it with the purpose of vilifying all non-Muslims. Simultaneously, the term has been appropriated by some Islamophobes who presented it as an Islamic idiom to convey hatred for the 'West' and all that it represents.

Not only that, among Muslims, there are some who belong to what is called *takfiri* groups, whose discourse relies on taking ownership of the term, thereby making a claim of exclusive interpretations of Islam which then renders others, including mainstream Muslims, to be labelled as wayward. Then, on a wider scale, the *Shī'as* might call the *Sunnīs* as *kāfir* or vice versa. Then, at the level of subgroups within these, there are groups who call the other *kāfir* based on the different interpretations of various articles of faith, interpretations of verses and other actions. Historically *takfīr* served as a counsel against intra-Islamic sectarianism and against conversion. However, nowadays, it also serves as a political strategy adopted by radical Islamists to reject undesirable viewpoints by declaring them un-Islamic (Raudvere, 2015: 24).

'Normative' traditional Islam takes the position that being a *kāfir* is a matter of conscience and of the heart. This is the domain about which only God alone fully knows. As an unknown state, no human should accuse and declare another fellow Muslim as being a *kāfir*, unless apparent and declared. Most contemporary scholars, like those of the past, warn their respective communities against the frivolous use of the term *kāfir*, based on a severe warning declared in a ***ḥadīth*** of the Prophet (ﷺ), where he said, 'If one accuses another of being a *kāfir* and the accused is not one, then the word will return to the accuser' (al-Bukhārī, 8:125).

The dictum often heard and used amongst jurists is that 'we do not declare anyone a *kāfir*, rather we point out the *kufr* in an individual'. In the religious and social contexts in which the term originated, the word is sensationalist in daily discourses. However, the problem arises when it is misappropriated and used for sinister and ulterior objectives.

Thus, the addressees and its purport also affect the application of the term. As noted above, it is used for non-Muslims with the intention of both demarcating them as a community and also accusing them of concealing the Truth. Internally, it is used to establish who has the correct interpretation of the faith.

Some pagan leaders of Makkah proposed a compromise between Islam and the ancient faith whereby the Prophet would concede to their gods an honourable place, so Chapter (112) indignantly repudiated all such suggestions (Daryabadī, 1991). Many Muslims in Britain recognise the liberal and pluralistic nature of their society and are cognisant of the freedom of conscience and belief, and often take recourse to these verses to present their case of tolerance of other faiths, which incidentally is called *The Disbelievers*:

> Say, 'O disbelievers,
>
> I do not worship what you worship.
>
> Nor are you worshippers of what I worship.
>
> Nor will I be a worshipper of what you worship.
>
> Nor will you be worshippers of what I worship.
>
> For you is your religion, and for me is my religion.' (109:1–6)

Shirk

In this final section about the foundations of faith in Islam, you will learn the definition and meaning of *Shirk*. Put simply, *Shirk* is the opposite of *Tawḥīd*. Literally, it means 'to share, make a partner or an equal'. It is usually translated as idolatry. It involves the denial of the fundamental principle of God's unity, which would dismantle the axiomatic primary foundation of the faith. It is unsurprising that it is declared the gravest and worst sin in Islam (4:48). It is a belief and act which God does not pardon, and its bearer is prohibited from entry into Paradise for rejecting and negating the Uniqueness of God – it is blasphemy of the highest order (Gwynne, 2018).

In terms of belief in God, *Tawḥīd* and *Shirk* are the two major opposing and oft-repeated themes of the Qur'ān. God will tolerate everything else but *Shirk* and *Kufr* as evident in the verse: 'Indeed, Allah does not forgive association with Him, but He forgives what is less than that for whom He wills. And he who associates others with Allah has certainly fabricated a tremendous sin' (4:48).

Holding someone or something equal to God entails a variety of things, which manifests in many different ways and to different degrees. The most severe and categorical would be to believe in the existence of more than one God. Then comes the attitudes, thoughts or actions towards another thing in those realms, which God has made exclusive for Himself. For example, associating other gods with God in worship (Ridgeon, 2009: 232). The pagans and some of the Makkans at the time of the Prophet (ﷺ) did not equate their deities with the One God in the fullest sense, for during the most troubled times they petitioned the One True God (6:63). In other words, they did, in fact, acknowledge differential powers between God and their gods. Their infidelity consisted of their devotion, divine service, prostration and sacrifices to their deities. It also involved entreating others, making offerings to them, supplicating, venerating, taking vows and oaths, taking others as omnipresent, and believing them to be intercessors with God, and placing faith in fortune-tellers, soothsayers and astrologers. They behaved towards others in ways that God had made exclusive for Himself (2:165). Nowadays, the rituals of divination and fortune reading are still popular even though they are contested and condemned by traditional theology (Raudvere, 2015: 224).

Muslim scholars have categorised *Shirk* in different ways. The greater *shirk* involves associating partners with Allah in those matters which are exclusively reserved for Him. In the terminology of Islamic jurisprudence (***Fiqh***) and theology, the implication for a Muslim who professes and indulges in *shirk* is to be excommunicated from the community. Should they repent and revert all is forgiven.

The Qur'ān dismisses the Christian belief in Trinity as it undermines the inner unity of godhead (5:17) and warns Muslim not to transgress the limits in relation to Prophet Muḥammad (ﷺ) as well, for he was human and not divine; even he is not to be petitioned directly. At its core, idolatry fails to appreciate the elusiveness and mystery that shrouds the divine face (Gwynne, 2018: 37). Similarly, during and after funeral prayers, actions which might be perceived as a representation of idolatry are circumvented (Gwynne, 2018: 136).

In the attempt to maintain and search original Islam, there exists opposition to what is deemed folk religion and local traditions. Historically, this has been a constant feature. The resistance can be articulated from both conservative standpoints and secular modernists (Raudvere, 2015: 151). For instance, some of the rituals connected with Sufi orders are prone to rejection, as they are perceived to be outside the fold of authentic teachings. Such criticisms do not necessarily come from the *Salafī/Wahhābī* positions and are not restricted to Sufism. According to a scholar, humankind becomes guilty of *Shirk* because they shun the teachings of the Prophets and rely on their own logic, false assumptions and biased interpretations (Mawdūdī , 2016: 66). Like *kufr,* there are two main categories of *shirk*; major/blatant (*jalīy*) and minor/subtle (*ḳhafī*) (Khan, 1994).

Case study 1.1 Creation story

Shamima was particularly interested in science and had opted for science modules to enhance her subject knowledge during her initial teacher training. She found her placement school, a two form entry, had had what she called a 'regimented' and 'tight' approach where there was little room for creativity and flexibility. After teaching in a couple of schools, she was appointed to her third school where she found creativity, innovation and autonomy were valued as part of their curriculum and ethos. She approached her deputy head and managed to acquire an incubator which she placed, with some eggs within, in her classroom for several weeks. In her science lesson, she explained to the pupils what she had done and asked what they expected to happen. With the exception of a few pupils, most of her 25 pupils would pass by it without much attention. Suddenly, one morning she noticed that the eggs had hatched. She anticipated considerable enthusiasm and got prepared for it. She decided

(Continued)

she would allocate 10 minutes for the pupils to absorb the excitement and make close observations of the little chicks. Some children courageously handled the chicks whilst others almost cringed. She was very impressed with the buzz. Once the pupils were satisfied she gathered them on the carpet and had a recap of what had happened. She then posed the question about which came first – the chick or the egg. She felt she could now move onto RE and teach them about Muslim beliefs about Allah and creation in Islam.

This case study reveals the different values and ethos in existence in a school. Shamima valued autonomy and flexibility.

- Consider the extent to which autonomy, creativity, flexibility and innovation are important to you.
- Reflect on the merits and potential challenges in using the method applied by Shamima to teach about creation.
- In Chapter 4 the story of the creation of Adam has been presented. Plan a lesson to teach the story to Year 3.

Summary

You have learnt that *Tawḥīd* is the belief in the Unity and Oneness of God and, for Muslims it is an organising principle in all walks of life. The antithesis of this fundamental belief is expressed through *Kufr* and *Shirk* which Muslims avoid. A detailed explanation about God has provided you with a clearer understanding about who God is to Muslims and what the relationship between humans and God is. You have also reflected on some of the beautiful names of God and how these influence Muslim spirituality. By examining three important chapters of the Qur'ān, you have understood the manner in which some Muslims use the Qur'ān and some of its themes.

Reflection tasks

- Analyse the concept and nature of *Tawḥīd* by drawing theological implications and considering how it affects Muslim life.

- How does knowing the names of God assist Muslims in recognising the nature of God and His relationship with the creation?
- How do you think Muslims might develop love of God?
- How and why might a Muslim avoid *Shirk* and *Kufr*?
- Identify the key themes in *Āyat al-Kursī*.
- How could you use *Al-Fātiḥah* to teach about Muslim beliefs and its significance in their life?

Further reading

Mawdudi, S.A.A. (2016) *Let Us Be Muslims* (new revised edn; K. Murad (ed.)). Leicester: The Islamic Foundation.

This is a highly influential book written by a leader of a contemporary movement. Originally delivered as sermons on Imān, Islam, the prayer, fasting, almsgiving, pilgrimage and Jihād.

Lawrence, B.B. (2015) *Who Is Allah?* Edinburgh: Edinburgh University Press.

This text offers how Muslims invoke, remember, define and debate Allah in seeking pietistic piety, including major facets of Muslim ritual life and intellectual traditions, both past and present.

2

THE WORD OF GOD

In this chapter you will:

- know some of the structural and organisational features of the Qur'ān
- understand the key beliefs held by Muslims regarding their Sacred Scripture
- reflect on how the Qur'ān is honoured and embodied in the lifeworld of Muslims
- become familiar with the sciences related to the Qur'ān
- examine a case study of a *ḥāfiẓ*.

Overview

Before you begin to consider the Qur'ān, it is important to recall that Muslims believe that there had been many messengers and revealed scriptures before Muḥammad (ﷺ) which will be covered in Chapter 4 and 5. In this chapter we will focus on the Qur'ān.

The Qur'ān is a bond between God and Muslims, and humanity in general. The word Qur'ān literally means 'recitation'. It is not always restricted to the written form as a book in existence today (Von Denffer, 2011). Some tend to refer to the written text as ***Muṣḥaf***. Religiously, it is a collection of the Divine revelation received by Muḥammad (ﷺ). For Muslims, the Qur'ān is a 'Light' which guides them from ignorance to knowledge and from darkness to enlightenment, simultaneously, it is a balm for spiritual ailments and social vices, which means that it is a manual for all walks of life.

The relationship between Muslims and the Qur'ān is multidimensional. Liturgically, it is recited during celebrations and solemn occasions such as weddings, funerals, religious and social gatherings, political campaigns and mourning. Aesthetically, it decorates their physical environments including their homes and streets with painted verses or wall frames just as it adorns their mosques, domes and minarets. Individually, you may notice some Muslims display specifically chosen verses, suiting their spiritual mood and emotions, as fridge magnets, car stickers and photo frames at work. They often listen to their favourite reciters on their way to work, whilst in the kitchen or at the gym. In the privacy of their homes and in a secluded corner of a mosque, you might also catch a glimpse of a devotee kissing the Qur'ān, out of love and sanctity, before and after reading it. It is often placed on an elevated position, though not necessary always on the highest shelf of a bookcase. Most will avoid putting anything on top of it, nevertheless. Thus they are connected to it so closely that it is everywhere in the world of phenomena (Ridgeon, 2009: 249). As a source of Divine blessings, spiritually, it is applied in warding off 'bad luck' and to exorcise evil spirits (*jinn*), sometimes in the form of amulets or by blowing on water to drink. Significantly, it is believed that its regular recitation cleanses the soul and heart from base characteristics and makes one become closer to God. Ontologically, the Qur'ān is the knowledge, language and point of reference to make sense of themselves, of God and of all else.

The Qur'ān in its own words

The Qur'ān refers to itself using a variety of terms which discloses its source, purpose, role and characteristics. Some Muslims infer from these names to suggest that Muslims are expected to imbue themselves with these descriptive characteristics. In class, it would be interesting to explore why it refers to itself as *the Qur'ān* and other titles. It calls itself:

- *al-Nūr* - the Light (7:157)
- *al-Dhikr* - the Reminder (15:9)
- *al-Tanzīl* - the Revelation (26:192)
- *al-Mubārak* – the Blessing (6:92)
- *al-Muṣaddiq* – the Confirmer of Truth (2:91)
- *al-Ḥakīm* – the Wisdom (54:5)
- *al-Ḥukm* - the Judgment (13:37)
- *al-Shīfā'* – the Healing (10:57)
- *al-Raḥmah* – the Mercy (7:52)
- *al-Ḥādī* - the Guide (17:9)
- *al-'Ilm* – the Knowledge (2:120)
- *al-Bashīr* - the Good News (16:102)
- *al-Nadhīr* - the Warner (41:4)
- *al-Muṭahhara* - the Purified (80:14)

Organisation of the Qur'ān

It is important to remember that the Qur'ān is not organised chronologically nor was it revealed in the order in which it is found in its current textual form. To appreciate the structure and practical usage of the Qur'ān in Muslim life, it is useful for you to become familiar with some essential terms. It should be noted, also, that some of these terms whilst universal, have local linguistic variations.

An *āyah* (pl. *āyāt*) literally is a sign or miracle of God and, technically, a single verse. *Sūrah* (pl. *suwar*), meaning 'enclosure', commonly denotes a chapter, of which there are 114 of varying lengths. Conventionally, these references are usually presented as *Sūrah* name: *āyah* number (Leaman, 2016). Each *Sūrah* is composed of verses and is organised approximately in descending order, with the shorter ones appearing towards the end, except for *Al-Fātiḥah*. Since the precise revelation of each verse is unknown, it cannot be organised chronologically (Mattson, 2013: 27). Nevertheless, it is said that the order of the arrangement of the *Sūrahs* (*Suwar*) was also revealed to the Prophet (ﷺ) (Mattson, 2013: 97). Each *Sūrah* shows the words 'Makkan' or 'Madinan' indicating ostensibly the period of the Prophet's life during which it was revealed; the majority of them in and around Makkah. All but one chapter begins with a *basmala*, meaning, the phrase 'In the name of Allah, the Entirely Merciful, the Especially Merciful.' This reminds Muslims about the nature of God and that these sacred words are an act of Divine mercy. Scholars have suggested there are some 6204–6236 verses – this range caused by the differing schemes of counting (Mattson, 2013) – and only 500 of these are about law (Rippin and Bernheimer, 2019).

Each chapter is titled based on a significant incident, verse, word, person, object and/or creature mentioned within the *Sūrah*. This facilitates referencing, learning and reading. Some have more than one title.

Table 2.1 Number and title of some *Sūrahs*

3. Al-'Imrān (The Family of Imran)	16. An-Naḥl (The Bee)	55. Al-Raḥmān (The Beneficent)
4. An-Nisā' (The Women)	17. Banī Isrā'īl (The Israelites)	62. Al-Jumu'ah (The Congregation)
5. Al-Mā'idah (The Table Spread)	19. Maryam (Mary)	63. Al-Munāfiqūn (The Hypocrites)
9. At-Taubah (The Repentance)	30. Ar-Rūm (The Romans)	68. Al-Qalam (The Pen)
12. Yūsuf (Joseph)	36. Yā Sīn (Ya Sin)	107. Al-Mā'un (Acts of Kindness)

For practical purposes the Qur'ān is divided in various ways, usually shown by symbols in the text or on margins. A *juz'* is a section, of which there are 30 to assist readers to complete it in a month. Another division is known as **manzil**, of which there are seven, perhaps to facilitate its completion in a week. A **rukū'** is a shorter segment to help with learning and reading in prayers. An *āyah* is a small sentence, *kalimah* is a word and *ḥarf* is a letter. Diacritical marks were a later addition to assist in its vocalisation both for grammatical accuracy and proficiency in elocution.

Key beliefs about the Qur'ān

The Qur'ān is not thought of being simply a 'book' in whose words Muslims have deep faith; such a view tends to omit the uniqueness of the Qur'ān in Muslim belief and life. To Muslims, it is the Divine law with words and sounds having perpetual existence. One of the attributes of Allah is speech, and therefore, the Qur'ān is God's eternal speech. The printed manuscripts, of course, are human products; but as Divine words, the content is eternal.

The Qur'ān is the final revelation from God to humanity revealed to the final Prophet Muḥammad (ﷺ) and it is believed to have remained exactly as received by the Prophet (ﷺ) through angel Jibrīl (Gabriel). This makes it unique in relation to other Holy Scriptures which were composed and revised by humans after the demise of their prophets and leaders. Significantly, you must know that the Qur'ān is not the work of Muḥammad (ﷺ) nor did he make any claims to its authorship. According to the Qur'ān, he did not speak from his own inclination but that it was a received revelation (53:3–4). The Qur'ān is not a history of Muslims either nor a record of the life of Muḥammad (ﷺ) (Mattson, 2013: 28). It is a text that is deeply concerned with the relationship between this world (*al-dunyā*) and the other world (*al-ākhirah*) (Lange, 2016).

Muslim scholarship has probed into the nature of the Qur'ān by questioning whether the Qur'ān is created or uncreated. The *Ahl al-Sunnah wal-Jamā'ah* orthodoxy considers it to be eternal and uncreated as it is the Word of God. However, some among the Mu'tazila considered it as created and separate from God; this was considered a deviant standpoint (Mattson, 2013: 145–147; Brown, 2017). The Ash'arite-Matūrīdī (*Ahl al-Sunnah*) standpoint finally triumphed and came to be considered orthodox as it was accepted by the majority of the community (Campanini, 2016: 14).

The revelation story

Prior to discovering the story of the revelation of the Qur'ān, it is useful to understand that the Arabic word '*waḥī*' is derived from the root word '*waḥa*'. It has many shades of meaning such as a divine indication or speech. In the parlance of Islam, it is defined as God's divine message conveyed in various ways to Allah's selected people to give knowledge of that which is beyond the physical realities of humankind. In the Qur'ān, *waḥy* is the technical term for revelation. (Buck, 2009: 22)

For several years, Muḥammad (ﷺ) habitually visited a cave known as Ḥirā, located some three miles outside Makkah. The Prophet (ﷺ) retreated here in solitude and meditation for many days, taking with him provisions, to engage in prolonged prayers, worship and fasting. As time progressed, he increased the duration of his solitude from days to weeks. In Ramaḍān of 610AH, when the Prophet (ﷺ), like other prophets, was 40-years-old, he sensed the presence of another being with him.

Angel Jibrīl instructed him: 'Read!' The Prophet (ﷺ) admitted: 'I am not a reader.' The angel pressed him hard, released him and repeated: 'Read!' The Prophet (ﷺ) replied: 'I am not a reader.' The angel pressed him hard for a third time and instructed:

> Recite in the name of your Lord who created -
>
> Created man from a clinging substance.
>
> Recite, and your Lord is the most Generous -
>
> Who taught by the pen -
>
> Taught man that which he knew not. (96:1–5)

As he had not been formally schooled, the Messenger (ﷺ) declared that he could not read.

This encounter would be the first in a long series which lasted until his demise. This initial auditory and visionary experience was, unsurprisingly, overwhelming. Once at home, he shared this experience with his wife Khadījah and close relatives who assured him and concluded that these were signs of being a prophet. These verses were to change the life of Muḥammad (ﷺ) and of Makkah and, eventually, the rest of the world.

The Qur'ān has some poetic features, metaphors and imagery. Labīd ibn Rabī'a was the greatest of Arabia's poets. Often, his poems were hung on the doors of Ka'bah as a sign of triumph. Peers dared to challenge him by hanging their verse besides Labīd's. The Prophet (ﷺ) was decried by the heathen Arabs as an magician and a deranged poet. A story is told that one day, some of his followers hung an excerpt from the second Sūrah of the Qur'ān and challenged Labīd to read it aloud. The king of poets laughed at their presumption. Out of idleness or in mockery, he condescended to recite them. Overwhelmed by their beauty, he professed Islam on the spot (Kermani, 2018: 1). It is not uncommon to observe contemporary Muslims cry out and weep whilst listening to the *qirā'ah* of the Qur'ān.

Modes of revelation

In addition to the above direct method, revelation came to the Prophet (ﷺ) through other modes. At times, it came from behind a screen or in the form of dreams; often it was infused directly into his heart or disclosed upon him as the sound of a bell, which was described by him to be the most difficult to endure, so much so that his brows would sweat and his face reddened. Commonly though, it was brought through Jibrīl who sometimes appeared in human form or in his true angelic form (al-Bukhārī, 1:2).

As noted above, according to its own testimony, the Qur'ān was revealed in Ramaḍān (2:185) during the Night of Power (97:1). However, Islamic history and the Qur'ān itself (17: 106) indicate that revelation took place in piecemeal over a period of some 22–23 years. The entire Qur'ān was revealed from the 'Preserved Tablet' (***al-lawḥ al-maḥfūẓ***) (85:22) to the earthly heaven on the Night of Power, and from there, through Jibrīl, it was revealed as needed over many years to the Prophet (ﷺ) in the earthly realm (Buck, 2009: 23).

It was revealed in parts to strengthen (Muḥammad's) heart (25:32) and to enable him to recite it to the people at intervals (17:106). A third wisdom is that, as the number of Muslims began to grow, they experienced different situations, circumstances and challenges, and so the Qur'ān was addressing these as they arose. In fact, often the Qur'ān was revealed in a direct response to specific questions, events, challenges and claims made both by Muslims and the wider non-Muslim community. The Qur'ān aimed to transform deep rooted customs, beliefs and ways of thinking and bring about a change in their moral, political, social, spiritual and religious facets of life. Thus, as a good teacher, the Qur'ān adopted a gradual and developmental approach. This method maintained a continuous dialogue between God, the Prophet (ﷺ) and the community with regular moral support, future successes and assurances being given to bolster them (25:106). Significantly, they witnessed revelation first-hand which heightened their faith and made it a reality.

Muslims and the Qur'ān

The parable of a believer who recites the Qur'ān and acts on it, is like a citrus fruit which tastes and smells nice, whereas the example of a believer who does not recite it but acts on it, is like a date which tastes good but has no scent. The example of a hypocrite who recites the Qur'ān is like a basil which smells good but tastes bitter and the example of a hypocrite who does not recite the Qur'ān is like a colocynth which tastes bitter and has a bad smell (al-Bukhārī, 6: 579).

As teachers you need to recognise that there are a myriad of reasons and intentions for the recitation and study of the Qur'ān. These offer a glimpse into the relationship that Muslims have with it. When they read it, some Muslims hope that it will intercede for them on the Day of Judgment (Muslim, 2:1757). The Prophet (ﷺ) promised that whoever recited a single letter from the Book of Allah, would have ten rewards for each letter (al-Tirmidhī, 5:2910). Hence, Muslims read it with the intention of increasing their rewards. Muslims believe that paradise has different gradations, about which you will learn in Chapter 5. One of the means of gaining a high stage in paradise is by reciting the Qur'ān as it will be said to its reciters: 'Read! Just as you used to recite it in the world and ascend; for you will find your place with the last verse you recite' (Abū Dāwūd, 1:1459).

In addition to these eschatological motivations, Muslims find solace and earthly benefits as well. For instance, spiritually, reciting and studying the Qur'ān affords them with being steadfast and firmer in their certitude (***yaqīn***). Peace and tranquillity (***sakīnah***) is said to descend when the Qur'ān is read in this world (Gade, 2009).

In Chapter 1, you read that *Al-Fātiḥah* is considered to be a cure. In fact, the whole Qur'ān is a cure for social and moral ills and spiritual ailments. Based on its spiritual message, some argue against the 'universality' of a culture of discrimination against women in all societies (Lamrabet, 2018). God sent it as 'a healing and a mercy for the believers' (17:82). Their hearts and souls find tranquillity and peace through it (13:28). Muslims who attach themselves with the Qur'ān join the various categories of chosen and special people of God (Ibn Mājah, 1:215). Importantly, it is a means of increasing their faith (*Imān*) and removing hypocrisy (9:124).

Some contemporary Muslims suggest it acts as an antidepressant which reduces sadness and distress in life and work, as in a supplication by the Messenger (ﷺ) he asks for the Qur'ān to be made the spring of his heart, the light of his chest, the banisher of his sadness, and the reliever of his distress (Ahmad, 3:3712). Since the Qur'ān claims to be a source of the knowledge of the seen and the metaphysical, some Muslims study it profusely to unlock the mysteries of God, the purpose of creation and to solve the problems faced by humanity. The ultimate aim, though, is to worship God through the Qur'ān. The Qur'ān is also evidence of the divine calling of Muḥammad (ﷺ) since it would be impossible for an illiterate person to produce such 'an exquisite and profound literary masterpiece without divine involvement' (Gwynne, 2018: 62).

Honouring and embodying the Qur'ān

The Qur'ān is the Word of God. As such, though it is often called a 'book', it is treated reverentially with the utmost respect and honour, as it is sacred and holy. When it is recited aloud, Muslims are expected to listen to it attentively and maintain silence to gain the mercy of God (7:204). Out of necessity, especially in crowded spaces in some communities, it may be placed on the floor temporarily, although such a practice would be rejected by most.

When reading it, many Muslims adopt a humble posture, generally by sitting on the floor facing the ***Qiblah*** with the head covered, lowered and in a state of ritual purity. Being sacred in nature, according to some scholars, anyone in a state of ritual impurity should not touch the Qur'ān (56:77–79; Ridgeon, 2009: 248; Sonn, 2009). It should not be carried below the waist or placed underneath other books (Brown, 2017). Some modernists who belittle belief in blessings (***barakah***) inherent in sacred objects place minimum, if any, restrictions on handling the Qur'ān by menstruating women, whereas Muslims, especially those following traditional schools of law and who have affinity with the sacrality of the text, tend to uphold prohibitions (Mattson, 2013: 164). In addition to other rituals, this is also the case among the Shīʿa (Momen, 2016).

Voice of a Muslimah

Qur'ān is full of messages to humanity. It teaches us how to be just, to understand other people that are different than us, kindness, helpful, respect each other, manage the time you have, be patient, charity, search knowledge, etc.... so many things. I normally put it in the bookcase together with other books but I have a section for Qur'ān. We will not put it on the floor while we are sitting. We normally have a small bench to put it or hold it on our lap when we read it. (Fāṭimah, mother, Indonesian, female)

Unlike the tendency of some modern and secular habits of thinking of a book in terms of conveying a message, it is worth appreciating that, since many Muslims do not understand Arabic, their experience of the Qur'ān is as an object of devotion and piety, a thing of beauty, and of spiritual value and power, independent of its discursive meaning (Brown, 2017). Hence it is kept close to their heart and memorised as such.

You might hear some Muslims uttering certain Arabic phrases as they go about their daily life, such as *In shā' Allah* (God willing; used when intending to do something), *Al-ḥamdū lil Allah* (praise be to God), *Subḥān Allah* (glory be to God) and *Mā shā Allah* (what God intends; usually to express surprise or success). These are examples of internalising the Qur'ān.

Exemplification of its contents

The life of a Muslim is meant to revolve around the teachings of the Qur'ān. Not only is it the basis of law providing guidance on matters such as marriage, divorce and inheritance but it is also a programme which promotes a life of virtue, piety and good human relations (Ridgeon, 2009: 248).

In the classroom a broader perspective on its content may be useful. The Qur'ān presents creation and life on earth as a revelation meaning that it implicates nature as part of a revelatory order. It talks at the biological level since Islam did not see any problem with science (21:30; 24:45). There are many verses which refer to geology, zoology, biology and astronomy. Verses of this kind in a religious text assist in explaining why Muslims enthusiastically embraced science in the Middle Ages (Saud, 2013a: 43). Ontologically, it claims to be a repository and exposition of all knowledge and human consciousness is expressed through its language.

The Qur'ān also contains guidelines to make ethical living possible among humans. In the absence of original sin, evil is a by-product of arrogance and ignorant choices made by humankind. It offers considerable provocations to facilitate a moral life as you will learn in Chapter 9. Simultaneously, the Qur'ān expects some practices to be performed which are designed to preserve spiritual integrity – commonly referred to as 'the Five Pillars' – which, in addition to the emphasis on reason, form the ascetic and social core of a Muslim's everyday life (Saud, 2013a: 47).

In general, the majority of *Makkan Sūrahs* are shorter and consist of teachings regarding the oneness of God, Afterlife and challenges to the beliefs and attitudes of the pagans, atheists, polytheists and idolaters. It also covers themes about Christian and Jewish scriptures and a critique of their standpoints.

The *Madinan Sūrahs* have edicts dealing with marriage, divorce, inheritance and criminal sanctions. Scattered across its pages, there are many historical events and stories of prophets of the past as sources of introspection. It has commands, parables and invitations to reflect on the purpose of life and the creation of the universe.

Preservation of the Qur'ān

One of the extraordinary characteristics of the Qur'ān is that it has been preserved not only in writing but also in the memories of thousands of individuals in every generation since its first revelation. This process began with the Prophet (ﷺ) himself and with many of those who were its first recipients. As soon as the revelation came, the Messenger (ﷺ) would hasten his tongue with its memorisation (***ḥifẓ***). God refrained him from doing this by promising that He would preserve it (75: 17) as it is also preserved in the '***al-lawḥ al-maḥfūẓ***' (The Preserved Tablet) (85: 21–22). It was indelibly inscribed in his heart (Buck, 2009: 23) and there were many scribes recording the revelation.

After a revelation, he would then recite and teach whatever was revealed to those around him, individually and collectively. In a mainly oral culture, these Companions (*Ṣaḥābah*) not only retained these verses in their memory but, with the scarcity of paper, they also recorded them on reeds, bones, stones, animal skin, bones, pottery, papyrus, parchments and other material (Buck, 2009: 23). They also practically implemented these verses and used them in their daily prayers (*Ṣalāh*) which aided their retention and understanding. Moreover, it was common for the Prophet (ﷺ) to listen to the Word of God from his Companions. In fact, during his last Ramaḍān, the Prophet (ﷺ) recited the entire text to angel Jibrīl twice; an act which inspires intense devotion to the Qur'ān in Ramaḍān for spiritual endeavours among contemporary Muslims as well. Consequently, a very large group (31) of these pious Companions, both male and female, had flawlessly memorised it in its entirety (Usmani, 2000). In the absence of printing press and widespread literacy, this was the most practical and reliable way of learning it.

In the second stage, Abū Bakr, the first *Khalīfah*, asked Zayd, a scribe of the Messenger (ﷺ), after the battle of Yamama where memorisers (*ḥuffāẓ*) had been martyred, to prepare an organised document with the collective endorsement of the community (Usmani, 2000). These transcripts remained throughout the period of 'Umar. When 'Uthmān became the third *Khalīfah*, Islam had spread to faraway lands. Since there were no dialectical variants in which the Qur'ān was recited by some of the Companions, people in these distant lands were learning to read the text in different ways. A concern developed that people might begin to declare their mode of recitation as the correct one. Hence, it was decided by 'Uthmān, with consultation of others, that a standard version should be adopted. This was to be based on the copy in Madīnah which was prepared by Zayd and whose custodian was Ḥafsah, the wife of the Messenger (ﷺ) (Mattson, 2013). Once a verified standard version was available, several copies were made and dispatched to various lands. Scholars tend to agree that the version in existence today was the official version commissioned by 'Uthmān and some Muslims claim that a copy of this exists in Madīnah and in Istanbul and Uzbekistan (Von Denffer, 2011). For this reason, some Muslims criticise a handful of people who discredit the Qur'ān and claim that the manuscripts are dated some 60 years after the Prophet's (ﷺ) death. Muslims respond by suggesting that prior to this it was received orally, practised, preserved in the minds of Muslims and in fragments until it was [fully] 'written down' (Ridgeon, 2009: 248). This would be unsurprising because the Arabs were renowned for their prowess in memorising large amounts of poetry, genealogy and names of animals. Ḥifẓ remains a continuous practice of Muslims.

The story of a *ḥāfiẓ*

A *ḥāfiẓ* (f. *ḥāfiẓah*) is one who has committed the entire Qur'ān to memory. *Ḥāfiẓ* literally means a preserver and guardian. *Taḥfiẓ* is protecting. Muslims believe that God is also *Al-Ḥāfiẓ* (15:9) – both of humans and of the Qur'ān – likewise, a *ḥāfiẓ* is a protector of the Qur'ān. Just as the Prophet (ﷺ) and many of his Companions had memorised it (Gaibie, 2017), all subsequent generations have been producing thousands of *ḥuffāẓ*; contemporary Muslims in all parts of the world continue with the practice of embodying the Qur'ān in their hearts. Memorisers are afforded a special status in the community out of respect for their accomplishment and for possessing it. It would not be an exaggeration to claim that it is the most memorised holy book in history. All Muslims are expected to learn to read the Qur'ān in Arabic and commit some portions to memory to enable them to execute prayers (*Ṣalāt*) properly and for liturgical purposes. Some children memorise it at home, at the madrasah or at Muslim boarding schools. There are many who memorised it whilst they were under ten.

Tafsīr – science of interpretation

Muslims claim, following the challenge of the Qur'ān itself, that it possesses the most eloquent and inimitable style of Arabic language that has never been paralleled. All translations are simply interpretations of its meaning and not the Qur'ān itself since it is 'sound' (Smart, 1992: 282). The Qur'ān is neither totally poetry nor fully prose. Some Muslims will readily inform you that it is not easy to understand the Qur'ān. It has content whose meaning may or may not be immediately clear to its readers and listeners.

Voice of a Muslimah

I started memorising the Qur'ān when I was in Year 9 and completed at 22. During this time I passed my GCSEs with flying colours. I then joined Sixth Form and studied history, government and politics, and maths which I also successfully passed. I enrolled in a university to read a degree in social sciences. I was also referring to the translation whilst I was memorising. This aided my memorisation as I could follow the stories and the themes. I also became familiar with the Arabic language. It is easy to learn new things but equally easy to forget, if not repeated. It makes you feel good when you remember it. (Hafṣah, researcher, British–Indian, female)

There are many sciences associated with the Qur'ān. The science of *Iḥsā'* involves counting the letters, words, sentences and other orthographic features. The first commentary was initially provided orally by the Prophet (ﷺ) and subsequently as ḥadīth and later generations based their commentaries on this. The term *tafsīr* is derived from '*f-s-r*' meaning 'to open', therefore, the science of the Qur'ān which deals with exposing and explaining the meanings of its verses is known as the *Science of Tafsīr* ('*Ilm al-tafsīr*). Within this science, another term is ***Ta'wīl*** (3:7). Some scholars suggest they are synonymous, whilst others think that *tafsīr* is the explanation of individual words whereas *ta'wīl* is about sentences. Others view *tafsīr* as the exposition of apparent meanings whilst *ta'wīl* explains their inherent interpretations (Usmani, 2000). In Shī'a belief there are many layers of hidden meanings in the Qur'ān which they attempt to uncover through *ta'wīl* (Steigerwald, 2009). Others attempt to decipher the meaning of some Qur'ānic references favouring equality (Lamrabet, 2018). On the other hand, some critics of Islam also look into the Qur'ān and stress selected parts and argue to show what is objectionable in the religion of Islam. Yet others use it to demonstrate long standing theoretical and philosophical issues (Leaman, 2016).

Briefly, some of the verses of the Qur'ān are clear to the extent that anyone knowing the language can easily understand their meaning; consequently the difference of opinion in such cases is very rare. Other verses are complex, ambiguous, legally intricate, and, therefore, they require much more than contextual information for their correct comprehension and application; thus, translations and mere knowledge of the Arabic language would be deemed insufficient. The Prophet (ﷺ) had severely counselled those who interpreted the Qur'ān insincerely without the prerequisite knowledge and merely relied on their personal views (al-Tirmidhī, 5:2950; 5:2951).

The *mufassirūn* (exegetes of the Qur'ān) have identified some of the sources of interpretation for the Qur'ān including: the Qur'ān itself, the prophetic traditions, sayings of the Companions, statements of their followers (***Tabi'ūn***), consensus (***Ijmā'***), Arabic lexicon, deliberation, deduction, common sense and knowledge of the causes of revelation (*asbāb al-nuzūl*) and of abrogation (*naskh*). Any person explaining the Qur'ān contrary to these or in conflict with another principle of Sharī'ah will have no credence (Usmani, 2000).

Over the years various kinds of commentaries (*tafāsīr*) have been written including those focussing on grammar and syntax, juristically orientated, spiritual dimensions, socio-ethical ideas, philosophical, historical, political and gender expositions. Since the Qur'ān exists for all times to come, every generation has produced commentaries relying on its knowledge and wisdom reflecting the needs and circumstances of the era to guide the Muslims of that time. These commentaries are a precious heritage in preserving the meaning of its Words and are the most significant works for understanding the Qur'ān which assist in contextualising and explaining it. As one of the most voluminous of Islamic literary genres, all generations of Muslims in nearly every Islamic land have consistently produced commentaries reflecting the outlook on fundamental issues confronting Muslim societies. This makes this genre a continuous record of what Muslims of different lands and different ages have thought on various topics, and, as such, *tafsīr* plays an important role in defining the religious outlook of Muslims (Saleh, 2017).

Tajwīd and *Qirā'ah* – the sciences of recitation

The sciences of ***tartīl***, ***tajwīd*** and *qirā'ah* deal with reading. Literally, ***tajwīd*** means to 'beautify something'. After the spread of Islam, especially among non-Arabic speaking people, Muslim scholars felt compelled to determine a set of rules that served as a reference point for these learners since dots and diacritical marks were initially absent. Therefore, *Tajwīd* aims to achieve the correct pronunciation of the Qur'ān and its subject matters are the points of articulation (*makhārij al-ḥurūf*), characteristics of letters (*ṣifāt al-ḥurf*) and other rules related to altering the sound of certain letters due to their position in the word. Muslims are expected to learn its proper articulation since local dialects of Arabic or individual ways of enunciation are impermissible (Gade, 2009; Gaibie, 2017).

Generally, children acquire this by imitating their teachers to know and practise how each letter sound is generated in the mouth and throat and where the tongue is positioned. When reciting, it is expected that they 'sound' it. The art of *tajwīd* assists Muslims to adopt a 'singing tone' as they enunciate each word. Significantly, Arabic grammar warrants the correct application of diacritical marks in pronunciation to avoid confusing, for example, the subject and predicate. Therefore, it is important for Muslims to know how verses are vocalised to avoid altering the meaning of the verse. Muslims adopt a melodious tone following the praise and encouragement of Prophet Muḥammad (ﷺ) to beautify the recitation of the Qur'ān (Ibn Mājah, 2:1342). At a higher sophistication, the most proficient ones may learn (*qirā'ah*) a valued and complex art form, which has seven or ten different modes of recitation. It is an honour for some Muslims who dedicate themselves to learning all seven and ten *Qirā'āt* (modes of readings) and to be linked through scholarly lineage (*sanad*) from contemporary times to illustrious personalities of the past who dedicated their lives to serve the Qur'ān (Gaibie, 2017). They are known as **Qurrā'**.

Calligraphy and art

Like the sound and embodiment of the Qur'ān which offers elements of identity, worship and psycho-spiritual benefits, over the centuries, these words have inspired visual contemplation and artwork in Muslim civilisation. Historically, various calligraphic styles developed to produce highly complex and exquisite handwritten and printed copies of the Qur'ān as sacred art and an act of piety and devotion.

Case study 2.1 The Qur'ān

Based on her own religious life experience, Ruth was fully aware of the significance of sacred scriptures in religious traditions. She was teaching about the Qur'ān to Year 6. Reflecting on her previous teaching, she had

(Continued)

detected that there existed some misconceptions among some children regarding Islam's holy book. She decided to address these first. Sensitive to her pupils, she felt a tactful and friendly approach would be most appropriate and more effective. Simultaneously, she decided to develop their talking and thinking skills. Using the interactive white board, she showed a few pre-prepared concept cartoons with some comments in speech bubbles. After reading these, using the think, pair and share strategy, she then invited the children to discuss their thoughts about the Qur'ān. She noticed that the speech bubbles in the cartoon acted as stimuli for her pupils to explore their own ideas and challenge each other's views about the Qur'ān. She went round listening and joined in their conversations. This technique of allowing children to question, listen and talk about their ideas had considerably reduced confusions, misconceptions and beliefs that they had previously held about the Qur'ān and sacred scriptures in general.

This case study highlights the importance of addressing misconceptions. There are many ways of doing this:

- think about two other strategies which you could use with different age groups
- reflect on the significance of addressing misconceptions before, during and after the lesson
- using a SWOT analysis identify the areas which you need to develop regarding your knowledge and understanding about the Qur'ān

Summary

In this chapter, you have analysed the major constitutional components of the Qur'ān. You have learnt that the Qur'ān is the Word of God which, as a final revelation, was revealed to the final Prophet Muḥammad (ﷺ). The Qur'ān is a dialogue between God and humanity and is a curriculum which has content related to their personal, social, moral, emotional, legal, spiritual, economic, political and aesthetic development. It has given rise to several religious sciences such as the sciences of *tajwīd, qirā'ah, ḥifẓ* and *tafsīr*. The impact of this comprehensive programme combined with the **Sunnah** is that Muslims try to follow its teachings in all walks of their personal and public life to keep them on the straight path.

Being a final revelation, you have become cognisant of the measures that have been taken for the preservation of its entire text; in turn, you have discovered how it has been transmitted, since it was first revealed, over the centuries in every generation. Linguistically and historically, the Qur'ān is a miracle in itself which was given to Muḥammad (ﷺ), among other miracles. This has led Muslims to claim that it is inimitable and has remained unchanged. As such, Muslims are expected to believe in its entirety without doubt otherwise a charge of disbelief (*kufr*) may be laid against them. As a sacred and holy scripture, in addition to its organisation, you have considered how Muslims honour and respect it, use it for worship, and how it is thought to be the most widely and frequently read divine scripture and a source of inspiration and guidance for Muslims all over the world.

Reflection tasks

- Describe what messages are conveyed to Muslims through the titles of the Qur'ān.
- Discuss the Muslim theology and attitude to the Qur'ān.
- Identify the benefits Muslims derive from reciting, studying and embodying the Qur'ān.
- Analyse the etiquettes adopted by Muslims to express love and sanctity of the Qur'ān.
- Critically evaluate the claim by Muslims that the Qur'ān has been preserved fully.
- Imagine you were teaching about the Qur'ān. How would you do this? What would you highlight?

Further reading

Mattson, I. (2013) *The Story of the Qur'an: Its History and Place in Muslim Life*. Chichester: Wiley-Blackwell.

An excellent scholarly text on the Qur'ān in the life and piety of Muslims and its impact on individuals, art, architecture, ethics, literature, culture, politics and important transmitters.

Von Denffer, A. (2011) *'Ulūm al Qur'ān: An Introduction to the Sciences of the Qur'ān*, 2nd revised edn. Markfield: The Islamic Foundation.

This has important features of Qur'ānic sciences such as Orientalists, compilation, translations, languages and reading. Useful to read such books first before studying the Qur'ān.

3

THE PROPHET OF GOD (ﷺ)

In this chapter you will:

- understand the terms *Sunnah* and *Sīrah*
- understand the concepts of obedience (*Iṭā'a*) and following (*Ittibā'*)
- know the significant events from the life of the Prophet (ﷺ)
- understand his status among Muslims
- consider how his life influences their behaviour.

Overview

To know and understand the Prophet **Muḥammad** (ﷺ) and the significant role that he continues to play in the grand scheme of God and in the life of Muslims, it is important to become aware of his life. This chapter offers some brief information about him.

The three main sources of information are the Qur'ān, ***Sīrah*** and *ḥadīth* literature. The *ḥadīth* literature consists of highly scrutinised narratives originating from the first community of Muslims who lived with him, observed his life on a daily basis and conveyed eye-witness accounts. As a corpus, this is commonly referred to as *Sunnah*, meaning 'conduct', 'practice' and 'method', covering all walks of his life. These have been preserved and collected as traditions, which you will study further in Chapter 10. His early biographical literature (*Sīrah*), compiled within about a century of his death, provides considerable details of his entire life in chronological sequence. Thus, the *Sīrah* refers to the genre of literature telling the life of Muḥammad (ﷺ) both as a historical person and as a prophet. The Sunnah and *ḥadīth* are mainly about how to live as a Muslim following the example of the Prophet (ﷺ); sometimes they are used interchangeably although among scholars technical distinctions exist (Brown, 2018).

The meticulous preservation of the Prophet's life was partly inspired by the declaration of the Qur'ān that the Messenger (ﷺ) is an excellent pattern for anyone whose hope is in Allah and the Last Day and [who] remembers Allah often (33:21). Thus, his example is considered the most beautiful example, which Muslims try to emulate.

Obedience to the Prophet (ﷺ)

Related to the above, there are two prominent concepts that you need to know so that the attachment that Muslims have to the Prophet (ﷺ) and the significant influence that he has on their way of life become apparent. The Qur'ān repeatedly emphasises his obedience (*Iṭā'a*): 'Obey Allah and the Messenger ...' (3:32; 5:92; 8:1). In many verses, this obedience has been required in parallel with the obedience to God. Thus, obeying the Prophet (ﷺ) embodies the obedience of Allah.

The second concept is 'to follow' (*Ittibā'*). Here again, the Qur'ān is unambiguous: 'Say, [O Muḥammad], "If you should love Allah, then follow me, [so] Allah will love you and forgive you your sins. And Allah is Forgiving and Merciful".' (3:31; 7:157; 12:108). Thus, believing in the Prophet (ﷺ) necessitates obeying and following him since he was sent as a guide and a universal messenger for the worlds. Muslims look into his life as an inspiring example of how to follow Qur'ānic guidance in every circumstance, regardless of how conditions change (Sonn, 2016). For you, as a teacher, knowing this is important, as you will better appreciate some of the behaviours and practices exhibited by Muslims from different cultural backgrounds.

Earliest sources

Muḥammad (ﷺ) delivered the revelation of the one true God to humanity. The annals of history prove that this prophet of Arabia fulfilled a role that united the responsibilities of an illustrious prophet, educator, reformer, statesman, father and husband (Gülen, 2006). Islam did not emerge in a religious vacuum. It ascended in some time more like a vortex wherein multiple faith traditions competed in the religious bazaar (DeLong-Bas, 2018). There were beliefs of many kinds and none.

Muḥammad's (ﷺ) message was rooted in religious belief but with the objective of achieving a profound moral, social, economic, and political transformation. In comparison to other prophets, for example, Abraham, Moses and Jesus about whom comprehensive knowledge is lacking and incomplete, the biographical accounts of Muḥammad's (ﷺ) life show that he is considered to be the first to live and preach in the full light of history (Largen, 2013). Historians, even some great critics of his biography and life, acknowledge that there is 'more information relating to his career than we have of his predecessors. His life by and large is not wrapped in mystery, and few tales have been woven around his personality' (Muir, 1923).

The main source of this biographical information is Ibn Isḥāq (85–151AH/704–767CE) who put forward the first biography which has been preserved through the classical version of the most important work of Ibn Hishām (d.219AH/834CE) (Crotty and Lovat, 2016). The most reliable information on his personality is the Qur'ān itself, as attested by his wife ʻĀishah. When questioned about his personality, she replied, 'His character (ethical and moral life) is the Qur'ān' (Abū Dāwūd, 1:1337) meaning that he implemented its teachings. However, you must appreciate that the Qur'ān is not about Muḥammad (ﷺ) and 'his life'; it is about God and humanity and events related to other prophets including Muḥammad (ﷺ) and His message. The careful documentation of his declarations and actions contributed in developing a tradition of social-scientific historiography (Saud, 2013a) as you will learn in Chapter 11. Moreover, since the Qur'ān was revealed during the historical context of his life, studying his biography is a fundamental part of understanding Islam (Saud, 2013a). You will now briefly learn about Prophet (ﷺ).

His birth and early life

Muḥammad (ﷺ) was born on 12 Rabīʻ al-Awwal 570/571, some suggest the 9th. He was the posthumous son of ʻAbdullah, a trader, and Āminah, who died when he was six. From his father's side, he descended from the house of Hāshim, among the Quraysh – the noblest of the leading aristocracy. On his mother's side, he was from the Najjār, a branch of Khazraj, a major tribe of **Yathrib** (later Madīnah). His grandfather, ʻAbd-al-Muṭṭalib, was a former custodian of the Kaʻbah and a leader of the Makkan confederation, who took charge of his upbringing when his mother died. After his grandfather died, his care was entrusted to his paternal uncle Abū Tālib. According to Makkan custom, he was handed over to a Bedouin foster-mother, Ḥalīmah, to be nursed (Salahi, 2002).

At birth, curiously, people enquired about the choice of **Muḥammad** as a name. His grandfather hoped that he would be praised on earth and by God in Heaven, for that is what it means (Salahi, 2002). Several names and titles are attributed to the Messenger (ﷺ) each alluding to a different aspect of his personality and together they enable devout Muslims to better understand his significance (Nasr, 1993:18). Although he belonged to the influential tribe of Quraysh, which should have guaranteed some privileges, as an orphan, he could not rely on family connections alone for social status and economic security. He proved himself through character and hard work (DeLong-Bas, 2018).

Voice of a Muslim

My eyes have not seen anything better than you. No woman gave birth to anything as beautiful as you. You were created free from all deficiencies. It is as though you were created as you wished. (Ḥassān **ibn** Thābit's [d.50AH/665CE] eulogy on Muḥammad [ﷺ], Ṣaḥābī poet, male)

His youth

As a boy, he accompanied his uncle Abū Ṭālib on trade caravans. During a trip to Shām (Syria), a hermit, Baḥīra, based on books he had diligently studied, recognised marks of prophethood on him such as the seal of prophethood. Baḥīra warned his uncle to protect him from harm (Brown, 2017). He grew up to be noble in lineage, reliable, a good neighbour and was removed from filthiness and corrupt morals, eventually becoming known as the trustworthy (al-Amīn) and truthful (al-Ṣādiq). He kept away from gambling, drinking, all things vulgar and the vice rampant around him. His excellent reputation attracted the attention of a wealthy businesswoman Khadījah, who employed him to trade as far as Damascus. On one journey, Khadījah's servant, Maysarah, observed two angels shading him as they travelled at midday. His trade and his character impressed Khadījah, a widow. So she proposed marriage. Her cousin, Waraqa, a Christian who was awaiting the coming of a prophet, approved of this and declared that the time of the expected prophet had arrived (Brown, 2017).

His family

There are different views among scholars about his family. Some suggest he had two sons, 'Abdullah and Qāsim from Khadījah, who died in infancy. Khadījah bore him four daughters: Zaynab, Ruqayya, Umm Kulthūm and Fātimah, whereas the Shī'a consider Fātimah as her only daughter (Gwynne, 2018). Other than Māriyah, the Coptic, from whom he had a son, Ibrāhīm, who died in his infancy, he did not have any child from any other wife. Muḥammad (ﷺ) did not take another wife until Khadīja's death (Cole, 2018).

His conflict resolution

Perhaps his first attempt to resolve conflict that historians record is known as *Ḥilf al-Fuḍūl*, a pact of chivalry (Lings, 2006) and an oath to resolve disorder within Makkan society. Later, at 35, he actually resolved a bloody conflict whilst rebuilding the Ka'bah. The different clans divided the task equally among themselves (Guillaume, 2007). Upon completion, a dispute arose regarding the resetting of the sacred Black Stone. All tribes claimed their exclusive right for the prestige. Some brought out bowls of blood and pledged to fight. After several days, a solution was proposed: the first person coming from the gate was to be the arbitrator (Salahi, 2002: 48). Next day, the first person was Muḥammad (ﷺ). People spontaneously accepted him as their arbitrator. After analysing the seriousness of the matter, he took a robe and placed the Black Stone at its centre. He then invited each elder from each tribe to hold the edges of the robe. Thereafter, everyone carried it to the Ka'bah and Muḥammad (ﷺ) set it in place. He settled a bloodshed and enhanced his reputation.

His city

Islam emerged in **Makkah**, a major commercial power in the region. Muḥammad (ﷺ) was growing up among city-dwellers rather than the desert-dwelling nomads. It was at the crossroads of trade routes between Africa, Middle East, China and Malaysia across the Indian Ocean and Mediterranean (Esposito, 2016). However, the monopoly of the wealthy and the injustices at all levels of Makkan society caused him much grief whereas in nomadic camps he observed generosity and goodwill. In Makkah, the wealthy reigned over the poor; the destitute were at the feet of the powerful; greed, selfishness and extortion ruled the markets; and infanticide was common. In his heart and mind, he was searching for answers to the religious, spiritual, social and moral crisis. Religiously, most people followed the old Semitic religion, with shrines and idols of various gods and goddesses, which they sometimes took with them on their journeys. As per the Qur'ān, they did believe in a 'higher' god, Allah (29:65; 30:33; 39:8). Some regarded angels as gods and intercessors whereas some tribes were Christian and Jewish (Esposito, 2016).

His call

After he received revelation at 40, he began calling people to the worship of the One True God, who was Merciful and Compassionate. Among the females were

Khadījah; his cousin 'Alī; his best friend Abū Bakr, a respected wealthy merchant; 'Uthmān and Ṭalḥah, well-to-do Makkans; and several poor citizens and slaves accepted this new faith. As soon as he went public, his fiercest opposition came from his uncles and near family, followed by the rest. At this stage he taught about the Oneness of God, Prophethood, resurrection, worship and purification of the soul – all these threatened the religious, socio-political and moral fabric of Makkan society.

His first revelation

Muḥammad (ﷺ) was born and lived among his people and over the years his integrity, trustworthiness and reliability was accepted by all. These qualities were in addition to his piety and love of solitude, for which he went out of Makkah to the Cave Ḥirā'. During one of his stays, according to Muslim belief, he started to receive revelation from Allah as narrated by 'Āishah.

The commencement of the Divine Inspiration to the Messenger (ﷺ) happened as good dreams, which came true like bright daylight. Then the love of seclusion was bestowed upon him. He went in the cave of Ḥirā' where he worshipped continuously for many days before he returned to see his family. He took food for his stay and returned to Khadījah. This continued until the day the Truth descended upon him. The angel came and asked him to read. The Prophet (ﷺ) replied, 'I do not know how to read.' The Prophet (ﷺ) added, 'The angel caught me and pressed me so hard that it was unbearable. He then released me and again asked me to read and I replied, !I do not know how to read." Thereupon he caught and pressed me a second time till I could not bear it anymore. He then released me and again asked me to read but again I replied, "I do not know how to read (or what shall I read)?" Thereupon he caught me for the third time and pressed me, and then released me and said, "Read in the name of your Lord, who has created (all that exists), created man from a clot. Read!" And your Lord is the Most Generous' (96:1–3). Then the Messenger (ﷺ) returned with the inspiration and with his heart beating severely. Then he went to Khadījah and said, 'Cover me! Cover me!' They covered him until his fear was over and after that, he told her everything that had happened and said, 'I fear that something may happen to me.' Khadījah replied, 'Never! By Allah, Allah will never disgrace you. You keep good relations with your kith and kin, help the poor and the destitute, serve your guests generously and assist the deserving calamity-afflicted ones' (al-Bukhārī, 1:3). When Khadījah took him to her cousin Waraqa, who had learnt to read the Gospels in their original language, Waraqa remarked, 'this is the Law (*nomos*) that was revealed to Moses' (Cole, 2018: 40).

His persecution

The new message challenged them to rethink and reject idol worship; it reminded them about the people of Noah and Moses and to return to the teachings of Abraham. Consequently, severe opposition grew because of the implications of the teachings of the Qur'ān. His followers began to be persecuted by his opponents – often they were their own relatives – making it impossible to live in peace and their torture was escalating. When the situation became unbearable for this nascent community, in the year 613CE he permitted a handful of Muslims to seek refuge in neighbouring **Abyssinia**, whose Christian king sympathetically viewed the message of Islam and declined to hand them over to their enemies from Makkah. At home, he was taunted as being soothsayer (***kāhin***, 69:42) and poet (*shā'ir*, 52:30).

His temptations

Persecution was failing, so the leaders of the Quraysh tribe sent a delegation to bribe Muḥammad (ﷺ) by offering to make him their wealthiest person, give him their prettiest daughters to marry, and also offering him to be their king, and to pay for his medical treatment should he be unwell – on the condition that he stopped his mission. As a person of principle, he rejected everything. They then proposed: 'We will worship your God one day and you worship our gods the following day'. Muḥammad (ﷺ) was not after material gain or political power, but as an advocate of truth, he also declined their offer of full partnership in governing Makkah (Salahi, 2002: 152). When their discussions failed, his uncle Abū Jahl promised to assassinate him. The following day, with a rock in hand, he walked to the Prophet (ﷺ) whilst he prostrated, but he could not proceed even as his supporters urged him. Upon enquiry, he told them that he had seen a fierce-looking camel, unlike any he had seen before, between him and the Prophet (ﷺ) (Salahi, 2002: 159).

His year of sorrow

The clan of Banū Hāshim protected the Prophet (ﷺ) so the Makkans boycotted them so that they would rescind their support. After about three years of hunger and suffering, the boycott failed. Soon Abū Ṭālib, the Prophet's (ﷺ) protector and uncle died and five weeks later another tragedy struck. In 620,

Khadījah his long-time supporter, comforter and the first one to understand his message passed away. In other words, in quick succession, he lost his internal and external supporters (Salahi, 2002). This resulted in some acts of public humiliation for the Prophet (ﷺ) whereby someone threw dust over his head at the instigation of his uncle, Abū Jahl, who later placed the intestines of a camel on his back as he prostrated in prayer (al-Bukhārī, 4:409; Salahi, 2002: 177). His neighbours tried to harm him too. This new situation led him to seek new avenues of support. He walked some 100 kilometres to a mountainous town called Ṭā'if. Here again, he was verbally abused, stoned by children and beaten so much so that he bled. He considered this one of his hardest days. At the command of God, angel Jibrīl appeared offering to crush the town (Salahi, 2002: 182). As he wiped blood off his face, he selflessly submitted: 'O God! Forgive my people, for they know not!' (al-Bukhārī, 9:63).

His Hijrah

Life in Makkah continued to be unbearable due to active persecution and hostilities especially for his followers. Initially, Muḥammad (ﷺ) sent some of his followers to Abyssinia where the Christian King gave them security. On the other side, the people of Yathrib (**Madīnah**), having received his message, invited him to settle there. His followers in Makkah began to escape from torture. He was among the very few remaining until God permitted him to leave, as the situation in Madīnah was safer. 'Alī, his cousin, remained in his house as a distraction, and Muḥammad (ﷺ) departed with his closest friend Abū Bakr. A bounty was offered for their heads. They were followed in this perilous journey constantly by their enemies but eventually reached Yathrib where some people hurried to offer them their home. The generosity was such that he left the decision of settlement to his camel, Al-Qaswah. Rather than accepting the place, he insisted on purchasing it, which then became his home and his mosque. The place became known as *Madīnat al-Nabi* – the city of the Prophet (ﷺ).

In Madīnah

In Madīnah, some 400km away from Makkah, the community began to be consolidated through the institutions of duties for themselves and rights for others; but they remained under the watchful eyes of the Makkans and local opposition, which was dormant when they first settled. The Qur'ān and the

Prophet (ﷺ) continued to nurture and train them in various ways to live as Muslims. Most of the Jews in Madīnah 'refused' to accept him as a prophet even though they were associated with his federation. They sometimes mocked parts of the Qur'ān and occasionally opposed the Muslims and so Muḥammad (ﷺ) expelled some of them from Madīnah. The hypocrites spread their mischief and behaved treacherously. There was fear and hatred in Makkah. In Madīnah it was different and more complex. It was a cosmopolitan city with different faiths, cultures and communities. Hence, the Prophet (ﷺ) was bound to face a variety of problems. Moulding the population of Madīnah into a united community could be achieved only through the force of faith, thus, the Prophet Muḥammad (ﷺ), who enjoyed God's support, was the only one able to achieve that unity at that particular time (Aleem, 2011; Salahi, 2002: 232).

His battles

Over the years, there were eight main battles and other skirmishes and expeditions. The Battle of Badr and also Uhud are considered to be among the most significant ones, as Divine intervention had been observed and these were successfully won despite considerable odds against them. There were many different causes and reasons for conducting these battles (***ghazawāt***).

Voice of a Muslimah

In terms of what the Prophet (pbuh) means to me: The Prophet (pbuh) is dearly loved and appears as a guide offering direction to my higher self. I performed Ḥajj in 2013 and was struck by the peace and tranquillity of Madīnah which permeated the city. I hadn't expected to like the country having heard so many awful things about it and so was pleasantly surprised by what I found. I visited the **Rawdah** frequently whilst there, and was privileged to stand and pray in the proximity of one so wonderful. The Prophet (pbuh) reminds me to be grateful for the many blessings bestowed on me, even through times of great difficulty, there is an awareness that others, including him, have maintained equanimity against all odds. I think his legacy is to remind us of our higher goals, to be loving to all of humanity, to be concerned with justice, the rights of the poor and oppressed and to approach life with compassion and mercy, and cultivate gratefulness and thankfulness. I think he embodies a unified approach to faith and religion which is encompassed within tawḥīd.

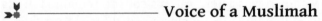

I feel blessed to have become a Muslim although only too aware of my frailties and human failings, and never quite sure of whether I can live up to what is expected of me by God. In terms of what the Prophet (pbuh) offers to humanity it is a personal programme for self-development and spiritual growth, one of community and societal improvement, a world-view that unites us and asks us to operate on the basis of love and concern for others, treating them well, as we would wish to be treated with dignity and respect, and trying to build a way of living that is inclusive and offers hope to all for the future, recognising the sparks of divinity that lie within each of us. We are all spiritual souls on a journey returning to God. (Munīrah, British citizen of an European Roman Catholic heritage, researcher, female)

His miracles

Miracles (*muʿjizāt*) have been a feature in the life of many prophets, like Moses and Jesus. Since his birth, authentic reports show miracles of various kinds performed by Muḥammad (ﷺ), sometimes at the demand of people. These manifested within the animate and inanimate kingdoms mainly to verify his claim to prophethood and God's existence. Thus, miracles served as psychological signs of prophethood (Azimabadi, 1993).

'Abdullah and others narrated that the moon had cleft asunder while they were with the Prophet (al-Bukhārī, 4:88); another report states that this was done following demands from some Makkans (al-Bukhārī, 6:390). The Qur'ān (60:1), related his miraculous night journey to Jerusalem.

Jābir reports that on the day of the Battle of **Al-Ḥudaybīyyah** people were thirsty and they approached the Messenger as their water-vessel had very little water. The Messenger (ﷺ) performed ablution. After that, he put his hand into the vessel and water began to pour forth between his fingers like springs. The people drank and performed ablution. They numbered 1500 (al-Bukhārī, Muslim, cf. Azimabadi, 1993: 29; *vide* al-Bukhārī, 4:779). On his marriage with Zaynab, Umm Salīm prepared a special dish and sent it to the Messenger's house. It was meant for a few people, but the Prophet (ﷺ) invited about 300 people. They ate it in tens at a time and the food remained unfinished (Azimabadi, 1993: 36–37). Once a shameless woman, who behaved like a child, asked for some food that God's Messenger (ﷺ) was eating. He gave her some. The woman insisted: 'No, I want a piece from your mouth.' He gave her a piece.

After eating the morsel, she became the most bashful and modest woman in Madīnah (Al-Yaḥsubī, 2011: 179–180).

A child, Muḥammad ibn al-Hātib, had been scalded. God's Messenger (ﷺ) touched his arm, spreading his saliva over it, and in the same instant he was healed (Al-Yaḥsubī, 2011: 179). At the Battle of **Khaybar**, 'Alī was suffering from ophthalmia. The Prophet (ﷺ) summoned him, applied his spittle and prayed for his success. His eyes were cured in no time (Azimabadi, 1993: 32).

His beloved city Makkah

In 630, Muḥammad (ﷺ) and the Muslims left from Madīnah with an army which by the time they reached Makkah numbered 10,000. There was obviously considerable consternation and fear among his enemies. To his army, he gave strict instructions that no blood was to be shed and not to fight unless attacked. As they entered the city, one of his Companions was heard as saying that it was a day for decisive war. However, the Prophet (ﷺ) had a different plan. Some of these people had divorced his daughters, mutilated his uncle, tortured his friends, boycotted his family, killed his followers and spread cruelty and barbarity (Mansoorpuri, 2002).

His mercy

Before entering Makkah he announced a general amnesty except to a few (Armstrong, 2007; Salahi, 2002). In fact, his arch enemy's house was declared a house of refuge. He was graceful, generous and merciful as that was what they expected of him. Consequently he won their hearts over.

His last sermon

In 632, Muḥammad (ﷺ) delivered his farewell sermon on 9 Dhūl Hijjah 10 AH (9 March 632) on Mount 'Arafāt. Being his first and last pilgrimage, it is a significant historical event and, today, the message is conveyed to Muslims everywhere. After praising Allah, some of his teachings include:

- The life and property of every Muslim is a sacred trust.
- Beware of Satan, for the safety of your religion. He has lost all hope in leading you astray in big things, so beware of following Satan in small things.

- You have certain rights over your women, but they also have rights over you.
- Worship Allah, perform prayers, fast, give alms and perform pilgrimage.
- All humankind is from Adam and Eve.
- No Arab has superiority over a non-Arab nor a non-Arab over an Arab; a white has no superiority over a black nor a black over a white except by piety and good action.
- Learn that every Muslim is a brother [sister] to every Muslim.
- Remember, you will appear before Allah and answer for your deeds.
- O People, no prophet or new faith will be born after me.
- I leave the Qur'ān and my Sunnah; follow these to avoid going astray.
- Those listening today pass on my words to others and they, in turn, to others again.
- Be my witness, O God, that I have conveyed your message to your people.

The discouragement and, for some, the prohibition of the visual depiction of the Prophet (ﷺ) stem from the centrality of monotheism. There are no known images during his lifetime as there is a fear that people will misunderstand such depictions and use them as icons or objects of worship (DeLong-Bas, 2018).

Death

In his final days, although his temperature rose high, he continued to lead prayers for 11 days. When he failed to stand, he sent Abū Bakr to lead 17 prayers (Salahi, 2002:800). On Sunday, he set his slaves free, gave away as a charity the seven ***dīnārs*** he owned and gave his belongings as a present to the Muslims. At night, his wife 'Ā'ishah borrowed some oil to light her oil-lantern. On Monday, the 12 Rabi' al-Awwal 11 AH, they performed the dawn prayer led by Abū Bakr. They were surprised to see the Messenger (ﷺ) raise the curtain of 'A'ishah's room. He looked at them in lines and smiled. He gestured to them to continue and went in. His pain intensified so that traces of poison he had at Khaybar became apparent. He then brushed his teeth, dipped his hands in water, and wiped his face. Then, raising his finger and looking upwards, he offered a prayer and breathed his last. On Tuesday, Al-'Abbās, 'Alī and others washed his body with his clothes on. They shrouded him in three white cotton cloths (al-Bukhārī, 2:361) and buried him in his own room. May God's peace and blessings be upon him.

His life vignettes

In both Muslim and non-Muslim circles, his character is an important factor, which attracts attention to Prophet Muḥammad (ﷺ). However, he himself claimed that God sent him to perfect good manners and do good deeds (Mālik, 2:1677). Some of his characteristics are discussed below so that you can supplement the historical information that is usually delivered in schools with these.

Educators, parents and others find in his life a model for positive human relationships. As a model father and community leader, Muslims look up to his kindness with children. They learn that he played with them to make them happy. Once he was out for a meal and Al-Ḥusaīn (his grandson) was playing in the street. The Prophet (ﷺ) came in front of the people and stretched out his hands. The child started to run here and there. The Prophet (ﷺ) made him laugh until he caught him, then he put one hand under his chin and the other on his head and kissed him, and said, 'Al-Husaīn is part of me and I am part of him. May Allah love those who love Al-Husaīn' (Ibn Mājah, 1:144).

In general, he smiled profusely (al-Tirmidhī, 6:3641). He cautioned people from being angry (al-Bukhārī, 8:137). He liked to make things light, easy, calm and not repulsive (al-Bukhārī, 8:146). Similarly, Muslims try to emulate his generosity. Of all people, he was the most generous in Ramaḍān and he was more generous than the strong uncontrollable wind (in readiness and haste to do charitable deeds) (al-Bukhārī, 1:5).

Muḥammad (ﷺ) is sometimes presented as a serious religious figure without a sense of humour. In contrast, his humour was dignified rather than demeaning. Anas, a close personal attendant for ten years, shared an example: once a man asked Muḥammad (ﷺ) for an animal to ride. He replied that he would receive the baby of a she-camel to ride on. Surprised, the man enquired: 'What would I do with a baby she-camel?' The Prophet (ﷺ) replied, 'Is there any camel which is not born of a she-camel?'

Another prominent personality trait was his modesty, never promoting any kind of vulgarity; instead, he was bashful and he encouraged modesty. He said that part of the teachings of the previous Prophets was, 'if one is not ashamed, then they would do whatever they liked' (al-Bukhārī, 8:141). This is taken as a principle to guide Muslims not only in their dress code but also, in conversations, achievements and material well-being where gratitude and modesty are kept at the forefront. He felt that whoever was deprived of gentleness was deprived of goodness (Ibn Mājah, 5:3687).

He gave value and dignity to females. He promised that anyone bringing up two girls till they came of age will be with him in the next world. He then joined his fingers to show proximity (Muslim, 4:6364). Subsequently, this statement, in part, refuted the contempt that some people had for females and, as such, not only did it make a huge attitudinal change at that time, but also, it continues to be used by scholars to challenge maltreatment of girls and to promote their education and care. Moreover, Muḥammad (ﷺ) showed concern for the whole society, especially for the less fortunate orphans and widows in particular. This and other such statements motivate charity projects and philanthropic activities among Muslims. Scholars are particularly sensitive in highlighting the need for the inheritance of orphans not to be usurped by surviving relatives.

Furthermore, as *Universal Mercy* (21:107), Muḥammad (ﷺ) expressed concern for animals, as creations of God. Muslims are taught that a prostitute was forgiven by God because she gave water using her shoe to a dog dying of thirst (al-Bukhārī, 4:538). Another woman was sent to hell because she left a cat to die of hunger (Muslim, 4:6638).

Moreover, some Companions, whilst on a journey with the Prophet (ﷺ), captured chicks of a bird. The bird returned and spread its wings. On return, the Messenger (ﷺ) asked who had caused it distress. He then asked them to return its young ones to it. He told his Companions that God had reproached an earlier Prophet for setting fire to a nest of ants (Abū Dāwūd, 3:5246; 3:5248). Muslims learn about the mercy of God and infer directives from this regarding the just treatment of animals for work and pleasure. He taught about public welfare, for example, a branch of a tree annoyed some people, so someone removed it, and for this they were admitted to Paradise (Ibn Mājah, 5:3682).

He was least concerned with material possessions; whatever he had was spent on others. History has recorded that he did not leave any gold or silver currency, or a slave, male or female, after his death. He only left behind his white mule, his weapons and a piece of land which he declared as charity for needy travellers (al-Bukhārī, 8:738). As the leader of Muslims, he died leaving very little showing the lifestyle he lived, which provides impetus to the pious and Sufi Orders to promote ascetic tendencies in life.

Loving Muḥammad (ﷺ)

Muslims believe that their faith is incomplete until their love for the Prophet (ﷺ) is more than their love for their children, parents and all humanity. In turn, no one can truly love Allah without loving His Prophet (ﷺ) who is designated the 'Beloved of Allah'. Muslims regularly participate and join in with God and the angels in sending salutations and blessings of peace upon him (33:56; 33:43). These salutations guide Muslims towards the characters and virtues of

Muḥammad (ﷺ). They hope for their sins to be forgiven and their life filled with blessings, grace, love and mercy from God. For some, this love is manifested in trying to follow his conduct and lifestyle in all personal and social matters. Muslims are often heard to say that the Prophet (ﷺ) lives in their heart.

Case study 3.1 Life of Muḥammad (ﷺ)

A teacher in a Year 4 class was aware that her pupils were soon going to leave for secondary school. The teacher wanted everyone leaving to know that all of them were special in their own way. This was important as some pupils, particularly those with specific education needs and disabilities, were often overlooked by a few pupils. The teacher declared to the class that each one had special abilities, talents, and different skills to excel in different ways. The children were asked to set up a 'profile' of their special characteristics so that they could all go to each other when they required any assistance. The teacher asked them to sketch an image of themselves with a costume and add a symbol. They were to list their top three special talents. The teacher collated all these and spread them on the three walls. The pupils were encouraged to use these 'profiles' and seek help from their peers. After a week, the teacher felt the class was ready to study a few lessons on the life of Muḥammad (ﷺ), what he means to Muslims and why he is considered to be the best model for them. The teacher was pleased as the pupils would learn from contemporary 'leaders' in their own class and a significant person in history.

You have been invited to make a class presentation at an inter-faith event.

- Reflect on what the key message of your class presentation might be
- Identify the core content that your pupils would deliver

Summary

In this chapter you have learnt that the life of Muḥammad (ﷺ) has been preserved in considerable detail covering all aspects of his personal and social life. This has been done both in practice and in literature so that Muslims are able to obey and follow him as a guide and model. You have also noted that Islam emerged from his life and experience; this has been both positive and challenging. His community accepted his trustworthiness and truthfulness prior to revelation. However, once he began to teach *Tawḥīd* and what it implied he and his followers faced persecution, which forced them to leave Makkah and settle in Madīnah. There the community flourished. He continued to receive revelation, which moulded the society, and after ten years, he passed away.

Reflection tasks

- Analyse the means and reasons for preserving the life history of Muḥammad (ﷺ).
- Evaluate the significance of the concepts of obedience (Iṭāʻa) and 'to follow' (Ittibāʻ) for Muslims.
- Discuss the relevance of the story of the Hijrah.
- Identify some miracles to use to teach about Muslim faith and Muḥammad (ﷺ).
- Evaluate the relevance of the life of Muḥammad (ﷺ) for Muslims and non-Muslims.
- Examine the life of Muḥammad (ﷺ) and create a character profile based on universal values.

Further reading

Nadwi, A.H.A (2014) *Prophet of Mercy*. London: Turath Publishing.

A translation of a comprehensive and scholarly work wherein the author addresses the modern mind-set and sensibilities. He used modern methods of research and discourse making the contents effective.

Ramadhan, T. (2009) *In the Footsteps of the Prophet: Lessons from the Life of Muhammad*. Oxford: Oxford University Press.

The book is by a leading contemporary thinker highlighting the ethical and spiritual teachings from the life of the Prophet with a focus on the significance of his example for some of the most controversial issues in the modern world. It is written for a wider audience.

4

THE STORIES OF PROPHETS

In this chapter you will:

- know and understand the role of stories in the Qur'ān
- learn about some important prophets and messengers in Islam
- consider the central beliefs about God held by these significant people
- reflect upon the key messages and main themes in these stories.

Overview

The Qur'ān frequently uses stories, parables, similes and allegories for a variety of purposes. Stories of early messengers are scattered throughout its pages and play an important role in conveying its messages including the unity of God, God's triumph and the continuity of God's message. The stories are not extensive but mainly summaries delivering the religious–moral point directly within the central message of Islam. For Muslims, these stories are not fairy tales and were revealed to Muḥammad (ﷺ), in part, to support his prophethood as he did not have access to unseen information, which was occasionally demanded by his adversaries. These primarily didactic stories also transmit reminders and warnings for Muslims to keep on the path of truth (*ḥaq*) regarding matters of life and spirituality. They are also warnings about the avoidance of errors of past nations. Significantly, they address the meaning and purpose of life: Where did I come from? Why am I here? Where am I going? Not only do they preach moral lessons to those who ponder, but they also motivate Muslims to attend to important matters. The inclusion of these stories is also considered an act of kindness to humanity as these prophets guided people towards that which was best for them. The syllabi taught to Muslim children worldwide consist of most of these stories.

According to the Qur'ān no narration was invented within it and it is a confirmation of what was before it and a detailed explanation of all things, and guidance and mercy for a people who believe (12:111).

As teachers, you need to know that much of the Qur'ān is devoted to prophets other than Muḥammad (ﷺ). The line of prophets ensured an uninterrupted communication with God and creation so that no nation could claim not to have heard from God (Wills, 2017). Among the Shī'a there is the idea that each prophet is accompanied by an Imām (Amir-Moezzi and Jaambet, 2018). There are at least 25 figures mentioned as being chosen by God as messengers (Mattson, 2013: 197). Yūsuf (Joseph) is the most cohesive narrative whereas others are scattered (Nickel and Rippin, 2008). In so doing, the Qur'ān encapsulates much of the sacred history that precedes it. The Qur'ān mentions that prophets were sent in different languages with the same message. There are stories about the struggles between good and evil and are narrated not with a view to historicity in the modern sense (Lumbard, 2015). Stories are presented non-chronologically and incomplete. Muḥammad (ﷺ) was informed about some messengers but not all (4:164). These stories demonstrate that to be God's envoy is to be mistreated and misunderstood, and the narratives of the endurance of previous messengers indirectly confirm Muḥammad (ﷺ) as being one of them (Kaltner and Mirza, 2018).

As you will read in Chapter 5, Muslims are required to have faith in all of them (2:177; 4:162). The Qur'ān mentions that the prophets and angels will intercede on behalf of believers on the Day of Judgement (20:109; 53:26). It is through them that part of God's mercy will manifest. The most prominent intercession will be conferred to the final Prophet Muḥammad (ﷺ) due to his praised station (17:79). It is common practice among Muslims to invoke blessings of peace after mentioning their name as a mark of respect and to show reverence.

There are other non-prophetic stories such as the Companions of the Cave (***aṣḥāb al kahf***, 18:9–26), the story of the person with two gardens (18:32), the mother of Mūsā (20:37–40; 28:7–14), **Dhū al-Qarnayn** and Gog (**Ya'jūj**) and Magog (**Ma'jūj**) (21:95–97; 18:83–98). The disciples of Jesus (**Ḥawāriyyūn**) (3:52; 5:111–115; 6:14), Eve (Ḥawwā') – though she is not mentioned by name (2:34–39; 7:19–25; 20:115–122) – and **Qābil** and **Hābil** (5:27–31) also feature. These are applied to make arguments and re-orient peoples' priorities and direction. Muslims derive much guidance from these verses about dealings with people. Mary is the only female after whom a chapter is named (Ibn Kathīr, 2011) and as with the male stories, this serves didactic purposes. 'The inclusion of positive and negative female and male characters indicates the broad human, rather than gendered, capacity of agency and choice' (DeLong-Bas, 2018: 219) and emphasises that each person will be held responsible for their own actions.

Characteristics

These stories portray some of the expected qualities and values of human beings in Islam, and as such, Muslims try to inculcate these and nurture them in their children. A synthesis of their main characteristics and disposition as reflected in the Qur'ān is presented in Table 4.1.

Table 4.1 Cumulative characteristics

Benefactors	Chaste	Compassionate	Deep concern for the people	Devoted to God
Eminent	Faithful	Forbearing	Gentle to the people	Given knowledge, wisdom and judgement
God-fearing	Good example	Glorify God	Grateful	Great character
Firm against the faithless	Honoured in the world and the Hereafter	Heart strengthened by God	Humble before God	Kind and considerate
Mercy to all the inhabitants of the world	Most kind and merciful to the faithful	Near to God	Noble	Obedient
Patient	Penitent	Pious	Pleasing to their Lord	Pure
Purified	Quick in performing good works	Righteous	Strong	Submissive to God
Tender-hearted	Trust in God	Trustworthy	Truthful	Upright

In Chapter 3 you read about the life of Muḥammad (ﷺ). In the section below, some edited and selected stories are presented. As you read them, you may want to consider how you would use them in your teaching.

Ādam

God announced to the angels the creation of a human being from clay. Since angels praise God, they asked why humans who would cause corruption and shed blood were being created. In defence of humanity, Allah declared that He knew what they did not. Thereafter, Allah taught Ādam the names of everything and asked them to name them. They realised their ignorance and so praised God and accepted that they did not know except what God had taught them as God is All-Knowing, the Wise. Allah invited Ādam to inform them. After informing them, Allah reminded them that He knew the unseen of the heavens and the earth and what they reveal and conceal.

Ādam and his wife were then told to dwell in Paradise and eat in ease and abundance from wherever they willed. They were instructed not to approach a tree, lest they became among the wrongdoers. Importantly Allah warned, 'O Ādam, this is an enemy to you and to your wife. Let him not remove you from Paradise otherwise you would suffer' (20:117). In Paradise, they were not hungry, unclothed, thirsty or hot. Later, Satan whispered, 'O Ādam, shall I direct you to the tree of eternity and possession that will not deteriorate?' (20:120). He misled them by alleging that God forbade them from the tree to prevent them becoming angels or immortal. He swore that he was their sincere advisor. Eventually, through deception, they tasted the tree and their private parts became apparent to them. They then began to cover themselves with the leaves of Paradise.

Ādam disobeyed his Lord and forgot. So, God reminded them, 'Did I not forbid you from that tree and tell you that Satan is your clear enemy?' (7:22). God then advised humanity not to let Satan tempt them just as he removed their parents from Paradise and stripped their clothing to show them their private parts and that Satan and his tribe see them from where they do not see them. Thereafter, Allah sent all of them down to earth to settle for a time as enemies to one another. Ādam then received some words of repentance from his Lord. His Lord accepted his forgiveness and guided him, since Allah is Accepting of repentance, the Merciful. Moreover, God promised that whosoever followed His guidance when it came to them would neither go astray in the world nor suffer in the Hereafter and whoever turns people away from His remembrance will have a distressed life.

- Discuss the key themes of the story of Adam.

Iblīs (Satan/Shayṭān)

To live on earth, Allah allowed humankind to eat from the good and lawful things and not follow the footsteps of Satan. As a clear enemy, Satan orders people to evil, immorality and to say about Allah what they do not know. Satan also threatens the children of Adam with poverty while Allah promises forgiveness and bounty. At the same time, Satan makes false promises and arouses desire in humans. Unfortunately, Satan does not promise anything except delusion.

After creating Ādam, Allah said to the angels, 'prostrate to Adam'. They prostrated, except for Iblīs who did not prostrate and declared, 'Never would I prostrate to a human whom You created out of clay' (15:33). Then Allah ordered Satan to descend from Paradise as it was inappropriate to be arrogant therein. Satan was cursed until the Day of Recompense. Iblīs pleaded to be reprieved until the Day of Resurrection. Allah granted reprieve as requested. After that, Iblīs claimed that since God had put him on earth in error, he would make disobedience attractive to humans and would mislead all of them.

Moreover, Iblīs made a challenge to Allah saying, 'Do You see this one whom You have honoured above me? If You delay me until the Day of Resurrection, I will surely destroy his descendants, except for a few.' Allah responded by warning, 'Go, for whoever of them follows you, indeed Hell will be the recompense of you' (17:63). Then Satan explained his plan promising to sit in wait for them on Allah's straight path. He said he would come to them from the front, behind, right and left and, as a result, God would not find most of them grateful except some of His chosen servants. Then, Allah ordered him to go out of Paradise and warned that whoever follows him will be filling Hell. Finally, Allah declared that the path of return to Allah is straight and Iblīs would not have authority over the true servant except those who follow him from the deviators.

To help humans, Allah taught that if Satan induces an evil suggestion, then they should seek refuge in Allah. Indeed, Allah is the Hearing, the Knowing. Allah also declared that whoever was blinded from the remembrance of the Most Merciful would have a devil appointed to be their companion. The devils would avert them from the way of guidance while they think that they are rightly guided. On the Day of Resurrection, Satan will speak, 'Allah had promised you the promise of truth. I promised you, but I betrayed you. I had no authority over you except that I invited you. You responded to me. So do not blame me; but blame yourselves. I cannot help you nor can you help me. Indeed, I deny your association of me with Allah. Indeed, for the wrongdoers is a painful punishment' (14:22).

- Identify the different ways through which Satan diverts people from God.

Ibrāhīm (Abraham)

The story of Ibrāhīm shows that he advised his father not to take idols as deities and that he saw him and his people in error. God had also shown Ibrāhīm the realm of the heavens and the earth to make his faith certain. One night, Ibrāhīm observed a star and declared, 'This is my lord.' However, when it set, he said he did not like those that disappeared. When he saw the moon rising, he declared again, 'This is my lord.' Like the star, the moon also disappeared so he admitted that unless God guided him, he would be among the people gone astray. Later, he looked at the sun rising and he announced, 'This is my lord; this is greater' (6:76–78). In the evening, when it set, he absolved himself from idolatry and what his community associated with Allah and turned himself toward He who created the heavens and the earth. Thereafter, his community started arguing with him. Ibrāhīm questioned why they were arguing with him concerning Allah, who had guided him. He told them that he was not afraid of those things which they associated with Allah and that he would not be harmed unless his Lord willed. He also responded by asking why he should fear what they associated with Allah while they did not fear the fact that they had associated with Allah something for which He had not sent down any authority. He then challenged them by asking which of the two parties had more right to security, if they knew; those who believed and did not mix their belief with injustice or others.

Ibrāhīm asked his father why he worshipped that which did not hear, see and benefit him at all. He informed his father that there had come to him knowledge which he did not have, and therefore, he should follow him. He also said, 'O my father, do not worship Satan. Indeed Satan has ever been, to the Most Merciful, disobedient.' Moreover, he informed his father that he feared a punishment from the Most Merciful would touch them and they would be accompanying Satan. His father warned him that he would stone him if he did not stop. Thereafter, Ibrāhīm said, 'Peace will be upon you. I will ask forgiveness for you of my Lord. Indeed, He is ever gracious to me. I will leave you and those you invoke other than Allah and will invoke my Lord. I expect that I will not be in invocation to my Lord unhappy' (19:48). So Ibrāhīm left them and those they worshipped other than Allah.

- Summarise the arguments presented by Ibrāhīm to express his belief and worship of One God.

Lūṭ (Lot)

After the angels gave Abraham and his wife the good news of a son, they informed him about the destruction of the city where Lūṭ resided. Abraham, being one who was forbearing and frequently turning to God, pleaded and argued against it. Thereupon, the angels told him to give up his plea as the command of his Lord had come.

Lūṭ declared to his people that they were committing an immorality which had not been preceded by anyone in the world. He reminded them that they approached men with desire instead of women and were leaving what their

Lord had created for them as mates. He told them that they were transgressing and behaving ignorantly. In defiance, they told Lūṭ if he did not stop then they would evict him. Lūṭ replied saying that he detested their deeds. As a result, his people announced the eviction of Lūṭ and those who followed him and declared that they were men who kept themselves pure. Some of his people came hastening to him who had been doing evil deeds. Lūṭ counselled them saying that they obstructed the road and committed evil in their meetings. The people did not pay heed and declared that he should bring the punishment of God, if he were truthful. Lūṭ prayed to God to support him against his corrupting people. Lūṭ also spoke with his people explaining that he was not asking for any payment from them and that his payment was only from the Lord.

When the angels came to Lūṭ, he was distressed. He offered to his people his daughters who he said were purer for them and reminded them to fear God and not to disgrace him among his guests. He pleaded with them to reason but they responded by insisting that they had no concern over his daughters and that he knew what they wanted. Thus, the people of Lūṭ denied him and disputed his warnings. The angels informed him that they were messengers of his Lord, and so the people would not get to them. Then, the angels stated that they had come regarding the matter which the people had been disputing. They told him to set out with his family during the night and not to let anyone look back, except his wife, who would be struck as well. Lūṭ supplicated, 'My Lord, save me and my family from [the consequence of] what they do.' Therefore, God saved them and conveyed to him the decree of the matter and that they would be eliminated by early morning.

God declared that, indeed they were, in their intoxication, wandering blindly (15:72). So the shriek seized them at sunrise (15:73) and God made the highest part of the city its lowest and rained stones upon them (11:82; 27:58). Indeed, in recalling this event there are signs for those who discern. These ruined cities are situated on an established road. Therein are signs for the believers. And those who passed by them in the morning and at night, were asked to reason.

- Discuss the impact of Lūṭ's admonition on the interpretation of the story.

Y'aqūb (Jacob) and Yūsuf (Joseph)

One night Yūsuf saw 11 stars, the sun and the moon prostrating to him in a dream. His father, Y'aqūb, advised him not to relate the dream to his brothers as he feared they would contrive a plan against him. He also reminded him that

Satan was a manifest enemy. He reassured him that Allah had chosen him and would teach him the interpretation of dreams.

One day, one of Yūsuf's brothers said that Yūsuf and his brother (Binyāmīn) were more beloved to their father than them. Thus, they felt their father was in error. A proposal was made to kill Yūsuf or to cast him out to another land. In so doing, the countenance of their father would become exclusive for them and, after that, they could be a righteous people. A speaker among them suggested against killing Yūsuf and to throw him into a well so that travellers would find him there.

After devising a plan, they asked their father to entrust them with Yūsuf as they were his sincere counsellors. They requested him to send Yūsuf with them so that he could eat well and play, and they would be his guardians. However, Y'aqūb was worried and informed them that he would be saddened if they should take him. He told them that he feared a wolf would eat Yūsuf while they were unaware. They retorted by saying how would a wolf eat him when they were a strong clan. They placed him in a well and came to their father at night, weeping. They announced, 'O our father, indeed we went racing each other and left Yūsuf with our possessions, and a wolf ate him. But you would not believe us, even if we were truthful.' They showed his shirt with false blood. Thereupon, Y'aqūb said that their souls had enticed them to do something, and, therefore, patience was most fitting for him.

Some travellers came and let down a bucket. Suddenly one of them shouted, 'Good news! Here is a boy.' The travellers concealed him and took him as merchandise. Allah was aware of what they were doing. Yūsuf was sold for a reduced price. The person from Egypt who bought him said to his wife, 'Make his residence comfortable. Perhaps he will benefit us, or we will adopt him as a son.' Thus, in this way Allah established Yūsuf in the land to teach him the interpretation of events. When Yūsuf reached maturity, Allah gave him judgment and knowledge. He later became a leader in Egypt. This is how Allah rewards the doers of good. Years later there was a drought in Egypt and his brothers came for assistance. Yūsuf gave them grains and other provisions without telling them who he was. They told him they had left another brother, Binyamīn, with their father. Yūsuf asked for him to be brought as well. When Binyamīn joined Yūsuf, he revealed his true identity to him and then to his other brothers, who were very sorry for what they had done to him. Yūsuf forgave them and asked them to return home and bring their parents to Egypt. When they arrived, all 11 brothers and the parents fell in prostration to Yūsuf. At this point Yūsuf informed his father that this was the interpretation of the dream he had seen as a child.

- Evaluate the potential of this story for character development.

Voice of a Muslimah

These stories help us illustrate complex problems and scenarios in a more easy to understand way. I don't have a favourite prophet; I can't wait to meet all of them in Jannah InshaaAllah! There's so much to learn from the stories of the prophets. Mūsā put up with a lot from his people and he still had patience and stuck by them. Yūsuf went to prison unjustly – that's particularly relevant for us in recent times. The amazing thing is, you might read one part of a story at different times and get two different morals from it depending on your situation. I think that's what's miraculous about the Qur'ān and the stories of the prophets. (Firdaus, Mauritian, language tutor, female)

Mūsā (Moses) and Al-Khiḍr

Mūsā is most frequently mentioned in the Qur'ān. There are many stories from his life. He was out in search of someone who had been granted knowledge so that he could learn from him. On his way, he told his boy-servant that they would travel until they reached the junction of the two seas or keep walking. When they reached that junction, they forgot their fish, which slipped away through the sea as if in a tunnel. After having walked further Mūsā requested their morning meal as they were suffering from fatigue. The boy recalled that they had forgotten it when they rested by the rock and that Satan had made him forget. The fish had taken its course into the sea in a strange way. Mūsā remarked: 'That is what we have been seeking.' So they went back retracing their footsteps.

Later, they found a person identified as **Al-Khiḍr** who had been bestowed with mercy and knowledge by Allah. Mūsā asked if he could follow him so that he could be taught something of the knowledge which he had been taught. He told Mūsā that he would not be able to have patience with him and how can he have patience about something which he did not know? Mūsā admitted that if Allah willed, he would find him patient and he would not disobey him. He (Al-Khiḍr) agreed on the condition that Mūsā was not to ask him about anything until he mentioned it himself. They both proceeded and embarked on a ship. He (Al-Khiḍr) scuttled it. Suddenly, Mūsā asked: 'Have you scuttled it in order to drown its people? You have committed a "bad" thing' (18:71). He (Al-Khiḍr) reminded Mūsā that he had been warned about not having patience. Mūsā apologised and pleaded not to be held to account for his forgetfulness and not to be hard upon him. They continued and met a boy. He (Al-Khiḍr) killed him. Mūsā queried why he had killed an innocent person which was a great prohibition. He (Al-Khiḍr) repeated that he had been warned about not having patience. Mūsā pleaded once more saying if he asked him anything after this, they could part company as he had received an excuse from him. Both proceeded until they came to a town and asked for food. The people refused to entertain them. As they walked, they found a wall about to collapse so he (Al-Khiḍr) set it up straight. At this point, Mūsā suggested that if he had wished, he could have taken a wage for it. He (Al-Khiḍr) then declared that they had to part and would tell him the interpretation of those actions over which Mūsā was unable to be patient.

The ship had belonged to poor people working in the sea and he wished to make it look defective since there was a king who seized every ship by force. The boy's parents were believers and it was feared that the child would later oppress them through rebellion and disbelief. The boy was replaced with another child who was more righteous and near to mercy. As for the wall, it belonged to two orphans in the town and beneath it was a treasure belonging to them. Their father was a righteous man and Allah intended that the orphans should attain their age of maturity and strength and then their treasure would be taken out as a mercy from Allah. He told Mūsā that he had not carried out these actions of his own accord.

- Discuss the nature of knowledge and the plan of God for people.

Qārūn (Korah)

Qārūn was a tyrant from the community of Mūsā. God had blessed him with so many treasures that the keys to these treasures required a whole band of strong men to carry them. One day his people advised him not to boast because God does not like the exultant. They also suggested that he should seek, through the wealth God had given, the home of the Hereafter. They proposed that he should do good just as God had done good to him and not to cause corruption as Allah does not like corrupters. Arrogantly, he claimed, 'I was only given it because of the knowledge I have' (28:78). But Qārūn did not know that Allah had destroyed before him generations of those who were greater than him in power and greater in the accumulation of wealth.

He came out before his people in his adornment. Those who desired the worldly life exclaimed, 'Oh, if only we had what was given to Qārūn. He is one with great fortune' (28:79). However, those people who had been given knowledge said that the reward of Allah is better for those who believe and do righteousness and no one is granted the reward of Allah except the patient. Then Allah caused the earth to swallow him and his home. There was no one to help him other than Allah nor could he defend himself. Those who had wished for his position and wealth the previous day, began to say, 'Oh, how Allah extends provision to whom He wills of His servants and restricts it! If Allah had conferred favour on us, then, He would have caused it to swallow us as well. Oh, how the disbelievers do not succeed!' (28:82).

Allah destroyed Qārūn, Pharaoh and Haman (Ar. Hāmān); Mūsā had come to them with clear evidences but they were arrogant and could not outrun the punishment. So each one was seized for their sin (29:39–40).

- Identify the main lesson from the story of Qārūn (Korah).

Sulaīmān (Solomon)

Solomon inherited David. He had control of the wind and a spring of liquid copper flowed for him. He had also been taught the language of birds. His soldiers included jinn, people and birds. One day, Solomon found the hoopoe absent and declared that he would punish it unless it brought a clear explanation. The hoopoe came and explained that it had acquired knowledge that Solomon had not encompassed. The hoopoe said it had come from Queen Sheba with certain news. It found a woman ruling them who had a great throne and had been given everything. It also found them prostrating to the sun instead of Allah and Satan had misguided them. Thereupon, Solomon said he would find out whether the hoopoe was truthful or a liar. He then gave it a letter to deliver to them and return.

The Queen said, 'O eminent ones, a noble letter has been delivered to me from Solomon. It reads: "In the name of Allah, the Entirely Merciful, the Especially Merciful. Be not haughty with me but come to me in submission"' (27:30–31). She sought their advice as she did not decide on a matter without their witness. So they suggested that they were people of strength and of great military might, but, ultimately, the command is hers. She responded by saying that when kings enter a city, they ruin it and render their honoured people humbled. However, she would send a gift and see what their messengers would return with. When they came to Solomon, he told them that they were providing him with wealth, whereas Allah had given him better than what He had given them. Therefore, he had the gift returned and declared that they would go to them with soldiers and expel them from there in humiliation.

Solomon then enquired from his assembly of jinns as to who would bring him her throne before they all came in submission to him. A strong, powerful and trustworthy jinn said he would bring it to him before he stood from his place. Another one, with knowledge about the Scripture declared, 'I will bring it to you before your glance returns to you' (27:40). When Solomon saw it placed before him, he admitted that this was a favour of his Lord to determine whether he would be grateful or ungrateful. Since whoever is grateful – their gratitude is only for the benefit of themselves and whoever is ungrateful – then indeed, his Lord is Free of need and Generous.

Solomon instructed them to disguise her throne to see whether she will be guided to the truth or will be of those who are not guided. So when she arrived, she was asked if the throne was like hers. She replied that it looked as though it was. Solomon remarked that he and his people were given knowledge before her and had been Muslims [in submission to Allah] and that which she was worshipping other than Allah had averted her from submission to Him. Indeed, she was from a disbelieving people.

Thereafter, she was told to enter the palace and when she saw it, she thought it was a body of water and uncovered her shins to wade through. He informed her that it was a palace whose floor was made smooth with glass. Once she realised this, she admitted that she had wronged herself and submitted with Solomon to Allah, Lord of the worlds.

- Analyse the story and discuss the nature of the relationship that God had with Solomon.

Maryam (Mary)

Scholars have debated the question of whether Mary was a prophet or not. It is generally considered that she was not since she did not receive a 'revelation' and was not tasked with the role of being a prophet. Nevertheless, she holds a high status and is considered a model of godliness, purity, reliance, faith and determination. She is the only woman mentioned by name in the Qur'ān and Chapter 19 is named after her. Like all prophets, companions and other pious personalities, salutation and prayer are also offered to Mary using the popular phrase, 'may the blessing be on her'.

The angels announced to Mary the good tidings of a Word from Allah and stated that his name will be the Messiah, Jesus, the son of Mary. He would be distinguished in this world and the Hereafter and be among those brought near to Allah. He would speak to the people in the cradle and in maturity and would be of the righteous. God would teach him writing and wisdom and the Torah and the Gospel.

Mary withdrew from her family to a place toward the east. She secluded herself from them using a screen. The angel was then sent to her who represented himself as a well-proportioned person. At this, she declared, 'I seek refuge in the Most Merciful from you, [so leave me] if you should be fearing of Allah' (19:18). The angel informed her that he was only a messenger of her Lord who came to give her the news of a pure boy. In surprise, she exclaimed how could she have a boy when no man had touched her and she had not been unchaste. The angel replied that that was how it was to be since her Lord had decreed it to be easy for Himself and He would make her son a sign to the people and a mercy from Him.

After conceiving, she withdrew with him to a remote place. The pains of childbirth drove her to the trunk of a palm tree. She called out 'Oh, I wish I had died before this and was in oblivion, forgotten' (19:23). To comfort her, the angel called her saying that she should not grieve as her Lord provided a stream for her. She was told to shake the trunk of the palm tree which would drop ripe and fresh dates. Thereafter, she ate, drank and became content. She was also instructed to inform anyone she met that she had vowed abstention to the Most Merciful and would not speak to any person on that day.

Later, she carried baby 'Īsā to her people. The people said to her that she had done something unprecedented and that her father was not a man of evil, nor was her mother unchaste. Mary pointed to him. The people enquired how could they speak to a child in the cradle. Thereupon, 'Īsā announced, 'I am the servant of Allah. He has given me the Scripture and made me a prophet. He has made me blessed wherever I am and has enjoined upon me prayer and zakāh as long as I remain alive' (19:27–31).

- Discuss the suggestion that Maryam/Mary was a prophet.

Voice of a Muslimah

In Islam a woman especially one who is blessed with a child holds the highest rank in importance. She is blessed by God with 'heaven under her feet', meaning if she is treated with respect and dignity by her child, they are granted heaven. (Yāsmīn, Yemeni, teacher, female)

‘Īsā (Jesus)

The Qur’ān states that Jesus, the son of Mary, was given clear proofs and supported with the Pure Spirit and made a messenger to the Children of Israel by Allah. Jesus informed them that he had come to them with a sign from His Lord. He would design a bird from clay and then breathe into it and it became a bird by the permission of Allah. He also cured the blind and lepers. He gave life to the dead by the permission of Allah. Jesus would also inform them of what they had eaten and stored. He posited that all these miracles were signs for them, if they were believers. Moreover, he had come to confirm the Torah and to make lawful for them some of what had been forbidden to them. His conclusion was that he was a sign from their Lord, and therefore they should fear Allah and obey him. Jesus declared that indeed Allah was his Lord and their Lord, hence, they should worship Him, for that was the straight path.

Allah told Jesus that he would take him and raise him to Himself and purify him from those who disbelieve. Allah would also make those who followed him [in submission to Allah alone] superior to those who disbelieve. Jesus was informed that everyone would return to Allah who will judge concerning that about which people used to differ. As for those who disbelieved, Allah would punish them in this world and the Hereafter, and they would not have any helpers. As for those who believed and did righteous deeds, Allah would give them their rewards in full, and Allah does not like the wrongdoers.

His mother, Mary, was a supporter of truth. They both used to eat food and lived as humans. Allah invites people to look at how He made such signs clear to them; yet they remain deluded. Furthermore, Allah mentioned that the example of Jesus to Allah is like that of Adam. He created Him from dust; then He said to him, ‘Be’, and he was. Jesus was also born without a father. Thus, Allah cursed people for their disbelief and their slander against Mary. And also for claiming, ‘Indeed, we have killed the Messiah, Jesus, the messenger of Allah’ (4:157). Allah said that they did not kill him, nor did they crucify him; but another person was made to resemble him.

In this story, the Qur’ān states that those who differ over the matter of Jesus are in doubt and have no knowledge of it except the following of assumption. It also predicts that the People of the Scripture will believe in Jesus and on the Day of Resurrection he will be a witness against them. To the end, Allah addresses, ‘O People of the Scripture, do not commit excess in your religion or say about Allah except the truth. The Messiah, Jesus, the son of Mary, was but a messenger of Allah and His word which He directed to Mary and a soul [created at a command] from Him.’ Thus, Allah encourages them to believe in Him and His messengers and to desist from saying ‘three’, as that is better for them. Indeed, Allah is but one God.

Exalted is He above having a son. To Him belongs whatever is in the heavens and whatever is on the earth. And sufficient is Allah as Disposer of affairs (4:171).

- Discuss your response to the Qur'ānic version of the story of 'Īsā (Jesus).

Luqmān

The general view among exegetes is that Luqmān was a sage and a wise person (31:12) and not a prophet. Luqmān was given immense wisdom. He made valuable counsels to his son as reported by the Qur'ān. These are used by parents, teachers, Imāms and others for character development. Luqmān addressed saying, O my son:

- do not associate [anything] with Allah
- association [with Allah] is great injustice
- we (Allah) have enjoined upon humans the care for their parents
- be grateful to Me (Allah) and to your parents
- if they (your parents) endeavour to make you associate with Me that of which you have no knowledge, do not obey them but accompany them in [this] world with appropriate kindness and follow the way of those who turn back to Me [in repentance]
- indeed if wrong should be the weight of a mustard seed and should be within a rock or [anywhere] in the heavens or in the earth, Allah will bring it forth
- establish prayer, enjoin what is right, forbid what is wrong
- be patient over what befalls you; indeed, all these matters [require] determination
- do not turn your cheek [in contempt] toward people
- do not walk through the earth exultantly; Allah does not like everyone self-deluded and boastful
- be moderate in your pace and lower your voice

Select and justify the most important advice you think Luqmān gave his son.

Case study 4.1 Stories of the Prophets

Mariam was a well-established and experienced teacher based in a well-performing Year 5 classroom. Following a staff meeting before the Christmas break, her Headteacher announced that developing writing across the school was going to be a target in the revised school improvement plan (SIP). In religious education, she was fully aware of the importance of using a wide range of teaching strategies which assisted her to accommodate the diverse learning needs of her pupils. In view of the importance of developing writing generally, and specifically for the SIP, she revisited the writing expectations of English in the National Curriculum. This would offer her opportunities for consolidation, progression and continuity. She also carried out a quick audit to ensure that she had covered different teaching strategies in the first and third term. She then decided that over twelve weeks of the second term she would set tasks based on a variety of writing experiences including writing a poem, story, blog posts, newspaper reports, diary accounts, biography, autobiography, letters, songs, explanations, descriptions, summaries and others. All at an age-appropriate level.

Mariam wanted her pupils to choose from the menu of writing experiences based on stories from the Qur'ān. She therefore created a carousel of activities. She set a challenge for her class. Over the three lessons of religious education each pupil was to use three different writing forms for the three prophets to be studied. She let them choose the form of writing as she believed it would enhance their autonomy, specific skills and motivation. She knew her pupils very well and recognised that some would require additional support. She already had posters on the wall which listed the specific features of some of the writing forms but now, with her new challenge, she recognised that some children would benefit from reminders of the other forms of writing. Therefore, she added these to her existing posters. She was now happy that all features of all forms of writing were accessible to all pupils. She encouraged them to continuously refer to them and to some pupils she provided appropriate writing frames.

Mariam has many years of experience. She seems to have drawn on this and linked her teaching in religious education with the SIP.

- Consider the implication of planning your teaching and linking it to the SIP.
- What are the advantages and limitations of using a cross-curricular approach?
- How can you ensure that the theological and religious import of sacred stories is maintained in your teaching?

Summary

In this chapter you have learnt about prophets in Islam and their essential role. You have understood that there were many chosen messengers that God sent to humanity for their guidance and salvation. Some of these messengers were given books whilst others were not. Miracles were performed at their hands with the Will of God for a variety of reasons. You have become familiar with some stories and key events in life stories. You have analysed the purposes of the Stories of Prophets in the Qur'ān.

Reflection tasks

- Discuss the relevance of the life of these prophets for contemporary times.
- Summarise the Muslim view of human nature.
- Select a story and identify the key lessons in that story which you could teach.
- Analyse the importance of the story of Ibrāhīm for Muslims.
- Evaluate the influence that the story of Satan has on Muslim lifestyles.

Further reading

Brannon, W. (2002) *Prophets in the Qur'an: An Introduction to the Qur'an and Muslim Exegesis.* London: Bloomsbury.

This in-depth text consists of original passages from the Qur'ān and other sources, draws on parallels with Biblical tradition and offers a detailed overview of prophets from Adam to Muhammad.

Yazicioglu, I. (2013) *Understanding the Qur'anic Miracle Stories in the Modern Age.* Pennsylvania: Penn State University Press.

The text makes connections between many stories from different times and cultures to understand miracle stories in the Qur'ān. A multi-layered investigation into possibilities of science, epistemology and scriptural hermeneutics.

5

FOUNDATIONS OF FAITH

In this chapter you will:

- know the components of faith in Islam and their impact on Muslims
- understand the relationship between angels, messengers and Islam
- explore the responses of Muslims to revelations from Allah
- reflect on the meaning of judgment day and its implications for Muslims
- examine beliefs about *al-qadr*, Satan, *jinn*, Heaven and Hell.

Overview

You will have discerned from the previous chapters that faith and belief in Islam is essentially ethical as well as religious. In other words, it is concerned with this world and life after it. You will study explicitly some of the ethical precepts later.

There has been a well-established tradition among Muslim theologians to systematise the fundamentals of faith, known as *'aqāid* (sing. *'aqīdah*), which are extracted from the primary sources and scholarly endeavours (Raudvere, 2015). These serve pedagogical purposes and instruments for determining the soundness of one's belief charter. Faith (*Imān*) is the core realm out of which emerges practice (*Islām*) and virtue (***Iḥsān***) as established through the important *Ḥadīth* of Jibrīl narrated in multiple ways.

In brief: one day while the Messenger (ﷺ) was sitting among people, a stranger came and enquired about what constituted belief (*Īmān*). The Messenger (ﷺ) recounted the articles of faith. He questioned about Islam. He (ﷺ) responded by articulating the five pillars. Thereafter he queried about *Iḥsān*. He (ﷺ) replied, '*Iḥsān* is to worship Allah as if you see Him, and if you do not achieve this state of devotion, then know that Allah sees you.' The man probed when the 'Hour' [Judgement Day] would be? The Messenger (ﷺ) replied, 'The one [Muḥammad] being asked about it does not know more than the questioner does.' Then the man left. The Messenger (ﷺ) then revealed to the people saying, 'That was Gabriel (the angel) who came to teach you your religion' (Muslim, 1:1).

The three components of *Īmān, Islām* and *Iḥsān* are interconnected and complement each other. The beliefs enumerated in this narration have since become the indispensable and absolute declarations which a Muslim must accept, as featured in (2:177) as well. This is taught to most Muslims as a 'doctrinal' statement popularly known as the Detailed Articles of Faith (*Al-Īmān al-Mufaṣṣal*): 'I belief in Allah, His angels, His books, His messengers, the final day, predestination and resurrection.' You studied beliefs about God in Chapter 1, the remaining are elaborated below.

Angels

The Arabic term for angel is *malak* (pl. *malā'ikah*). Often, they feature as the second constituent of faith next only to belief in God (2:277; 2:285; 4:146), demonstrating, thereby, the significance of believing in their existence as celestial beings.

There are many aspects of Islamic angelology. It is believed that angels are created from light (***nūr***), some having two or more wings (35:1). Exactly when they were created is unknown; however, Muslims know from the creation narrative that they existed before Adam (2:30) as honoured servants of God (22:75). As spiritual beings, they are normally invisible, but, as noted above, they can appear in human form as they have subtle bodies (Hewer, 2006). Muslims will resoundingly reveal to you that their abundance is such that only God knows their precise number. Some are helpful, powerful and beautiful (12:31). Importantly, angels are neither male nor female, and significantly, they do not possess free will, unlike humans. It would appear that they have a constant state of faith. To reject a contemporaneous belief, the Qur'ān asserts that they are neither God's daughters nor objects to be deified (34:40) and their knowledge is limited (2:32). Their nature means they are ideal messengers from the transcendent world to the created world (Hewer, 2006).

In the spiritual and temporal worlds, the function of angels is similar: they work as mediators in accomplishing the will of God. In the former domain, they are involved in continuous worship, glorification, praise and prostration before God, in awe and fear, and, in the latter, they bring about the development of creation. According to *ḥadīth* literature, angels are closely related with the life-events of human beings, from breathing the soul in the womb to the moment of their death and beyond (Burge, 2012), sometimes as guardian angels (13:10).

Hierarchically, they rank below the prophets. There are four archangels:

- Jibrīl: the highest who delivered messages to prophets who has an epithet of Holy Spirit (*Rūh ul-qudus*, 16:102, vide 26:193)
- Mikā'il (Michael): responsible for events of nature

- ‘Izrā’īl: common name for the one who ‘extracts’ souls (*malak ul-māwt*, 28:88)
- Isrāfīl: awaits to sound the trumpet to usher in the Last Day

Angels are assigned specific missions (Burge, 2012), for example, *Riḍwān* safeguards the Heavens, whereas *Mālik* is the gatekeeper of Hell (39:71). Therefore, Muslims are expected to be ever conscious of their actions throughout their lives. This belief has implications in inspiring them to remain steadfast on Islam and to follow the example of Prophet Muḥammad (ﷺ).

Prophet Muḥammad (ﷺ) explained the methodology:

> Whoever intended a good deed, but did not do it, has it written as a complete good deed. If performed, then it is recorded as ten good deeds, or up to seven hundred times or more. However, if a person intends an evil act, but does not do it, has it written as a good deed, but once it’s acted upon, it is written as a single evil deed. (al-Būkhārī, 8:498)

It is also believed that some angels continuously encircle the **Ka‘bah** just as the throne of God is surrounded by an entourage of angels (39:75). Moreover, angels visit the most Frequented House (*Al-Bayt al-Ma‘mūr*) which is directly above the Ka‘bah, making it the spiritual axis of the universe, and perform the ***Ṭawāf*** there, just as Muslims circle (*Ṭawāf*) the Ka‘bah on earth (52:4; al-Bukhārī, 4:429). Angels implore forgiveness (40:7–9) and intercede for sinners (21:28). Angels are powerful in repelling evil (37:1–2), inspiring humans to righteousness and strengthening the hearts of the righteous (41:30). Thus, those who oppose angels are admonished (2:98).

As you can see, Muslims believe there is a mutual relationship between angels and humans. Ordinarily they remain unseen. However, they can, if God wills, adopt any form so that some people may see them at times of ‘crisis’ and others sense their presence during intense prayer, meditation and dreams (Maqsood, 2010). Indeed, angels visit the house in which the Qur’ān is recited (Rippin, 2006). Some scholars disagree on the use of the names of angels (Al-Jawziyyah, 2008). Still, Muslims use Mikā’il and Jibrīl, and among some Persians, Firishta and for Turkish women Melek is popular. Riḍwān proffers the name to men and, with a feminine ending, to women, Riḍwāna (Schimmel, 1997).

Faith in angels is a fundamental belief in Islam; their rejection constitutes unbelief (***kufr***) (Burge, 2012). Their multidimensional and multifaceted roles in the temporal and spiritual domains are connected in some ways with the operation of the entire universe and with the spiritual life of humans. In essence, angels are servants duty-bound to God. It is through angels that God ‘governs’ the universe. Muslims aim to adopt their traits. Some Sufi masters inspire their tutees to do so; perhaps a reason for requiring this belief is that they learn to be submitted and devoted to God like angels.

Sacred scriptures

Muslims think that Allah, out of mercy and to remove ignorance, repeatedly sent revelations. Kutub, meaning books (sing. *kitāb*), is derived from the root *k-t-b* meaning 'to write'. The substantive ones are called *kutub* (books) whereas the minor ones are scrolls (sing. *ṣaḥīfah*, pl. *ṣaḥā'if* or *ṣuḥuf*).

There is little certainty about their exact number; however, all but four perished. These revealed books represented God's blueprint for people to live according to God's law (Riddell, 2018). Since the Qur'ān has remained intact (15:9), it is the last repository of truth supplanting all other revelations (Riddell, 2018). Simultaneously, it is the criterion to judge (*Al-Furqān*) all previous and current books.

The Torah (Ar. *Al-Tawrāt*) was given to Mūsā (Moses) through divine inspiration and direct communication at Mount Sinai and elsewhere, as a true revelation preceding the Qur'ān and Injīl. The Qur'ān characterises this scripture as being a mercy (46:12), instruction (5:46), an enlightenment (28:43) and a light based upon which the prophets who submitted [to God] judged by it for the Jews, as did the Rabbis and scholars who were entrusted with the Scripture of Allah (5:44).

However, the charge against the Torah is that some of it was distorted (2:75), misinterpreted from its [proper] usages (4:46) and some forgotten (5:13). Therefore, from the perspective of the Qur'ān and Muslim scholarship, its reliability is questioned. Thus, whilst some Muslims would accept that there may be much preserved in the current Torah, it remains incomplete and misinterpreted.

The Zabūr (Psalms) was revealed to King David (17:55). Little is known about this revelation in Islam. The word echoes the Hebrew *Zamīr* (song) and *Mizmōr* (melody) (Glassé, 2013). Traditions confirm that they were recited much like poetry or hymns. After defeating Goliath, Dāwūd glorified Allah to which plants, birds, beasts, and even the mountains responded to his voice glorifying Allah (38:18–20). Over the years, the Psalms have had later additions, thus, Muslims would consider this as an admission of alteration and an absence of the original hymnbook of the Temple of Jerusalem. This means that though the Psalms might have some of the original Zabūr, it is unreliable for guiding humankind as it is not entirely preserved (Hewer, 2006).

The single Gospel (*Injīl*), according to Muslims, was revealed to Jesus. Some contents of the Gospel of Barnabas would resonate with some Muslim beliefs, otherwise, mostly it is overlooked (Glassé, 2013). Moreover, the Qur'ān charges it with corruption (*taḥrīf*) (5:15). Therefore, it corrects the Christian Gospel on several accounts including the nature of Jesus and his death.

The Qur'ān refers to the Ṣuḥuf of Ibrāhīm and Mūsā (87:18–19) which are extinct. They contained parables and wisdom (Shafī', 1995). Other exegetes suggest that the contents of Chapter 87 of the Qur'ān were included therein (Pānipatī, 1991).

For Muslims, this means that respect, to avoid being guilty of irreverence, is to be given to these books as revelations from God, albeit not preserved. Muslim children are taught about these books as part of their faith education and are expected to believe in them. As regards their content, matters confirmed by Qur'ān are confirmed whereas matters denied by the Qur'ān but affirmed by them are rejected and for matters which are neither confirmed nor denied, it is permissible to mention them; however, religious tenets cannot be based on them (Usmani, 2000). There may be no harm in mentioning them although silence is preferred, in case the revealed portion is inadvertently rejected.

Prophethood (Risālah and Nubūwwah)

God, the All-Wise, in His infinite wisdom decided to make known His guidance through chosen individuals called Messengers (*rasūl* pl. *rusul*) and Prophets (*nabī* pl. *anbiyā'*). Muslims believe they were all humans with the highest characters, protected from sin (*ma'ṣūm*) and sent with the message of *Tawḥīd*. Shī'ism views their **Imāms** as being sinless and infallible (Momen, 1985). Messengers and Prophets performed miracles to challenge the most advanced knowledge and skills of their respective times, to convince their people of their veracity and to meet their demands of proving they were appointed by God (as you learnt in Chapter 4).

Every 'community' was sent a guide (16:36) but not all of them were given a scripture. Muslim tradition stresses the distinction of the terms *nabī* and *rasūl* (Stewart, 2010). The Arabic term for prophet is *nabī*, derived from *naba'*, meaning a significant announcement. Rasūl is derived from *r-s-l* 'to compare', which gives *irsāl* meaning 'to send' and *mursal* 'the one sent', thus, a *rasūl* is an ambassador.

Some scholars see no difference and use them interchangeably based on (2:285) which mentions *rusul* only but refers to all. However, others differentiate, because a report mentions that there were 124,000 prophets, of which 313 were messengers (Shafī', 1995; Rāzī, 23:49–50). They also refer to verses where these two words appear separately (22:52) and posit that in Arabic grammar when the letter '*waw*' [و] appears between two similar things mentioned together, then, it highlights a difference. On this basis, Imām Fakhruddin Rāzī (543–606AH/1149–1209CE), a historian and philosopher, explained that a *rasūl* performed miracles, received a new Divine book to establish a new code (Sharī'ah) and abrogated the previous one. He visibly sees the angel and is commanded to invite people towards the religion, whereas a *nabī* is not given a new scripture, but establishes the book revealed to the *rasūl* before him. He does not abrogate the book and law in practice before him. He sees the angel in a dream or the current *rasūl* informs him that he has been chosen as a *nabī* (Rāzī, 23:50). Therefore all *rusul* were *anbiyā'* but not all were *rusul*.

These guides were sent to all different people and nations throughout the ages as bringers of good news and to warn (35:24). The reason for this is that God would not take a people to task unless it was made clear to them what His expectations were. God is Kind and Merciful and His mercy is manifested in the form of prophets sent as reminders to the forgetful to return to God (Brown, 2017).

In their nature, the Qur'ān makes no distinction (2:285). However, some of their functions depended on the temperament and needs of their respective times. Some of their laws differed from one another because Divine Knowledge entailed that the circumstance and needs of the people necessitated such differences. In addition, they interpreted and applied that message so that people took them as models to live a life of faith. Messengers freed people from the bondage of humans to the love of God. They showed their followers how to behave, to overcome the barriers of sin and evil to achieve moral and spiritual heights.

Though prophets were deputised to all nations, for some, their message was particularistic and, sometimes, nationalistic and generational. However, Prophet Muḥammad (ﷺ) was appointed universally to lead people to the Oneness of God and oneness of humanity. Moreover, in this chain of prophets selected by God, Muḥammad (ﷺ) is the final messenger sealing any claims of new prophecy (33:40) except for the Aḥmadiyya about whom you will read in Chapter 12. For Muslims, this means the example of Prophet Muḥammad (ﷺ) is final. Anyone claiming to be a prophet of God is deemed to be out of the fold of Islam and opposed for making a false claim. All God-sent prophets are respected, expressed by the phrase 'peace be upon them' after uttering their names.

Death

Death is an uncontroverted reality and, as such, it is a subject which most Muslims would be less reticent to discuss openly. The Qur'ān, ḥadīth literature and many scholars have written on it extensively in a range of rich contexts of Islamic discourse through interdisciplinary prisms as it relates to ritual, spiritual and intellectual sensibilities (Buturovic, 2010). Muslims are reminded that every soul will taste death (3:185), that it is impossible to die except by God's will at a decree determined (3:145) and no soul perceives where it will die (31:34). Importantly, when the time arrives, no one can remain behind nor precede it (16:61). However, God can defer death as the story of 'Uzayr shows who passed by a ruined city and wondered how God would resurrect life. He was shown a township brought back to life after a hundred years (2:259; *vide* Seven Sleepers 18:9–17). These verses have had a huge impact on how Muslims understand death, its rituals and the relationship of the soul, spirit and body; and with matters eschatological and worldly, through moral, philosophical and spiritual genres. It is a common practice to recite Sūrah Yā Sīn (36) near a dying person and at death the phrase: 'Indeed we belong to Allah, and indeed to Him we will return' (2:156). The ***muḥaddīth*** Al-Tabrīzī (740–816AH/1341–1413) wrote:

> The heart rusts, just as iron does, proclaimed the Messenger (ﷺ). On being asked what could cleanse it, he counselled 'much remembrance of death and recitation of Qur'ān'. (Tabrīzī, 2:2168)

For some Muslims, there are three purposes of remembering death. First, a negligent person absorbed in the world disparages death and regrets being deprived of its vanities. Second, a repentant becomes firmer in their repentance; remorse proceeds from the heart and becomes devoted to repair the past. Finally, the gnostic constantly remembers death since a lover contemplates on the promise of the sight of the Beloved (Al-Ghazālī, 2009). Death can be a painful and easy experience as an indication of what might be coming ahead (Smith and Haddad, 2002). Thus, Muslims expect to die hoping only good from Allah (Muslim, 4:6877).

Voice of a Muslim

In my career I observe the frequency of cross county lines' sale of alcohol misuse, a large number of Muslim domestic violence cases and much more. This has given me the opportunity to step back, reflect and be grateful for the stability and calm in my own personal life and to realise that normal is something different to us all. This helps me to be grateful for even the smallest things in life such as my younger brother returning home from school safe daily and using his time to go to the *masjid* and spending time in Islamic and everyday acceptable teenage activities. There has been no domestic violence between my parents, and a lack of poverty in my home. I strongly believe Islam and social work not only co-exist but are also entwined and support each other. This helps me to feel complete as an individual and to strive to achieve the best for the community and in my professional and personal roles. (Idrīs, Libyan, social worker, male)

The unseen

Broadly, you will find three stages of human-life mentioned. The first, known as ***ʻĀlam al-arwāh*** (abode of souls) is where all souls confirmed the Lordship of God (7:172). Then, the life on earth (*ʻĀlam al-dunyā*) followed by life in the Hereafter (*ʻĀlam al-ākhirah*). Thus, there is a seen and the unseen world (*ʻĀlam al-**ghayb***), which is discussed below.

The waiting stage

Death is a bridge from this temporal life to the next stage of life in the grave. The journey of the Afterlife starts immediately after death. The intervening period between death and Resurrection Day is called *Al-Barzakh* (lit. a barrier) (23:100). It is a prelude through which 'humans' must pass just as they passed sometime in the womb (Nomānī, 1971). Here, two angels, *Munkar* and *Nakīr,* interrogate individuals to reveal the reality of the condition of their soul by using questions such as: 'Who is your Lord? What is your religion? Who is your prophet?' (al-Tirmidhī, 5:3120). In Shīʻism, questioning also includes: 'Who is your Imām?' (Bayram, 2013). Responses to these determine a person's eternal destiny (Gwynne, 2018) but there is a prior taste of pleasures or pain as the *barzakh* is a form of spatio-temporal hiatus (Buturovic, 2010). The Khawārij, Jahmīyyah and some Muʻtazilah contend that humans become nothing after death and there is neither suffering nor delight until resurrection. However, Al-Ghazālī (450–505AH/1058–1111CE) from the ***Ahl al-Sunnah wal-Jamāʻat,*** considered these views as unsound based on the Qur'ān, and traditions, and intellectually stated that death indicates a change in state and that the spirit survives after leaving the body to feel torment or bliss (Al-Ghazālī, 1989). Being matters of belief, Muslims accept these as intricate matters beyond the perception of human senses; they are only truly known after death.

Afterlife

When you study Islam, you will observe lifelike descriptions of the Hereafter intended to arouse hope, consciousness of God and a true desire to prepare for the ultimate life. There are several transcendental truths, which the Qur'ān requires Muslims to uphold as a matter of *modus operandi.* Of these, the belief concerning the Hereafter holds a status next in significance only to *Tawḥīd* and *Risālah* (Nomānī, 1971). Some obscure minor sects deny the Resurrection (Al-Ghazālī, 1989). Nevertheless, the existential question of the Hereafter, being of fundamental significance to religion, was revealed by God in all sacred scriptures and by all God's appointed messengers to invite their respective followers to have unreserved faith in the Afterlife, since this world is but a plantation.

The Qur'ān states that just as God exists and God's existence is regarded as a reality, even though the senses do not perceive God, without doubt, after the earthly life, another permanent existence will come; unsurprisingly this important subject matter is covered extensively in a variety of persuasive ways and from a range of perspectives. Muslims consider this exposition as an act of mercy from God, since the exams, answers are given and people know results in advance, leaving humans to choose their destination. Importantly, the Qur'ān advances rationales (*vide* 17:49–51) for the necessity of such a belief and how, from the viewpoint of the Qur'ān, it would be irrational and mistaken to deny it (Nomānī, 1971).

> And they say, 'When we are bones and crumbled particles, will we [truly] be resurrected as a new creation?' Say, 'Be you stones or iron. Or [any] creation of that which is great within your breasts.' And they will say, 'Who will restore us?' Say, 'He who brought you forth the first time'. (17:49–51)

The Final Day

The existence of another life implies this world has to end; its precise time is unknown except to God. However, *ḥadīth* literature discloses some major and minor signs to herald its nearness. In brief, these include an increase in sin, prevalence of religious ignorance, widespread disobedience to parental authority, disrespect to elders, increase in debauchery, increase of women vis-à-vis men, and incompetent people assuming leadership positions. Others include the abundance of chaos, the disappearance of the Ka'bah, the rising of the sun from the west, the appearance of **Yā'jūj and Mā'jūj** (Gog and Magog) and **Dajjāl** ('anti-Christ') (al-Bukhārī, 1:56; 1:81; Muslim, 4:6881; 4:6924; 4:6931–7057). Also the descent of Imām **Al-Mahdī** (Abū Dāwūd, 3:4272), who will rule for 40 years after which the world will experience chaos again. To the Shī'a, Al-Mahdī is in occultation (Daftary, 2013). Thereafter, Prophet 'Isā will descend to restore justice (al-Bukhārī, 3:656). God will instruct the angel Isrāfīl to blow the trumpet to bring an end to the universe.

The Day of Resurrection

Isrāfīl will blow the trumpet again to resurrect everyone and assemble before God. Many verses counsel Muslims and humanity in general, of the impending Day of Reckoning (*Yawm al-**ḥisāb***) (Mattson, 2013). On this Day, accountability will be based according to sincere repentance and the measurement of deeds (Riddell, 2018). The Qur'ān sketches the scene revealing that the successful receive their books in their right hand, whereas others will do so in the left. Each person will examine their book and respond accordingly; others will enter without questions (Pānipatī, 1991). The great balance (***Al-mīzān***) will be the measuring instrument and their respective destination announced (Smith and Haddad, 2002). People will plead to Prophet Muḥammad (ﷺ) to intercede. God will accept his intercession (***Shafā'ah***) after which judgement will be finalised. There will be a bridge (*Al-ṣirāṭ*) to walk past, those falling would perish, the others would succeed (Ibn Mājah, 5:4307–4311; 5:4279). There will be the pond granted to the Prophet (ﷺ) (108:1) from which his followers will drink.

Divine decree and foreknowledge

Belief in ***Al-qaḍā' wa al-qadar*** (decree and foreknowledge; also predestination) is perhaps the most perplexing article, so much so that Muslims are advised to keep its deep deliberation at bay. Put simply, it means that God knows everything and that before He created the universe, every action that was to happen was recorded. In matters of faith, this means that God permits people to choose to believe and submit to Him. In essence, God controls the past, the present and the future (Riddell, 2018).

The concept of 'predestination' is notoriously challenging to reconcile with the concept of free will, but Islam should not be considered a fatalistic religion.

Messengers were sent to give people free choice and human life is a test (Maqsood, 2010). Such a belief raises the question of who is responsible for evil and wrongdoing, while believing that God has absolute power. Some other related questions include: How can God be considered just if He is the one who made individuals do the actions? If God knows everything, why did He not stop someone from carrying out a harmful action? If God knows someone was going to do evil deeds, why did He create them in the first place and why did He not kill them to stop those horrible actions? If God is absolute, why should individuals be blamed for the actions that they do, should it not be God who is to be blamed (Hewer, 2006: 81)?

Over the centuries, Muslim scholarship has debated these and other similar questions, which has resulted historically in theological schools emerging as you will learn in Chapter 11. Among some Shīʿa, the concept of the changeability of God's will (*badā*) meant that He could change the course of events (Momen, 1985). The Muʿtazila and Qadariyyah believe that humans have complete control of their actions. Some Muʿtazila look to the Hereafter and opine that humans are responsible for their actions since judgement is to be made on the basis of human actions, therefore people have free will. Judgement can only be made when an individual is held responsible. God gave humans free will and it is their decision of what they do in this world. Having applied logic to the issue, they eventually denied *Al-Qadar*. The Jabariyyah believed that humans have absolutely no control of their actions; whatever they do is not through their choice. Therefore, they believed that humans will not be punished for their evil acts, but will be rewarded for good actions. The *Ahl al-Sunnah wal-Jamāʿah* declare both these beliefs as deviant because humans do not have the ability to create their own actions. They argue that it is impossible for humans to bring something non-existent into existence. Moreover, these orthodox theologians respond by reconciling *Al-Qadar* and free will. To them, God knows what humans are going to do before they act, but their free will assists them to decide whether to do what God wants or not. It is also argued that although God knows everything, it does not mean that He forces humans to believe or disbelieve (Saud, 2013a; Brown, 2017).

Satan

Muslims acknowledge the existence of spiritual beings besides angels. God, after creating Adam, commanded the angels and Iblīs to prostrate before Adam in his honour but Iblīs refused. After being banished, he vowed to take revenge (7:11–24), as you read in Chapter 4.

Thus, the main objective of Iblīs (Ar. Shayṭān, pl. Shayāṭīn, [Satan]) and his party is to make humans forgetful and disobedient to God by using all efforts and allurements (35:6). Satan influences all human affairs and has a 'touch' by which people are threatened to reject the truth, to fear poverty and to perform outrageous actions (Ashour, 1989). His chief weapon is to whisper in the bosoms of humans (114:5). Thus, the force of good is God and the force of evil is Satan, both existing side by side (7:14–16).

Both God and the Prophet (ﷺ) have warned people against the ploys of Satan and his clear enmity (2:168). Their influence primarily lies in exploiting human weaknesses and seducing them from righteousness, to incite hatred and sow dissension (5:91; 15:39–40; 17:53). However, on Judgement Day, Iblīs will exonerate himself by informing those who fell into his deception:

> Indeed, God had promised you the promise of truth. And I promised you, but I betrayed you. But I had no authority over you except that I invited you, and you responded to me. So do not blame me; but blame yourselves. I cannot be called to your aid, nor can you be called to my aid. Indeed, I deny your association of me [with God] before ... .(14:22)

The belief in Satan considerably effects all walks of Muslim life from business to spiritual matters. You will now recognise why Muslims follow the teachings of Islam. They believe it offers them guidance and protection from the mischief of Satan. Simultaneously, they are encouraged to seek refuge in Allah from their promptings (23:97–98) and to recite the Qur'ān (16:98–99), since it is a healer for what is in their chests (10:57). Moreover, Muslims repent and ask forgiveness, refrain from excesses, increase their knowledge and hold onto the community and good company. They try to refrain from pride and jealousy, as these were Satan's main traits.

Since the instruction to prostrate to Adam was made to angels (7:11), questions are often asked about who Satan actually is. Some maintain he was an angel. However, according to (18:50), Satan is a *jinn* and was in the company of angels when God commanded them to prostrate before Adam. That he disobeyed further makes him a *jinn,* since angels are incapable of disobedience (66:6). Moreover, he said about himself to God that he had been created from fire whereas, according to a *ḥadīth*, angels are created from light.

Jinn

The word *jinn* literally means hidden, and is linked with both physical and metaphorical darkness. Theologically, the *jinn* are a creation of God concealed (*ijtinān*) from sight and who existed before humans (15:26–27; 7:27). The *jinn* have free will (Hussain, 2016). Therefore, they, unlike angels, may or may not obey God (51:56) making them similar to humans in this respect, but their nature is different (Ramadan, 2017). Like humans, they are created to worship God (51:56) which means they will be brought to account (37:158). The jurists (***fuqahā'***), Imām Mālik, Aḥmad and Al-Shāfi'ī maintain that they are rewarded for their obedience and punished for disobedience, whereas Imām Abū Ḥanīfah upheld that their reward is to be saved from punishment (Ashour, 1989). Messengers are sent to both *jinns* and humankind (6:130). Therefore, Prophet Muḥammad (ﷺ), being a universal messenger, was sent to them too (Pānipatī, 1991).

The *jinns* are created from smokeless fire (55:15). Human origin is from clay but they are not actually clay; similarly the origin of *jinn* is fire but they are not actually fire. This leads some scholars to maintain that they have bodies whereas others deny it (Ashour, 1989). A commentator of the Qur'ān, Qāḍhī Thanā'ullah Pānipatī (d.1125AH/1810AD) maintains that they are intelligent with procreative ability and have their own communities (Pānipatī, 1991). They visited the Messenger (ﷺ) to listen to the Qur'ān and subsequently some believed in it (72:1–3) and others remained unjust (72:14–15).

They can possess humans and cause mischief in their lives. Tradition has it that they tend to inhabit unclean sites, graveyards, ruins and human dwellings (Ashour, 1989). Imām Ibn Taymiyyah (661–728AH/1263–1328CE) maintained that there is consensus among scholars of *Ahl al-Sunnah wal-Jamā'ah* regarding their ability to possess humans out of hatred, revenge or to harm them (Ashour, 1989). For some people, this possession is empirically observed especially during exorcism. The Spanish exegete **Al-Qurṭubī** (d.671AH/1273CE) mentioned that the verse (2:275) contains evidence against those who deny the *jinn's* effect on human beings (Al-Qurṭubī, 2003).

The Prophet (ﷺ) cautioned Muslims against their harm and he suggested that they regularly read certain prayers (Muslim, 2:1757; 4:6541), Chapters 113, 114 and verses (23:97–98). Moreover, some Muslims utilise **amulets** (*ruqyah*) as means of protection from *jinns* and 'evil eyes'. This practice is shunned by some authorities altogether, whereas others permit them on the condition that it exclusively contains the verses of the Qur'ān as it is an antidote (17:82) and consists of God's names and attributes. Since there is much folklore associated with such practices, Muslims are expected to have faith that these objects in themselves have no power since God is the ultimate Curer.

A tiny minority denies their existence claiming that *jinn* refers to the souls, whereas some philosophers claim they are the evil inclinations in humankind just as angels are good inclinations. For Muslims, however, the *jinn* are another type of being, apart from angels and humans. They are intelligent with subtle bodies, and not philosophical accidents or microorganisms, and are responsible for their actions. For Muslims, the acceptance of their existence is an essential part of faith. Those who deny the *jinn* deny the Qur'ān (Ashour, 1989).

Destination

If one receives favour from God on Judgement Day, inspired by righteous actions, correct belief and sincere repentance, then Paradise is their everlasting abode. In contrast, associating partners in worship to God, leads to Hell (Hewer, 2006). All the messengers sent by God and all revealed sacred texts stressed this belief. In Heaven, the perfect manifestation of the attributes of the Most Merciful occur, whereas Hell finds the gravest expression of the attributes of God's displeasure. The consensus of the Muslim community, in general, is that these are literal and will occur as revealed (Nomānī, 1971). They are in existence rather than being symbolic as substantiated by numerous verses and narrations.

Voice of a Muslimah

Rābi'ah Basriyyah (95–185AH/713–801CE) was once seen hurrying through the streets of Basra carrying a torch in one hand and a bucket of water in the other. She was asked what was happening; she replied that I want to pour water on Hell, and burn down Paradise. They block the way to God. I do not want to worship from fear of punishment or for the promise of reward, but simply for the love of God. (Saud, 2013a)

Paradise

Heaven (*Jannah*) is frequently mentioned as a motivator for good actions and deterrent from vice. It also answers for the existence of people and the universe and assists humans in determining their ultimate destination, consequently, Muslims ruminate its details as an act of grace and mercy. The material culture of the Qur'ānic paradise is rich whereas the landscape of Hell is more developed and detailed (Lange, 2016).

In brief, Heaven is depicted with multiple synonyms including a home of everlasting peace (10:25). The parable of paradise, which the virtuous are promised, is that it has rivers of water unaltered, of milk the taste of which never changes, of wine delicious to those who drink, and of purified honey, and dwellers receive all kinds of fruits and forgiveness from their Lord (47:15). It is a place of unrestricted enjoyment where food and drink can be had without fear of intoxication (69:24). It is an eternal abode to live in security and tranquillity (2:82). The most sought after garden is **Al-Firdaws**, where prophets, martyrs and the most truthful and pious will reside (23:11). Muslims often invoke for their deceased to be placed in it. However, there will be something better than this. The pinnacle reward will be the pleasure of Allah (3:15) and God's announcement of 'peace'. Hence, Muslims plead for God to be happy with them but the greatest reward will be viewing the countenance of Allah (75:22).

The realm of Heaven is beyond human comprehension. Its reality starts where human perception ends. These are symbolisms to convey the truth and the blessings are real, whose true nature is known to God alone (Ansari, 1994). Their nature is beyond imagination. Prophet Muḥammad (ﷺ) revealed that Allah promised: 'I have prepared for my righteous slaves (such excellent things) as no eye has ever seen, nor an ear has ever heard, nor heart perceive' (al-Bukhārī, 9:589). In other words, qualitatively, spatially and perceptively it is different to this world.

Muslims are taught to petition for God's grace for entry into Heaven and attempt to perform as many good actions as possible with sincerity to gain the pleasure of God. They try their best to fulfil all the obligations and carry out additional meritorious actions following the model of the Prophet (ﷺ) and the pious. They offer thanks for all the favours blessed to them, exercise patience when faced with adversity, seek God's mercy and carry out acts which deserve perpetual merits. They also try to focus and increase their devotion of those specific actions which are promised to take them to Heaven.

Hell

In brief, Hell (*Jahannam*), with its variant names, is characterised as an abode where sinners receive punishment in a wretched place (3:197). Often, wherever Heaven is mentioned as a pleasurable reward, Hell is contrasted as being a fiery place. For some actions, the displeasure of God will be such that He will ignore people (23:108). Consequently, some people will offer in ransom the whole of the earth in gold but it will be rejected, as they will have no helpers (3:91). In fact, the curse of God and of the angels and the people, all together will be upon them (2:162). Ultimately, out of regret, some people will wish to return to earth to do good and not have denied the signs of their Lord (6:27). Others will wish for a second chance to disassociate themselves from wrongdoing (2:167).

Those who may end up in Hell include idolaters and polytheists (50:26), hypocrites, the arrogant, those who treat religion frivolously, those who break treaties, mockers of God's Messengers and the reality of Resurrection, murderers, slanderers of chaste women, those misappropriating inheritance especially of orphans, those claiming divinity for themselves and rejecters of Truth, earners of evil and wrong doers (2:81).

Both Heaven and Hell have many different levels subject to good and bad actions and beliefs held in life (Smith and Haddad, 2002). These are differentiated into various levels according to how well one abided or lapsed in following the rules of God. Muslims are taught to seek refuge from Hell and from all those actions which may displease God. They try their best to live as per the Will of God. They also seek His forgiveness from their shortcomings and try to settle all matters both with God and fellow humans as quickly as possible here on earth and hope that His mercy will envelop them just as a womb envelops a foetus.

The philosophy underpinning these details is to promote reflection among Muslims and to stir their souls to be wise and make wise decisions. Some earthly pain is bearable, unlike perpetual pain. Similarly, some earthly pleasures can be squandered, but not eternal ones. Therefore, they constantly think about the future.

Case study 5.1 Five pillars

A student teacher was expected by a class teacher to teach a lesson to 7–8-year olds in Year 3 about the basics of the five pillars of Islam in a faith school. The student teacher's learning objectives were for the pupils to:

- listen to words in Arabic and their equivalent in English
- draw five pillars for a house
- complete colouring the pillars and the house.

The student teacher decided that the pupils would be successful if they had:

- repeated the Arabic words and their equivalent in English
- completed drawing all the five pillars for a house
- used different pencil crayons to colour the five pillars and the house.

(Continued)

The student teacher's plan was to teach the pupils the five pillars of Islam, what they were and briefly, at their own level, about how Muslims expressed them. Next, the meaning of the first pillar would be explained to them, after which the pupils would be given a sheet of A4 paper and some pencil crayons in order to colour a house with five pillars. At the end of the lesson, the drawing would be collected and the neatest would be displayed.

After the lesson, the student teacher wrote the following for their assessment:

- The pupils liked the lesson. All of them repeated the Arabic and their equivalent in English. The majority of them drew the five pillars of Islam. All of them coloured their work with many producing very neat work. For the next lesson, I will teach them about prayer and its importance in Islam.

The student teacher recorded the following as part of their self-evaluation and reflection:

- The pupils enjoyed the lesson. They all listened to me. They managed to finish their colouring. I managed to go around and praised their neatness. A few, the usual ones, were talkative. Once they were all engrossed with their colouring, I was able to organise my next lesson on history. I feel this was good organisation. In future, I will make sure I give some pupils a cut and paste activity because in my class some prefer practical work. I will also reduce the talkativeness of the circle group.

In reviewing the lesson with a university tutor, the student teacher was rather surprised to discover that the tutor, who was not an RE specialist, was very concerned about the planning and progress of the class. If you were this student teacher's university tutor, and based on what you have read on the five pillars in this chapter, what feedback would you offer to the student about:

- learning aims and objectives
- evidence of knowledge and understanding of the five pillars
- the delivery of the lesson

- assessment of learning
- self-evaluation and reflection
- what targets would you share with your student teacher for the future?

Summary

In this chapter, you have analysed the major components of the belief system in Islam about the physical and unseen world. You explored in good detail their beliefs about angels, Divine scriptures, prophets and messengers, death, the waiting stage, the necessity for life after death, signs of the Final Day, the Day of Resurrection and Judgement Day, predestination and the expositions of Hell and Paradise. You have found out more about Satan and the *jinn* and recognised the correct Islamic beliefs and the requirements for Muslims and, thereby, developed an understanding of some matters which may invalidate faith. You have also become aware of the complexity of the differences that exist in some of these matters. This chapter has demonstrated to you the significance of faith and disbelief and its consequences in this world and in the Hereafter for Muslims.

Reflection tasks

- Critically evaluate the arguments for and against the need for messengers to guide people.
- Describe angelology in Islam; consider how it might help Muslims live a pious life.
- Imagine you were explaining the main articles of faith in Islam to a child. How would you do this? Which points would you choose and why?
- Islam stresses metaphysical beliefs – would it, therefore, be an attractive option for those living in secular societies?
- What arguments are presented by Islam for the existence of the Afterlife?

(Continued)

- How do these articles of faith assist Muslims to pursue their personal salvation?
- Do you think Muslims should act to please God or to gain entry into paradise?

Further reading

Jaques, R.K. (2010) 'Beliefs', in J. Elias (ed.), *Key Themes for the Study of Islam*. Oxford: Oneworld, pp. 51–71.

This is a useful chapter in showing the inadequacy and limited capacity of the term 'belief' in expressing the study of Muslim tradition. It argues that at the macro and micro level it does not account for the scope of the integrated concept of *tawḥīd*.

Smith, J.I. and Haddad, Y.Y. (2002) *The Islamic Understanding of Death and Resurrection.* Oxford: Oxford University Press.

This is an in-depth scholarly study of Islamic **eschatology** based on classical and modern Muslim writers. It is an invaluable source on this important subject. It devotes a special chapter to women and children in the Afterlife.

6

OBLIGATIONS OF FAITH

In this chapter you will:

- identify the five significant devotional obligations instituted by the teachings of Islam
- assess the importance of worship for contemporary Muslims
- understand the practical manifestations and implications of these five pillars
- appreciate what it means to be a Muslim today
- understand the moral, social and spiritual meanings of these religious practices.

Overview

You will recall from the previous chapter the angel Jibrīl asking about Islam. The Messenger (ﷺ) had answered that Islam is to declare that there is no god but God and Muḥammad (ﷺ) is the messenger of Allah, to establish **Ṣalāh**, give Zakāh, observe Ṣawm and perform Ḥajj. Thus in five short sentences the entire edifice of Islam was enumerated as an expectation of the relationship between God and creation.

The Qur'ān sees all humans as religious beings. Often, Muslims are reminded that people and *jinns* have been created for worship alone (51:56–58). You will encounter the word *'abd* frequently in Muslim literature, as in *'Abd'* of Allah for 'Abdullah – this is a single term denoting the dual meanings of 'servant' and 'worshipper'. Therefore, Muslims will often self-define themselves as the servants of Allah. The implication of this is that life is meant to be lived under the command of God and through this submission peace is to be achieved, since the Sharī'ah touches all aspects of Muslim life (Crotty and Lovat, 2016). According to Imām Al-Ghazālī, to attain salvation, the actions of a person must accord with both his faith and knowledge ('Umaruddin, 1996). At the core of these pillars lies humility which is the greatest virtue in acquiring ultimate felicity and it depends on it (Walī Allah, 2017).

The Five Pillars are preliminaries for understanding Muslim practices, although they are not the totality of their beliefs and practice. All Muslims respect and are expected to observe them, but some are more dedicated to their complete fulfilment than others. Nevertheless, even when Muslims fall short, the Five Pillars represent the ideal that Muslims should strive to achieve (DeLong-Bas, 2018).

Islam

The terms *islām, salām*, ***taslīm***, *muslim* all share the same trilateral root *s-l-m*. A Muslim is one who has submitted (*taslīm*) to the Will of Allah (*islām*) through which peace (*salām*) is intended to be attained.

For the manifestation of this submission, there is a definitive system of worship that is central to Islam and is expected from Muslims. These focus on individual Muslims so that the Islamic collectivity consists of healthy units (Hathout, 2008). There are five minimum obligations related to worship, described as pillars (sing. *rukn*, pl. *arkān*) by the Prophet (ﷺ) himself (Muslim, 1:20). Needless, to say that buildings do not consist of pillars; rather, pillars exist to support whole buildings (Hathout, 2008). However, there may be a tendency by some to adopt a reductionist stance to Islam and relate it to ritual worship only. Therefore, worship in Islam requires an understanding of its comprehensive and multifaceted nature, otherwise the purpose that these acts of worship are meant to serve in moulding the character of the worshipper may be overlooked, since any lawful act performed with the intention of pleasing God is considered worship of God (Hathout, 2008). This includes the removal of a harmful object from the path, planting a tree and smiling – all actions directed and practised by the Prophet (ﷺ) himself. Abū Barza asked the Prophet what he could do to benefit himself. The Prophet said: remove harmful objects from the paths (Ibn Mājah, 5:3681) as such actions can lead to Paradise (Ibn Mājah, 5:3682). In essence, all actions, subject to their intentions, are potentially acts of worship.

Shahādah

The ***Shahādah*** is the testimony of faith: 'I bear witness that there is no god but Allah; I bear witness that Muḥammad is the Messenger of God' (Ramadan, 2017). In Shī'ism, there is a third part: 'and 'Ali is the Walī (Friend) of Allah'. This refers to the fourth ***Khalīfah*** of the Sunnī and first Imām of the Shī'a. You will learn about the roots and obligations of Shī'ism in Chapter 10.

Despite diverse practices, these five pillars remain the common denominator (Esposito, 2016). The testimony is the foundation upon which Islam and the totality of its teaching rests. This is all that is required to become a Muslim in the presence of witnesses. By declaring this, a Muslim then commits oneself to obey God and follow the Prophet (ﷺ). It is an exceptionally popular phrase in Arabic, which features in the daily *Adhān, Iqāmah, Ṣalāh,* and is on the lips of Muslims frequently, informally or as a formal remembrance (*dhikr*). Significantly, it is expected to be uttered before death (Muslim, 2:1996). You will observe its calligraphy appearing in religious buildings, paintings, gravestones and elsewhere. It is attributed great value on Judgement Day.

For example, a person will be summoned and 99 enormous scrolls (of misdeeds) will be presented. Allah will ask: 'Do you deny anything of this?' The person will reply: 'No, my Lord.' Then, Allah will ask: 'Have My scribes been unfair?' Then Allah will say: 'Do you have a good deed?' The anxious person will admit: 'No.' Allah will say: 'Your good deeds are with Us. You will not be treated unjustly today.' Then a card bearing the *Ṣhahādah* will be shown. The person will (whilst undermining it) say: 'O Lord, what is this card compared with these scrolls?' Then both will be put on a balance. The scrolls will go up and the card will go down' (Ibn Mājah, 5:4300). As a result, there will be mercy and pardon due to this testimony.

Ṭahārah (purity)

Acts of worship tend to be preceded by adhering to the matters of ritual purity, both physical and spiritual. Thus, scholars have penned a plethora of manuals as guides detailing the laws for purification (*Ṭahārah*) for Muslims. From a very young age, Muslims, at home, are introduced to the concept of purity and impurity. Thereafter, they formally learn, at the *madrasah* ('mosque school'), the categories, types, rulings and how these affect their daily life and particular situations. Then, through observation and practical demonstrations, they learn how to perform *wuḍū'* (ablution), its compulsory acts, how it is nullified, which acts of worship require it and how it is spiritually cleansing.

Ablution entails using water to clean the mouth, nostrils, face, forearms, dabbing part of the head, wiping the ears and washing feet up to the ankles according to (5:6). Jurists differ regarding the nullification of ablution and considerable details feature in manuals on purity. A single ablution may take a person through more than one prayer but must be repeated following minor impurities (***ḥadath***) like passing urine, stool, flatus, vomit, bleeding or sleep (Nyazee, 2006).

It may be easy to conclude that the requirement for ablution is absolute, but travellers, the sick and others are given conditional dispensations. The crucial matter here is obedience to Allah's specific requirements rather than cleanliness per se (Brown, 2017). For instance, in the absence of the availability of water, an alternative is to use clean earth instead to fulfil the requirements of ritual purity (*tayammum*). However, personal supplication and remembrance, glorification and praise of God (*dhikr*) do not require formal purification. Dispensation may be applied in severe icy situations too.

Once the worshipper has fulfilled the physical ritual purity, God is concerned with their inner consciousness. The Prophet (ﷺ) declared that actions are determined by their intentions (al-Bukhārī, 1:1). Thus, all acts are preceded with a specific intent to conduct it for Allah. In other words, the first stage of purity involves the purification of the external organs from physical filths. The second is the purification of the bodily organs from sins. The third is the purification of the heart from evil traits and vices. The fourth stage is the purification of the inner self from everything except Allah. This is the stage of the prophets, friends of God and saints (Al-Ghazālī, 2009).

Adhān

The call to prayer (*Adhān*), creates a sense of discipline to leave everything aside and assemble for prayer. It is a uniform announcement extended to Muslims globally five times daily evoking emotions of piety and serenity. Its initiation has an interesting story.

After the emigration (*Hijrah*) to Madīnah, Muslims habitually assembled for prayers and used to approximate the time for it. Consequently, they discussed the matter and several suggestions were proposed: to hoist a flag, ring a bell like the Christians, blow a *shofār* like the Jews or light a fire like the Zoroastrians. In the night, ʻAbd Allah ibn Zayd saw a dream about calling people. Accordingly, the next day the Messenger (ﷺ) instructed an Abyssinian named Bilāl, previously a slave, to pronounce it for prayers (Abū Dāwūd, 1:498). Since then it has been instituted as a universal practice.

The minarets, as tall structures, are used by skilful ***mu'adhdhin*** for projecting their voices further. In recent times, an attempt, with little success, was made in Cairo to transform the famous soundscape of this ancient city so that one *adhān* was offered for the metropolis. In the UK, many mosques relay it via their radio receivers to homes; a few mosques, during legally permitted hours, use public address systems. Many adults and children have their own style, whilst some copy their local caller or other popular ones by imitating the elongation of vowels and making their tunes melodious.

Historically, it was also deployed for announcing deaths, warning against fires, or demanding justice and when one is afflicted with epilepsy (Jazīrī, 2009). In July 2016, many mosques in Turkey incanted it outside of ritual time inviting the public to gather in open squares to resist the coup.

Prayer (*Ṣalāh*)

Individual Muslims, as worshippers, are situated within a worshipping community. The Sharī'ah codifies and organises these practices in many different collective forms. The main act of establishing this regular communal form of worship is *Ṣalāh*, which is obligatory on every adult and sane Muslim five times a day. Acts of worship become obligatory upon individuals who fulfil certain criteria and the commands are derived from the Lawgiver on the basis of decisive evidence (Hasan, 2007). An obligatory act is known as *farḍ* (pl. *farā'iḍ*) or *wājib (pl. wājibāt).*

Muslims execute *Ṣalāh* after fulfilling certain priori conditions such as the purity of the body, clothes, space, covering the body, appropriate time, facing the *Qiblah*, having the intention and declaring the ***Takbīr*** (Allahu Akbar). This liturgical prayer occupies the most significant position and is given maximum prominence in the Qur'ān. From the viewpoint of its status, *Ṣalāh* can be *farḍ*, ***sunnah*** (prophetic habit) and *nafl* (optional).

Organisationally, it can be offered congregationally and individually and, when necessary, you will observe Muslims offering their *Ṣalāh* on different modes of transport including aeroplanes, ships and on animals. *Ṣalāh* may be offered at any ritually clean place, home, park, mosque or office. However, *Ṣalāh* performed in congregation (*Ṣalāh bil jamā'ah*) is more meritorious and is highly recommended at the mosque (al-Bukhārī, 1:618). Where women attend, they tend to occupy the rear lines as was the practice during the prophetic times (Ibn Mājah, 2:1000). It is also suggested that it addresses uncomfortable situations of men performing behind women during their movements of bowing and prostrating (Hathout, 2008), since the import is to turn to God after having turned away from all evil thoughts and worldly matters (Al-Ghazālī, 1993). It is also reported that it is more excellent for a woman to pray in her house than in her courtyard, and more excellent for her to pray in her private chamber within her house (Abū Dāwūd, 1:570).

Muslims stand facing a common direction of the **Ka'bah** in Makkah from any part of the world which is known as the *Qiblah*. The Ka'bah is considered to be the first House [of worship] established for humankind (3:96). As such, it provides a unique emotional and spiritual unity on a universal scale. The concentric circle is only visible around the Ka'bah in Makkah, otherwise, across the globe it is usually straight lines bringing uniformity in the Muslim body globally, in terms of direction and intention (Chittick, 2012: 24). However, in certain circumstances this requirement is waived like being out at sea without a navigating gadget. In a mosque the *Qiblah* is indicated by a semi-circular recess called the *miḥrāb* (niche). However, when Muslims find themselves in unfamiliar locations at the time of prayer, most jurists agree that they should make an effort in locating the direction (*Taḥarrī*), and pray in that direction. *Qiblah* apps are now used to determine the direction.

Having fulfilled these external requirements, to announce the commencement of prayer, the *Iqāmah* is called. Muslims will assemble at the mosque, home, workplace or service stations usually behind an Imām to have an audience with Allah. Each mandatory *Ṣalāh* is made up of two, three or four units called ***rak'ah*** (pl. *raka'āt*).

The sequence in which these different postures are performed follows a natural order and embodies servitude and humility. Standing shoulder to shoulder with one another minimises the distinctions of wealth, race, status and other differentials within the community so that they gain a sense of being equal in the presence of Allah. In congregation, Muslims judiciously follow the Imām as a single body endorsing its submission before Allah as a collective. These uniform motions develop a notable spirit of unity in body, mind and soul (Al-Ghazālī, 1993). Moreover, for most contemporary Muslims, angels are a pervasive meta-reality which is acknowledged within these prayers (Hussain, 2016).

The number of units differ according to the prayer. Most mosques publish a timetable showing the beginning and termination times with other information to make it convenient to congregate. The times and actions are not specified in the Qur'ān but were established by Muḥammad (ﷺ) (Esposito, 2016). The precise duration of each prayer period is a matter of some discussion among scholars. Table 6.1 shows the general duration of compulsory prayers.

Table 6.1 General duration of compulsory prayers

Ṣalāh	Compulsory units	Earliest start time	End time
Fajr	2	After dawn	Prior to sunrise
Ẓuhr	4	After zenith	An object's shadow equal to or twice its length
'Asr	4	End of Ẓuhr	Immediately before sunset
Maghrib	3	After sunset	Disappearance of twilight
'Ishā'	4	End of Maghrib	Start of dawn

Being created for the worship of Allah does not imply abandoning families, work and living a life of seclusion since the reality of worship is to obey Allah in all everyday matters. Islam acknowledges that humans are by nature weak

(4:28) and forgetful, thus they need a regular reminder especially when Satan is continuously whispering insinuations making them unmindful of Allah. The urgings of the self in numerous façades keep on 'whispering' to make them preoccupied with other matters. This demands a constant reminder of who Muslims are. Thus, God in His Infinite Wisdom ordained *Ṣalāh* as a blessing to assist Muslims to remember and develop this mind frame of being conscious (Mawdūdī, 2016).

It is among the first actions to be questioned on the Day of Judgment (Abū Dāwūd, 1:863). As the most frequent practice affecting the daily lives of Muslims, they are encouraged to seek help through patience and *Ṣalāh* (2:153). Muslims consider it a shield as it prohibits immorality and wrongdoing (29:45). Therefore, if *Ṣhaḥādah* is the oral acknowledgment of surrender to God's love and mercy, the *Ṣalāh* adds the bodily activity most recommended by God (Chittick, 2012). The Messenger (ﷺ) encouraged, "'If there existed a river at the door of anyone of you, and you took a bath therein five times a day, would you notice any dirt being left on you?" They said, "No dirt would be left." The Prophet said, "That is the parable of the five prayers by which Allah removes sins"' (al-Bukhārī, 1:506).

There are distinct features and instructions elaborated for Friday congregational prayers, prayers on a journey, prayers during wartime, prayers by the sick, and prayers during solar and lunar eclipses. There are other optional ones offered at different times such as the late night (***Tahajjud*** *Ṣalāh*) which is usually part of the routine of the more devout. These are all established by the regular practice of the Prophet (ﷺ). They compensate for the deficiencies in the compulsory prayers (Nadwi, 2011) and are a source of virtue and spiritual advancement. Furthermore, there exists specific prayers for seeking rain and personal needs. These are set topics, which every teacher of Islamic law deals with, and curricula discuss in detail. You should be aware that several actions could render the prayer invalid including speaking, laughing, exposing parts of the body which require covering, and bleeding. However, it is permissible to ward off harm (Brown, 2017). Table 6.2 shows the distinctions and selected features of three common prayers.

Fasting (*Ṣawm*)

Ramaḍān is the ninth month of the *Hijrah* calendar (*Hijrī*). The word *ra-ma-ḍa* literally means 'to burn', implying that a person endeavours to burn evil inclinations and negative propensities. According to the Qur'ān, fasting was ordained in the Laws (Sharī'ah) of many previous prophets (2:183). However,

Table 6.2 Features of the prayers for the deceased, Friday and 'Īd

For the deceased (Janāzah)	Friday prayer (Jumu'ah)	'Īd prayers
Seek forgiveness for adults	Fulfilment of personal duty	Fulfilment of personal duty
No Adhān	Two: call for prayer and before commencing sermon	No Adhān
No Iqāmah before prayer	Iqāmah before prayer	Iqāmah before prayer
Facing Qiblah	Facing Qiblah	Facing Qiblah
As soon as possible	After zenith	Early or mid-morning
No recitation of Qur'ān	Recitation of Qur'ān	Recitation of Qur'ān
No bowing, no prostration	Bowing and prostration	Bowing and prostration
No sermon	Sermon before prayer	Sermon after prayer
Sometimes advice given	Speech before sermon in some communities	Speech before sermon in some communities
Four proclamations of ***takbīr***	Many proclamations	Many proclamations
Usually led by local Imām	Led by Imām/senior	Led by Imām/senior
Communal obligation	Individual duty	Individual duty
For all, other than stillbirths, to be a reward, treasure and intercessor for parents	Not compulsory on travellers, terminally ill, women and children	Not compulsory on travellers, terminally ill, women and children
Prohibited times avoided	Replaces *Ẓuhr* of the day	Does not replace *Ẓuhr*
At the mosque or cemetery; if needed single prayer for mass burials	Collectively performed in mosque or public space	Collectively performed in mosque or public space
Coffin/body usually in front	Imām in front	Imām in front
Could be performed in absentia, according to some	At airports, hospitals, prisons and universities	In prisons but less likely in airports and hospitals
Sometimes offered after burial, if not previously done	Cannot be offered after *Ẓuhr* time ends, but compensatory	Could be postponed to the next day/s
Ends with salām	Ends with salām	Ends with salām

their rules, number and duration varied; so Muslims find comfort from knowing that others had fasted and are grateful for the opportunity to express their devotion through such a major act of worship.

Commonly, fasting is defined as giving up eating, drinking and sexual intercourse from dawn to sunset. However, in essence, it encompasses all the senses and thoughts including backbiting, verbal and physical abuse, anger, jealousy and dishonesty, and, economically, the hands abstain from encroaching the belongings of others and illegal financial activity. If one does not give up speaking falsehood and acting by it, God does not require them to give up eating and drinking (al-Bukhārī, 3:127); rather than absolving the fast, this *ḥadīth* draws attention to its 'bigger picture'. According to the Hanafī school, kissing does not break the fast, although it is discouraged so as not to lead to intercourse or ejaculation, whereas vomiting a mouthful intentionally invalidates the fast and swallowing the saliva of one's wife after kissing too, according to many scholars (Shurunbulali, 2007).

Fasting is compulsory upon every Muslim, male and female, who is physically well and mature. It is to be preceded by an intention. The infirm, terminally ill, travellers, pregnant women subject to their condition, may opt in or out of the fast. All these are to make up for their missed fasts, except the terminally ill who, in lieu of the missed fasts, give a ***fidyah*** to the poor, whereas the travellers and pregnant women make up for their fasts later.

Minors, meaning those who, according to Islam, have not yet reached maturity (*bulūgh*) which is usually biologically determined rather than age, are not obligated to fast. However, many children do participate and parents often recommend that they do so to train them and to join in family and communal devotions. It is also part of their physical, emotional, moral and spiritual development and creates God-consciousness.

Fasting is a private worship, in the sense that the others consist of some outward manifestation unlike fasting; which unless an individual declares so, no one except the All-Knowing Allah would know about it. Hence, faith in God is strengthened and, undoubtedly, it is seen as a test in integrity and a programme for discipline in searching for higher goals and meaning in life (Mawdūdī, 2016).

Imām Al-Ghazālī examined fasting deeply and proposed three degrees: namely, (i) abstinence from the satisfaction of the belly and private parts, of which the common people are capable, (ii) abstinence from sins associated with the ear, eye, tongue, legs and hands, which the elite are capable of and (iii) abstinence from the sins of the heart and mind. Only the elite and most pious people fulfil this last condition. All worldly thoughts are to be banished. Only the thought of God should remain since the object of fasting is to achieve mastery over desires and to attain spiritual kinship with the nearness of God (Sway, 2017).

Voice of a Muslim

On Tuesday 7 May 2019, it was my first fast. I woke up early for *suhūr*, had cereal and went to sleep. Then at 8:15 I got ready to go to school. I did all the lessons, break and more lessons, then it was lunch time. You have to go to a Year 6 classroom and do colouring. Then we go in and do more lessons, then it is home time. I walked home with my friend. When I got home I learnt my books and went upstairs, did my *wuḍū'* and went to mosque class. In Ramaḍān mosque is only for one hour. Normally it is for two hours. When mosque finishes I go home with a different friend. At home I baked a cake with lots of sprinkles and icing. Then I went to sleep and woke up at 7:30. Then I started to help my mum with the food for *iftār* and I had made a big cheese ball. Then I played on the computer till 8:40. When it was time to break our fast I had lots of samosas, dates, my big cheese ball, watermelon and a glass of rose flavoured milk. Everybody wanted the cake so I cut it and shared it. After that I went with my dad to the masjid for *maghrib*. After we came back, I opened my Ramaḍān chocolate calendar and on the flap it had Arabic and English words. The first day it revealed patience (*ṣabr*) which is what I had done all day! After that I had rice and *dhāl* with chicken and went to sleep. I fasted because it is Ramaḍān and to feel how it is for the people without food and for Allah. I hope to get lots of reward. I felt hungry during the day at teatime and in the evening. At the end I felt very full. It has stopped a lot of bad habits. It was the best day of my life. When I grow up it will be easy for me because my sisters said that when they were small the fasts were from 6:30 to 16:00 which is very easy. (Muṣṭafā, British, 10 year old, male)

Personal and social benefits

Unlike Ṣalāh, Zakāh and Ḥajj, fasting enables Muslims to express obedience for a sustained period during the day and at night, voluntarily.

You might observe a very real change in the environment as a whole; there is a propensity to avoid sin and undesirable acts within an atmosphere of righteousness and piety. Muslims will readily inform you that there is a noticeable change in the increase of charity, sharing, expression of gratitude and contribution to goodness in all forms. In other words, with the physical discipline, a change in the social behaviour of the whole community is expected for the month. The pace of life slows down and there is time for reflection to reaffirm social relationships, reconciliation and to express solidarity of the community (Kerr, 2018b).

The inspiration originates from the Prophet (ﷺ) himself as the embodiment of such virtues. As regards the reward of fasting, God says, 'fasting is exclusively for Me. I reward for it as much as I wish' (Muslim, 2:2566). This is because only Allah knows about it. One wears an inner armour of detachment against passions of the outside which requires asceticism and interior discipline which come about through inner *jihād* (Nasr, 2012). Religiously and spiritually, other purposes and motivation of fasting include:

- To (learn how to) attain God-consciousness (*taqwā*) (2:183)
- Fasting is a shield (from succumbing to low desires) (Muslim, 2:2565)
- It gets all past sins (minor) forgiven (al-Bukhārī, 1:34)
- A fasting person's supplication is not rejected (al-Tirmidhī, 6:3598)
- The gates of the Heaven are opened and Hell is closed (Ibn Mājah, 3:1642)

Onset of Ramaḍān

The onset of the months in the Islamic (***Hijrī***) calendar depends on the sighting of the crescent following a new moon, whose visibility is dependent on clear skies and other atmospheric factors; thus, the precise date for the first day of Ramaḍān cannot be predicted with absolute certainty. Moreover, since the crescent is not visible in all regions of the world at once and local dates can be different from one country to another, Ramaḍān may start on different dates according to a country's geography. In the UK, Muslims have generated several formulae; hence, the controversy for the start and end of Ramaḍān and two 'Īd. Briefly, some attempt local sighting and, in its absence, follow sighting in Morocco. Some accept European or African sightings. Others rely exclusively on Saudi Arabia. A third view takes calculations from the observatory and the possibility of any sighting from the east of the UK. Consequently, some families begin observing Ramaḍān and 'Īd on different days.

Suḥūr and Ifṭār

Muslims would have a pre-dawn meal (*Suḥūr*) for in it lies blessings (al-Bukhārī, 3:146) and, at dawn, fasting commences which ends with the partaking of something to eat or drink (*Ifṭār*) at sunset. Many prefer to break their fast with dates as recommended by the Prophet (ﷺ) (al-Tirmidhī, 2:696), others opt for *zamzam* or anything of their liking such as milkshake, water, stews, soups or rice, bread and chapatti with a curry. After breaking fast and the subsequent meal, some will have family time, take a stroll, and smoke a cigarette whilst others may begin preparing for the night prayers.

The duration of the fast will depend on the location of the country and time of the year. You might want to compare the timetables shown in Table 6.3 and Table 6.4 from a city in the UK.

Table 6.3 Ramaḍān in Spring

Ramaḍān	Date	Suḥūr	Fajr	Ẓuhr	'Asr	Iftār and Maghrib	'Ishā' and Tarawīh
1	16 May	3:19 am	3:34	1:30 pm	6:45	8:50	10:45 pm
2	17 May	3:17 am	3:32	1:30 pm	6:45	8:52	10:45 pm
3	18 May	3:16 am	3:31	1:30 pm	6:45	8:53	10:45 pm
4	19 May	3:13 am	3:28	1:30 pm	6:45	8:55	10:45 pm
5	20 May	3:12 am	3:27	1:30 pm	6:45	8:56	10:45 pm

Table 6.4 Ramaḍān in Winter

Ramaḍān	Date	Suḥūr	Fajr	Ẓuhr	'Asr	Iftār and Maghrib	'Ishā' and Tarāwīh
1	18 Dec	6:45 am	7:15	1:15 pm	2:45	3:57	6:30 pm
2	19 Dec	6:46 am	7:15	1:15 pm	2:45	3:57	6:30 pm
3	20 Dec	6:46 am	7:15	1:15 pm	2:45	3:57	6:30 pm
4	21 Dec	6:46 am	7:15	1:15 pm	2:45	3:58	6:30 pm
5	22 Dec	6:47 am	7:15	1:15 pm	2:45	3:58	6:30 pm

Night of Power

The Qur'ān was revealed in Ramaḍān, hence, there is strong attachment with it during this period. For instance, after the 'Ishā prayer, in Ramaḍān, you may hear children refer to 'a special long prayer'; this is called *Tarāwiḥ* consisting of 20 units in total offered in congregation; a minority performs eight. In these prayers, it is common for the entire Qur'ān to be recited during the month; an opportunity seized by many. The night commemorates the descent of the Qur'ān (97:1–5). Some try to complete a full recital on a daily basis.

Ṣadaqat al-Fiṭr

Before offering the ***'Īd al-Fiṭr** prayer*, a special alms, called *Ṣadaqat al-Fiṭr* (also *Zakāh-al-Fiṭr),* is distributed as a mark of gratitude, to show an end to Ramaḍān and to assist the poor and needy to join in and have a happier day. The head of each family must give a specified amount of barley, dates, wheat or raisins or its equivalent as staple food. However, in the UK many opt to give money. If sent overseas, Muslims try to do so in advance so that the recipients receive it before 'Īd day, otherwise the objective may be defeated.

Giving for God

You need to be familiar with several terms for understanding 'charitable' acts in Islam. The concept *Infāq* denotes spending compassionately for any cause; this type of giving has no limits but to seek the pleasure of Allah (*Lillāh*), such as giving to street beggars.

Ṣadaqah is derived from the root '*ṣidq*' meaning truth, righteousness or sincerity, and signifies a charitable deed usually with a purpose. There is no fixed rate of the general *ṣaqadah* and a person may give it at any time, place, and whatever amount either openly or secretly as a concern for humanity or for themselves, for example, to ward off personal calamities or to express gratitude. However, *Ṣadaqat-al-fiṭr* has a stipulated amount, and time as stated above.

Another type is when an individual makes an oath (*Nadhr*) of giving charity; then it becomes mandatory. A compensation (*Fidyah*) for missing prayer or fasting is mandatory for one unable to perform them due to a terminal illness or a mishap in *Ḥajj*, which is also a kind of *ṣadaqah. Kaffarah* is a substantial compensation, also a kind of mandated *ṣadaqah* which applies in situations such as breaking a fast intentionally, killing someone or breaking an oath, when it becomes binding as a form of redemption.

Another type is perpetual charity (*Ṣadaqah Jāriyah*). In reality, this is any voluntary *ṣadaqah* given to a cause for long-term benefit. Parents leaving a pious child who prays for them is included in this. Muslims in the UK, like elsewhere, take advantage of this and build wells, hospitals, orphanages, schools, mosques, *madāris* and other social projects which can all fall under this category so that after death they continue to be credited with rewards (Abū Dāwūd, 2:2874). It is similar to endowment (*waqf*).

Voice of a Muslim

Shaykh 'Abdul Qādir Jilānī (470–561AH/1077–1166CE), a universally acclaimed spiritual master and ascetic, once declared, there is a hole in my palm. Nothing stays in it, if I had even a thousand dirhams, they would be spent before dusk. (Nadwi, 2011)

In many verses (2:245), Allah asks who is willing to give God a goodly loan (*Qarḍ Ḥasan*); obviously Allah is not in need of it, so the purport is to encourage giving willingly a gratuitous loan to someone whose current need can be fulfilled for a set time without taking interest. The root *q-r-ḍ* denotes 'to cut' something, since one takes a part of their wealth or belongings to give to another. This is also an optional type of *ṣadaqah*. Many mosques, schools and local institutions in the UK tend to begin their projects with such loans, which are sometimes waived.

The quality of giving is emphasised since, when it is given with the intention of seeking God's pleasure and for self-purification, it is likened to a garden on a hill; the rainstorm smites it and it brings forth its fruit twofold (Kerr, 2018b). Being an act designed to cure the spiritual malady and because the heart of the giver is prone to show, giving *ṣadaqah* secretly is encouraged as a powerful remedy for both. Indeed, discretion is preferred to ostentation, and reproach on the part of the giver makes the action worthless. Importantly, it is a mercy to the giver as much as to the recipient. Like fasting, it is a means to atone for sins, which are motivated by human self-centeredness, or by irresponsible stewardship of possessions (Kerr, 2018b: 78).

Within this framework, it is useful to keep in mind that the giving and receiving of interest/usury is explicitly forbidden (2:275). Thus, the interest accumulated in a bank account presents a challenge to many Muslims. Since it is impermissible to use it for personal benefit, some give the interest money to general public charitable works, without intending any reward and avoiding the consumption of something severely disliked by God.

Zakāh

Zakāh is a technical term which literally means 'to grow' or 'to purify'. It is an obligation (*farḍ*) set by the Qur'ān and is regulated in terms of its quantity, types of commodities, time, recipients and condition of individuals. It is eligible on mature and sane persons who meet the quantum (***niṣāb***) threshold. Zakāh is the act of removing a portion of one's total wealth for the specified eight categories of people stipulated in the Qur'ān: the poor, needy, collectors [of Zakāh] and for bringing hearts together [for Islam] and for freeing captives [or slaves] and for those in debt and for the cause of Allah and for the [stranded] traveller (9:60). This is a form of *jihād* as one must fight the covetousness of one's carnal soul and establish economic justice (Nasr, 2012). The amounts of Zakāh to be given on different types of possessions are precisely set. However, contemporary practice simplifies the amount to 2.5 per cent of one's total wealth (Kerr, 2018b).

You should now be able to recognise its significance. It is through 'giving' to others that a Muslims' wealth is purified. Importantly, the 'self' (*nafs*) is also cleansed of greed, love of wealth and selfishness. On the contrary, anyone negligent to execute it renders their wealth and inner state impure. In other words, the heart is void of generosity, empathy, gratitude and social activism. To attain the nearness, love and friendship of God, in light of the Qur'ān, Muslims believe that they have to part with their treasured wealth and sacrifice some of their luxuries (3:92). Thus, Zakāh is a balm for stinginess (59:9), a means to show magnanimity (24:22) and is given for selfless reasons (76:8–9). Finally, the heart should be pure to give (2:267). Concurrently, the recalcitrant of *Zakāh* have been severely warned (9:34–35). In general, giving is not restricted to good times (63:9) because even in hard times, helping the cause of Allah and humanity should continue (3:133). Accordingly, almsgiving and charity are integral to society just as prayer, fasting and pilgrimage are integral to Allah. In Chapter 10 you will learn about Khums in Shī'ism. Table 6.5 is an example of how to calculate Zakāh.

Table 6.5 A typical chart used for calculating Zakāh

Zakāh calculation chart	
Cash in hand (any currency acceptable in the market)	£
Cash at bank (in any type of account)	£
Value of gold/silver (jewellery, ornaments, cutlery, coins)	£
Livestock	£
Creditors (add money owed to you)	£
Shares and stocks	£

Zakāh calculation chart	
Pensions and retirement plans	£
Trusts	£
Business goods	£
Total (add all the above)	£
Debts (deduct money you owe to others)	£
Total amount eligible for Zakāh	£
2.5% of the above amount is to be given as Zakāh	£

In view of the fact that wealth is a means of enjoying the pleasure of the world and that people find it most difficult to part with money, *Zakāh* is one of the most crucial tests of a person's real love of Allah ('Umaruddin, 1996). There has evolved considerable discussion among contemporary jurists (*fuqahā'*) on various modern issues related to Zakāh. For some there are no clear answers, so qualified scholars resort to *ijtihād* where each school has its reasoning for the positions held; some apply the principle of public benefit (*maslahah al-'āmma*).

Voice of a Muslim

There are many types of martyrs. Those who died in the way of Allah. Those dying of plague, diseases of the stomach or intestines; drowning, being crushed by a collapsing building; being killed defending property, life and family and dying in fire. Also a woman who dies from complications of pregnancy and delivery and one who speaks to a tyrannical leader and is killed. One falling passionately in love but remains chaste. Interesting also *dhātul-janb* [swelling of membrane under the rib], maybe this is cancer. This is a sign of Allah's mercy. (Fokhrul, Muftī, Bengali, male)

Ḥajj (pilgrimage)

Ḥajj assists in moulding the life of a Muslim to surrender to God. Literally it means 'to set out on a journey'; otherwise, it is to visit Makkah to execute the rites of pilgrimage seeking the pleasure of God. Unlike the constancy of the four obligations above, *Ḥajj* is only required once in a lifetime by the physically and financially capable, sane, adults who can safely go there. Some do make multiple visits, even though the Prophet (ﷺ) made a single pilgrimage; those physically unable may send a substitute.

Ḥajj is significant as it offers an opportunity for pilgrims to overlook their country, comforts, kith and kin, friends and wealth and completely submit to the Divine command. In the state of *Iḥrām* during pilgrimage, sexual relations, disobedience and disputes must be avoided (2:197). As a blessing, pilgrims are promised a return in a pure and sinless state as they were at birth (al-Bukhārī, 2:596). Their sins are removed in the same way as the furnace removes the impurities of gold, silver and iron and the reward for a sincere *Ḥajj* is paradise (Al-Nasā'ī, 3:2632).

The *Ḥajj* (Greater Pilgrimage) occurs over five days in the twelfth month (*Dhul al-Ḥijjah*). A visit for pilgrimage at any other time during the year is known as *'Umrah* (the Lesser Pilgrimage). This makes Makkah eventful throughout the year; *Ḥajj* is time-specific but both are spatially confined.

Pilgrims will adorn themselves in simple pilgrimage clothing (*Iḥrām*), usually white in colour for men and women have a choice. This represents the state of ritual purification and dropping socio-economical distinctions. This is done before crossing the border (***Mīqāt***) either at an airport, while in flight or on land at the various crossing points. Then they offer two units of prayer, make their intention of *Ḥajj* and declare: 'Here I am, My Lord, Here I am' (*Talbiyyah*). Once they arrive in Makkah, they enter the Holy Precinct (*Ḥaram*) and circumambulate the Ka'bah seven times (*Ṭawāf*) in a counter-clockwise direction. This is followed by two units of prayer around the station of Ibrāhīm, drinking *zamzam* and then they proceed to a walkway which encompasses two hillocks where they walk (*Sa'ī*) except in the middle section when they adopt a brisk pace to commemorate the predicament of **Hagar** (Ḥajrah). Subject to the type of *Ḥajj,* they either trim or shave their hair. This act would complete the *'Umrah*, as it is a visitation but does not accomplish the *Ḥajj*.

On the eighth day (the Day of Reflection) some will put on a fresh *Iḥrām* for *Ḥajj* and, after sunrise, proceed to Mina in the outskirts of Makkah. There, they spend the night in personal supplications, voluntary prayer, remembrance of God's name, glorifying, praising and thanking Allah and recitation of the Qur'ān. It is also known as Yawm al-Tarwiyah (the Day of Quenching Thirst) as pilgrims and their animals ensured they had enough to drink and prepared for their travels.

On the ninth day (Day of Standing/'Arafāt) after offering the Morning Prayer, they wait for sunrise and then they move *en masse* to another plain known as 'Arafāt, where the *Ḥajj* reaches its climax, and being in this space renders the *Ḥajj* fulfilled, otherwise not. This is a scene reminiscent of the Judgement Day. Here pilgrims stay in penitence, reflection, forgiveness, worship and other devotions.

After sunset, from 'Arafāt they go to the plain of Muzdalifah where they stay overnight or be there at least from dawn to sunrise and collect pebbles. Just before sunrise of the following day, the tenth (Day of Sacrifice), they return to Minā. From there they go to fling pebbles (*Ramī al-jimār*) to the pillars (*Jamarāt*) representing the position of Satan who tempted Ibrāhīm on his way to sacrifice Ismā'īl. Then they sacrifice an animal (***Hadī***). Pilgrims then proceed to Makkah where they perform the *Ṭawāf Ziyarah, Sa'y* and shave their hair, and return to Minā. This frees them from the *Iḥrām* and completes the *Ḥajj*. The lapidation of the pillars is usually completed on the eleventh and twelfth day.

Zamzam

Most, if not all pilgrims, will bring along *zamzam* to share with their family and friends as blessings and cure. Ḥājrah (Hagar) was frantically running up and down two hillocks searching support and sustenance for her baby, Ismā'īl, who was near the Ka'bah. The child was blessed with a miraculous spring of water, which had broken through the desert sands. Ḥājrah arrived and, according to some whispered, '*zam zam*' flow slowly; others suggest it refers to the sound it made, or the gathering of sand around it (Mubarakpuri, 2002). Henceforth, this well and water acquired its honoured name. The *Sa'y*, mentioned above, represents this run from *Al-Safā* to *Al-Marwah* and these eminences are among the symbols of Allah (2:158).

Station of Abraham

If you look closely in the precinct of the Ka'bah, you will notice a golden case-like structure. The Qur'ān proposes that there are clear signs in it (3:97); one being its greatness both material and spiritual, it being the permanent all-world centre of the monotheists (Daryābādi, 1991), and also the Station of Ibrāhīm (Maqām Ibrāhīm) which is a place of prayer (2:125). The case has a stone (the *maqām*) with the footmarks of Ibrāhīm which were ingrained as he built the Ka'bah (Pānipatī, 1991).

Black Stone

On one corner of the Ka'bah, you will also observe a silver casing. In it is what is called the Black Stone (*Al-Ḥajar al-Aswad*) which is a stone reported to be from

Heaven (Al-Nasā'ī, 3:2938). In every circuit, pilgrims execute the ritual of *Istilām* which is an attempt to kiss it, emulating the kiss of Muḥammad (ﷺ) (al-Bukhārī, 2:673), or, if inaccessible, they raise their hands towards it and kiss their palm and declare in Arabic: 'In the name of God, Allah is Greater'. However, it is important to recollect that Muslims do not worship it.

A Muslim completing a *Ḥajj* tends to receive an honorific title; ***Ḥāji*** for males and ***Ḥajjah*** for females. It denotes a degree of social reputation and, eventually, it may be adopted as a family name or title. It constitutes one of the five pillars of Islam, and in Shī'ism, one of its ten branches of religion. Pilgrims from across the globe converge in Makkah providing a unique opportunity for those of different cultures, languages and ethnicities to meet one another to express a strong sense of duty and commitment.

Case study 6.1 Jihād

Jamīl completed his first degree in British and Irish history. As a newly qualified PGCE teacher he knew that battles and wars have been a constant trait in the history of the British Isles. Recently the topic of *jihād* had become a regular feature in the media. He heard children talking about it in the playground. He felt that pupils in his own classroom and beyond would benefit from learning about this topic. However he had a dilemma because he was not fully acquainted with the subject matter. So he approached the year group coordinator who agreed and suggested that he spoke with and found out more from an Imām, which he did. He shared his findings with his coordinator. In class he wanted to focus on knowledge and understanding. To facilitate this he chose to use the K, W, H, L grid. He provided the children with an A3 sheet of paper divided into three columns with K, W, H and L at the top of each column. He then asked the pupils to identify what they already knew (K) or had heard about *jihād*, what they wanted (W) to find out, how (H) they would find this out and what they expected to learn (L). Using this information he was able to identify some concepts, content knowledge and misunderstandings, and plan his future activities. He was impressed with this and decided to cite it as example during his next progress review meeting with his NQT mentor. At the meeting the mentor was very pleased and suggested that Jamīl present a summary of this at the next staff meeting.

This case study encapsulates teaching of contemporary and controversial issues.

- Consider how you can make a religious education lesson relevant and have meaning in your class.
- Having read the case study, what implications does it have for your own development about *jihād* and how to teach it?

Summary

In this chapter, you have learnt that Muslims believe that humans have been created to worship God. In Islam, worship has a broad meaning and it manifests in diverse ways. You have analysed the significance of the main devotional acts of Shahādah, Ṣalāh, Ṣawm and Ḥajj which are the foundations of the edifice of the religion. You have also recognised the role that these play in the moral and social development, and in providing spiritual contentment, to the universal Muslim community. You have appreciated how Muslims show their devotion to God through worship and how they fulfil their religious obligations towards fellow humans. The detailed description of a range of Muslim practices has made you aware of the complexities and diverse ways in which these are executed in everyday situations. At the core of all these acts, there exists a yearning to gain the love and pleasure of Allah.

Reflection tasks

- How significant are the five pillars of Islam for contemporary Muslims?
- Why is the concept of submission and humility so pervasive in Islam?
- What is Shahādah and what are the implications of believing in it?
- Explain the role of Ṣalāh in the spiritual, moral, personal and social development of a Muslim.
- What are the aims and purposes of Ṣawm?
- Explain the importance of the social role that Zakāh plays in society.
- Why is Ḥajj important in Islam?

Further reading

Kreinath, J. (2012) *The Anthropology of Islam Reader*. Abingdon: Routledge.

This collection examines the ways in which religious, ethical and theological teachings operate within the social world. It offers a conceptual framework on the anthropology of Islam as well.

Nadwi, A.H.A. (2011) *The Four Pillars of Islam*. Malaysia: Islamic Book Trust.

Written by an erudite scholar, this publication elucidates the four pillars, their legal position and significance, and covers rich Islamic literature by previous scholars and their representation in other religions.

7

EXPRESSIONS OF PRACTICE

In this chapter you will:

- know about the honoured institutions in Islam
- understand the significant stages in the life of a Muslim
- reflect on the major events as represented in the *Hijri* calendar
- identify some of the collective pietistic, religious and social behaviours.

Overview

The manifestation of Islam is observed in the arena of everyday life. Granted, there are shortcomings among some Muslims as in other communities; nevertheless, Islam continues to be about daily living, both on an individual and communal level. It has a vibrancy that continues to provide meaning to their life even at a time when hostilities to its fundamental principles and attacks to its core teachings are high.

The Muslim is an individual unit with a direct and personal relationship with God. However, this unit connects with many other Muslims in different ways. This relationship is important for teachers to understand individuals, as they are located within the global Muslim community and humanity at large. The concepts of identity, belonging, community, culture and citizenship play a key role in living as a Muslim since they live their faith under different civic laws and constitutions. The teachings of Islam and the model of the Prophet (ﷺ) provide meaning for existence and, therefore, some rituals and rites are significant milestones along the journey of life. The sections on birth, marriage and death raise your awareness of how Muslims celebrate and interpret the beginning and end of human life. The section on the Muslim calendar discusses the main events providing you with the transcendent meanings of these practices.

Family life

The Qur'ān and the traditions of the Prophet (ﷺ) attach considerable importance to the family, since the continuity of humankind depends, in part, on the mutual support, compassion and care that exist between family members and, therefore, it acts as a safeguard for a secure and stable, moral and spiritual upbringing of children and a stronger society. A Muslim family is established through marriage (Gabriel, 2018).

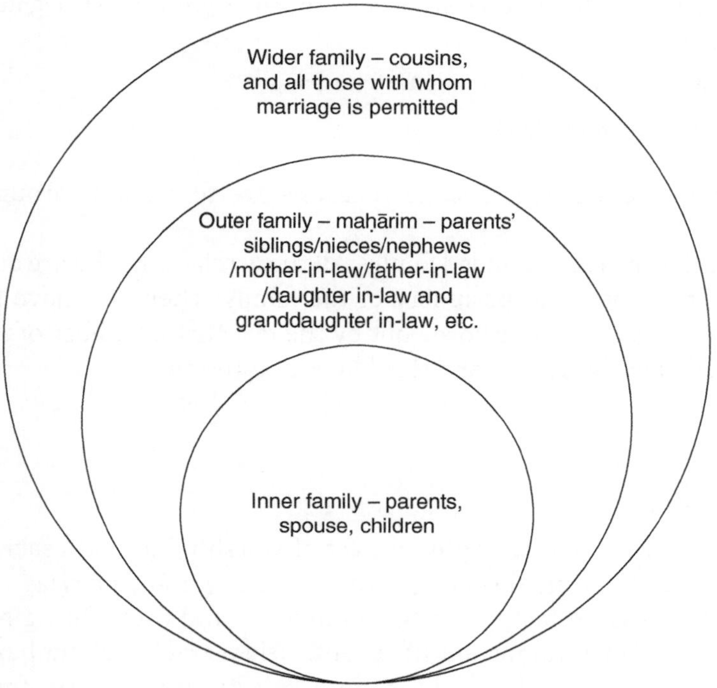

Figure 7.1 The interconnectedness of a Muslim family

The family structure in Figure 7.1 shows three layers. The first comprises of the husband, wife, their parents and their children. The second entails a number of close relatives, who have privileges on each other and who move freely within the family. Marriage between them is forbidden, as they are ***maḥārim***, based on blood relationships, marital ties or breastfeeding and there is no observance of *hijāb* (veil) in their presence. They are also beneficiaries in matters of inheritance. These relationships emerge from consanguinity, affinity and foster-nursing (Abd Al-Ati, 1995). This relationship includes:

a. father, mother, grandfather, grandmother and other direct ascendants
b. direct descendants, that is, sons, daughters, grandsons, granddaughters, etc.
c. relations of the second degree (such as brothers, sisters and their descendants)
d. father's or mother's sisters (not their daughters or other descendants).

Those based on affinity include:

a. mother-in-law, father-in-law, grandmother-in-law, grandfather-in-law
b. wife's daughters, husband's sons or their grand or great granddaughters or sons respectively
c. son's wife, grandson's wife, daughter's husband
d. step-mothers (step-father).

With some exceptions, the same relations are forbidden through foster-nursing.

The third is the real extended family. All those relations who are outside this fold constitute the outer periphery of the family. They, too, have their own rights and obligations, as is borne out by the fact that a number of them have been included in the second and third lines of inheritors.

Marriage

Marriage is a virtuous and righteous act of worship but not a sacrament, as it is dissolvable. From the perspective of the Qur'ān, marriage does not impede godliness. In fact, marriage, family life and the upbringing of children are regarded as important life events. Islam teaches about bashfulness, modesty and control of self-desire and rejects promiscuity, fornication, debauchery and adultery (***Zinā***). Marriage is important as a protective institution from immorality and, through marriage, many social teachings are implemented. It is a gift, gives comfort and is a divine sign: 'And of His signs is that He created for you from yourselves mates that you may find tranquillity in them; and He placed between you affection and mercy. Indeed in that are signs for a people who give thought' (30:21). Therefore, marriage encompasses the satisfaction of the natural sexual appetite, enjoyment and procreation (2:223; 7:189; 16:72). A beautiful imagery depicts the relationship between a husband and wife, 'It has been made permissible for you the night preceding fasting to go to your wives (for sexual relations). They are clothing for you and you are clothing for them … So now, have relations with them and seek that which Allah has decreed for you' (2:187). Thus, in marriage, Muslims find solace for their spiritual, psychological, emotional, moral, physical and social needs (Siddiqi, 2010).

In general, individuals and their guardians are responsible for ensuring they are married (al-Nasā'ī, 4:3212). There is no sanction for forced marriages or honour killings in the teachings of Islam. The method of arranged marriages, for practical and faith reasons, is one way of finding a prospective suitor since marriage brings two families as well as two individuals together. However, an increasing number of Muslim youth are taking the initiative to make the initial introduction, whilst bringing parents through a process of negotiation; thus the outcome is a family consensus (Nielsen and Otterbeck, 2016). Thereafter, a get-together is organised between the two and their respective families. The couples will exchange information, find out about their backgrounds and explore aspects of mutual interests. Once they are happy, before making the final decision, they may offer a prayer (***Ṣalāt al-Istikḥārah***) seeking Allah's guidance and goodness. Following this, a formal acceptance or rejection is shared, as per their feelings.

The week leading to the marriage is very busy with a range of activities depending on cultural and family traditions. The ***mehndi*** **(henna)** ceremony is common to most communities where the bride gathers her friends, relatives, neighbours and guests.

Nikāḥ

The *nikāḥ* (marriage ceremony) is supposed to be a simple process and event. In reality though, in many cases it is very different and flamboyant, due to many customs and social pressures. It is not necessary for the *nikāḥ* to be held in a mosque and presided by an Imām; nevertheless, many Muslims prefer these on a religious basis. In the UK, as elsewhere, the ceremony is also conducted in community and banqueting halls, stately homes, hotels, family homes or any place chosen by the couple or their families.

At the solemnising ceremony, it is traditional, as part of the ***khuṭbah***, to initially counsel them on being God-conscious, respectful, pure, loving and responsible. The presider then confirms consent from the bride. In some families, this consent is obtained through her representative, normally at a family ceremony. Following this, the groom is presented with the proposal and accepts it in the presence of at least two witnesses and the gathering. The validity of the marriage depends on the proposition (*Ījāb*) and acceptance (*Qubūl*), either directly between the parties, or through a representative (***Wakīl/Walī***). Thereafter, prayers for the union of the families and the couple's health, prosperity and spiritual well-being are offered and everyone is congratulated. Some will issue a *nikāḥ* and a civil marriage certificate as evidence of the lawful Muslim relationship.

The bridal gift

It is a right for the woman to be gifted (*mahr*) something from her husband according to his capacity and her status (2:236; 4:4; 4:24). This bridal nuptial gift, which is mutually agreed, may be given prior, during the *nikāḥ* or deferred, and used at her discretion, even when divorce occurs. However, should the divorce be initiated by her, she would be expected to return it. *Mahr* is not essential for the validity of a marriage but is not waived. The use of the term 'dowry' is a misappropriation of the concept of *mahr* (Maqsood, 2010). Bride prices (dowry/*jahaz*) play no part in Islam. This is when the family and the groom ask for money or belongings from the bride and her family, as a condition for accepting the woman (Maqsood, 2005).

Walīmah

Usually, after consummation, a celebratory feast is organised. For some, this includes a lavish wedding in a hall and entertainment with drums, fireworks, dance, and car entourages; but these are not sanctioned by Islam, as it places an unreasonable financial burden, some going as far as incurring large debts. Unsurprisingly, some Muslims tend to be critical of them, saying that they contradict the spirit of Islam. Nevertheless, as a means of informing the public and thanksgiving, families invite people to a meal (*Walimah*), as a religious event, encouraged by the Messenger (ﷺ) to be simple (Muslim, 2:3321) and inclusive of the poor.

Divorce

Talāq is the Arabic term for divorce meaning 'letting go' or 'undoing a knot'. Technically, for the jurists, it signifies the dissolution of marriage usually by declaring certain words. Sacredness is a characteristic of marriage; even then, Islam takes a pragmatic view and recognises that the union might be temporary for a variety of reasons. Islam recognises its need when marital relations make a peaceful home life impossible (Siddiqi, 2010). Therefore, divorce is not forbidden, rather it is discouraged. In fact, it is the last resort, after all steps of reconciliation, within families and externally, have been fully exhausted. The Qur'ān expects arbiters to be appointed from both sides (4:35). The Prophet (ﷺ) counselled, 'The most detestable of all permissible actions to Allah is divorce'

(Abū Dāwūd, 2:2173). Nevertheless, cultural influences lead many Muslims including some in the UK to frown upon it and it remains a stigmatised subject in some communities (Scourfield et al., 2013), despite the apparent increase in divorce rates.

There are various methods of separation and nullification of a marriage and the juristic ruling for these can be complex (Siddiqi, 2010). Therefore, for Muslims, it is very important that the divorce is pronounced in the correct manner as it may have detrimental consequences on the couples and their families as the type of separation chosen affects various factors within their marriage. You will appreciate that this is a very complex matter discussed in all books of law by jurists with intricate details, and therefore most Muslims will seek guidance from qualified scholars on this issue.

Voice of a Muslim

Islam ordains the provision of divorce because I feel Allah does not want to burden people to be in a loveless or inadequate/mismatched relationship and the fact that divorce is created means that divorce cases will always exist, exercised by both men and women. So long as all options of reconciliation have been exhausted then one can pursue the correct manner of divorce. In my own experience, I always felt that Allah has given me this right, and after consulting qualified 'Ulama, I exercised this right duly without feeling guilty.

From my perspective, divorce in the UK is increasing. I do not have a conclusive explanation or stats to quantify this. It's only through the circle of people I come across that I judge my opinion. Nobody when entering into a marriage wishes for their marriage to be dissolved but in mainstream society these situations do arise for various reasons; some simple and others due to complex reasons. I feel it can be reduced by the couples having a voluntary pre-training course (like we do for ḥajj) to instil the meaning of marriage in Islam as marriage is a contract and a journey. I once attended a nikāḥ at a masjid and this late Imām (may Allah bless his soul) said something really profound and until today has stuck on my mind. He said now that you are married you must forbear things about your wife. By accepting this you overlook so many things and look for the better qualities your spouse has. Islam offers reconciliation and to involve trustworthy persons to deal with the discrepancies/issues between the couple. If it cannot be worked and divorce is the only solution then the

(Continued)

couple are presented with the option of divorce. Also one must seek spiritual help from Allah for guidance and my own personal experience was certainly based on ultimate faith in Allah no matter what was thrown in my direction. It kept me going and I now feel I am settled for the better and have learnt from previous experiences to keep your relationship going especially when you have found the right one and I feel my fate took me thousands of miles to find the match for me.

We, Muslims, are part of society and part of this world and tribulations will also be felt by us as the Qur'ān is a living guidance for all problems. The solution is there but we sometimes look for the answers elsewhere. Islam wants you to be happy and places great responsibility even during divorce to treat the other person with respect and to provide maintenance if she has a child, etc. The Companions also experienced divorce and we should draw inspiration from this when going through such difficult situations. I always used to pray *Inna ma al usri yusran* [with difficulty there is ease] and this kept me strong and a belief in Allah that things will get better! (Dāniyāl, British Asian Indian, housing professional, male)

'Iddah

After the divorce, there is a waiting period (*'Iddah*) during which women cannot marry. Subject to the type of divorce issued, it allows time for reconciliation and ascertaining conception. The waiting period lasts three menstrual cycles or with birth when divorced in pregnancy (2:228). There will be no waiting period when the marriage is not consummated (33:49). A waiting period is also required on the death of a husband (2:234).

Polygyny

Polygyny has been practised throughout human history in eastern and western lands and many civilisations. Currently, in many parts of the world, it is practised in different ways. Currently it seems to be most often identified with Islam, whereas the Qur'ān regulated its number rather than give an open license (Esposito, 2016). In principle, it is permitted, according to the verse (4:3). Thus, permission has been granted for a man to marry up to a maximum of four wives at one time, but only if one can treat them all with justice and afforded full status, otherwise a person should marry only one. It is not a license for uncontrolled promiscuity but a concession, through legitimate and dignified *nikāḥ*, unlike keeping mistresses and having affairs, which are prohibited. **Polyandry** is prohibited. The Prophet (ﷺ) led a life of celibacy, then at the age around 25 he wed Khadījah, a twice married widow, and remained in this monogamous relationship until she died when he was 50 (Salahi, 2002). Only after that did he remarry.

In general, it is also important to be aware that not all polygamous marriages are the same across different cultural and religions traditions. It is important to note that polygyny is not imposed by Sharīʿah and is certainly not compulsory, but available as an option and Sunnah. Some of the circumstances which may lead to another marriage, include the first wife being incapable of bearing children, being incapable of vaginal sexual intercourse, and minimising the opportunities of prostitution. In some countries, where Muslims are in the majority, the law forbids it; in others, it is hardly practised at all. In traditional Islamic societies in the right circumstances, polygyny was a supportive measure and offered dignity to women who would otherwise be unmarried, as well as to children who would otherwise be born outside marriage (Noibi and Haleem, 1999). The above verse was revealed after the Battle of Badr when about 700 people were killed leaving many orphans and widows, in addition to female captives (Kheri, 2008). Therefore, it attempted to ensure the welfare of single women and widows in a diminishing male population (Esposito, 2016). Along similar lines, in contemporary times, it is worth reflecting over the role of multiple marriages in situations created by genocides in Bosnia, Rwanda and Chechnya where very large numbers of men died. There are some women who support their husband in taking another wife to enable them both to live as per the Sunnah. Other women see it as being divinely sanctioned and are happy to enter such a relationship and are not restricted because it is perceived to be contrary to modern sensibilities. Others are against it on feminist grounds.

Interracial and interfaith marriages

To begin with, Islam does not discourage interracial marriages, as long as the two are Muslim. Muslim males may marry women of other faiths on the condition that they believe in God and a revealed religion, by this, according to some scholars, it means monotheistic Christianity and Judaism, and implies conversion. At an individual level, such marriages do take place (Nielsen and Otterbeck, 2016). A Muslim female must marry a Muslim male

(2:221). You should note that radical changes following urbanisation, globalisation, international migration, internal religious reforms that stress civil liberties and popular culture influence the personal choices of some Muslims and their expectations regarding marriage (Raudvere, 2015). Within Muslim countries and, for example in the UK, interracial marriages also encompass interethnic marriages with the obsession of caste-affiliation and ethnic affiliation declining to a degree. However, in some places, it continues to be an important consideration.

Children

Children are a gift and a test concurrently. The primary responsibility for their provision rests with the father. Parents are invited to be grateful for being blessed with children. Prior to Islam, some people rejoiced with the birth of a male and expressed frustration with females. This attitude became unacceptable in Islam, whether it was out of fear of poverty or disgrace. The Qur'ān rejected both behaviours (16:58–59). Simultaneously infanticide is forbidden (6:151; 60:12) as Islam declares children as favours from Allah (42:49–50).

Rites of passage

In diverse ways, often coloured by local customs, Muslims acknowledge births, marriages and death as part of the holistic nature of life itself. They see this as part of God's Will (*Qadr*) operating in the temporal existence.

Birth

Most Muslims try to ensure the first sound their baby hears is the call to prayer (*Adhān*), whispered in the right ear, and the *Iqāmah* in the left by an Imām, pious person, father or elder of the family. It is a welcome into the universal community of Islam and a reminder of its Creator. It is also a ritual of incorporation and welcoming the child to the human experience (Scourfield et al., 2013). Thereafter, the lips of the newborn are smeared with honey or something sweet (*Taḥnīk*). Most will prefer to rub dates, which are softened by mastication, on the palate with the hope that the child will become prosperous, pious, obedient and sweet. This practice is rooted in the lifestyle of the Messenger (ﷺ) (al-Bukhārī, 7:378).

'Aqīqah

On the seventh day, usually at home, the baby's hair is removed (*Ḥalaq*), perhaps reflecting the idea of detachment or transition as in Ḥajj (Gwynne, 2018). The equivalent of its weight in silver or cash is given as *ṣadaqah* (alms) to the poor. To express thanks, a sheep or goat is slaughtered (***'Aqīqah***) to symbolise the aversion of misfortune (Ibn Mājah, 4:3165). The meat is shared among families, neighbours and the poor to mark the happy occasion; as such, it acts as an announcement. The Prophet (ﷺ) offered it for his grandsons (al-Nasā'ī, 5:4218). People wish the newborn a healthy and pious life. For the parents, prayers are offered for the child to be a source of mercy and coolness of their eyes. Nowadays, *'Aqīqah* ceremonial parties, hosted outside the home, have become a feature in some families. A name is given which is often rooted in Arabic culture, Muslim history, Islamic traditions and local conventions. You may notice that they are often permutations of the 99 names of Allah. Thus, it would be inappropriate to enquire about their 'Christian names'. Though Muslims themselves are prone to using 'Abdul', in reality there is no such name, since 'Abd' means servant and 'al' is the definitive article (the servant). However, as you read previously, 'Abd' is used in conjunction with another attribute of God to form a name, for example, 'Abd-al-Raḥmān, servant of the Most Gracious'. Sometimes, names are changed if perceived to be religiously inappropriate or having negative connotations (Hawramani, 2018).

Circumcision

Prophet Abraham was circumcised (al-Bukhārī, 8:313). In the UK, this is usually carried out by the local GP or at the hospital. Most, if not all, boys are circumcised (khitān). The age at which this is carried out varies in different parts of the world. In some countries, it is marked as a special event where the child is adorned in elaborate costumes. It is not a condition for the acceptance of Islam. It symbolises purification, belonging and identity. It is also both a ritual of separation, through removal and a symbol of incorporation into the community of the faithful (Scourfield et al., 2013). Female genital mutilation is regarded as a cultural phenomenon and though the authenticity of the ḥadīth in question is debated, the strongest trend is against it.

Breastfeeding

The Qur'ān encourages breastfeeding for numerous benefits. Mothers shall breastfeed their children for two whole years, for those who wish to complete the term (2:233). However, if for any reason, parents decide on weaning, by mutual consent, and after due consultation, there is no blame on them. Moreover, if they decide on a foster-mother for their offspring, there is no blame on them, provided they pay (the foster-mother) what they offer, on equitable terms. In public, modesty is exercised by covering the chest, although some women in the privacy of their home (***Ḥarīm/Harem***) or amongst other women might nurse openly, for it is viewed as a natural part of mothering.

Voice of a Muslimah

Childbirth within the Yemeni community is seen as a moment of celebration. The first 40 days after childbirth the new mother and child are to remain at the mother's family home where she recovers and relaxes. She is to usually stay with her family away from the husband; however, he can come to visit, but she will mostly be surrounded by her family and their support. Within the first seven days, the baby's head is to be shaved to cleanse away impurities, and if the baby is a boy he must be circumcised for long-term health benefits. Once the 40 days are up the woman and child are to return to her husband. This is celebrated with an extravagant party similar to a wedding as she is returning to her married life but with the most precious gift. (Yāsmin, Yemeni, teacher, female)

Youth and adolescence

This is a significant phase in the life of a Muslim, as obligations need to be fulfilled. The Prophet (ﷺ) valued and respected the youth. The majority of his early followers were young people. They were brought to the forefront of the community and given responsibilities of various kinds. Mu'ādh ibn Jabal, for example, became a great scholar and jurist, who was appointed the governor of Yemen at 27. The Prophet (ﷺ) advised everyone to value their time before poor health and old age overcame them.

Seniority in age

Muslims are instructed to be respectful and serve their parents, particularly their mothers (Ibn Mājah, 4:2781). Children are educated to obey and honour their parents (31:14–5). Children should care for their parents and be patient with them. Addressing offspring, Allah says 'to parents, [give] good treatment. Whether one or both of them reach old age [while] with you, say not to them [so much as], "uff," and do not repel them but speak to them a noble word. And lower to them the wing of humility out of mercy and say, "My Lord, have mercy upon them as they brought me up [when I was] small"' (17:23–24).

When parents pass away, their children and grandchildren usually pray for them and express kindness to their relatives and friends. Children take it upon themselves to fulfil their parents' outstanding religious and personal obligations, such as giving Zakāt and returning debts.

Death

Death is not to be feared for it is believed that God has determined it. Since the era of the Prophet (ﷺ) the remembrance of death is a foundational spiritual practice among Muslims (Yusuf, 2017). There is discouragement on excessive grieving and mourning, since this might be construed as being unhappy with God's Will. The corpse is given a bath (***Ghusl***) and shrouded in white sheets before being placed in a coffin, should it be used, and buried as soon as possible. Others prefer to be buried without a coffin. The grave is dug parallel to Makkah and the face is inclined towards the *Qiblah*. In many cemeteries of the UK, a section is allocated for Muslim burials. It is the right of the next of kin to lead the prayer although in practice it is delegated to the local Imām or a pious person of their choosing.

Ṣalāt al-Janāzah

A few people's presence for this prayer absolves the rest of the community from its duty. The body must be washed by the same gender. It is shrouded in three pieces of white cloth for the male and five for the female, if affordable, otherwise whatever is available suffices. After the prayer, the cortège is usually taken on foot to the grave on people's shoulders. The corpse is entered feet first. Those around will sprinkle cusps full of soil whilst saying the words of verse (20:55). The grave is usually filled using as much soil as possible. Once full, a little mound is made to make it visibly recognisable as a grave. Simple headstones are erected; others may prefer elaborate ones although these and associated tomb structures are not necessary nor religiously sanctioned, hence some avoid them altogether.

Cremation

Cremation dishonours the dignity of a body created in the image of God (Muslim, 4:6325), hence it is avoided and because fire is seen as symbolic of hell-fire. As a legal necessity, post-mortem is reluctantly accepted, although many now prefer imaging as an alternative to autopsy in the diagnosis of deaths.

The Muslim calendar

Every day is an important day for the Muslim who is conscious of the limited nature of existence on earth and who utilises every opportunity to get closer to God through good actions and devotions of various kinds. In turn, God, as an act of kindness and mercy, has made some actions, moments, places and times more virtuous than others for the benefit of humans. Of all places, according to some scholars, Makkah is superior; others suggest it is Madīnah, as the Prophet's (ﷺ) body rests there. Of all months, Ramaḍān is most blessed. Of all days, Friday is the best day. Of all the nights, the Night of Power is excellent. Daily, the time between *'Asr* and *Maghrib* prayers, is most precious. The mosque is better than the marketplace. Since there is no inhibition in Islam for individuals to pursue their own salvation, some annual events offer Muslims opportunities to be diligent about preserving their salvation and the state of *fitrah* - the inherent disposition toward God, which is cultivated through good works and by being conscious of *Tawḥīd* (Saud, 2013a).

Jumu'ah

In some Muslim countries, Friday as a holy day is combined with Thursday or Saturday. In other places, although government offices might be closed, it is the most dynamic day of the week for social and economic activities. After the prayer, the Qur'ān expects Muslims 'to disperse within the land and seek from the bounty of Allah' (62:10). The sermon (*Khuṭbah*) is the most significant feature delivered from the pulpit (*Minbar*) (Esposito, 2016).

Religiously, Friday is significant, as it is believed that it is the best day on which the sun rises. It is the day Adam was created, was expelled from Heaven and died. Also, it is believed that the Day of Resurrection will take place on a Friday, although no one knows the specific time and date. Sins are forgiven, rewards for charity are multiplied, and it has a moment in which God answers supplications (Abū Dāwūd, 1:1044; Ibn Mājah, 2:1084, 1086). Friday is better than ***'Īd*** and there are certain recommended devotional acts which many Muslims will carry out. It is also a day when abundant salutations and blessings of peace upon the Prophet (ﷺ) are said, as it is believed that these are presented to him on this day (al-Nasā'ī, 2:1377).

Hijrah

The Islamic calendar is based on the lunar system, and, unlike others, it is not adjusted to synchronise with the solar year (Breuilly et al., 2007). This means the solar year is ten or eleven days longer than the lunar one, and as a result the dates change constantly in relation to the Gregorian calendar.

The calendar has its origins with the migration of Prophet Muḥammad (ﷺ) which took place in 622 CE. 'Umar, the second *Khalīfah* chose the *Hijrah* as it marked the establishment of the nascent Muslim community and for being a truly historic event and joyous occasion. Thus, AH means after *Hijrah* or in the year of the *Hijrah*. There are twelve months, of which four are known as forbidden months (***Al-Ashhur al-Ḥurum***) (9:36). Each month may be 29 or 30 days. Most Muslim countries use the Gregorian calendar for civic purposes and the *Hijrī* calendar to establish the Islamic holy months. The mathematical formula for calculating corresponding dates common to Muslim or Christian dates is AH = (33/32) x (CE – 622), or conversely CE = (32AH/33) + 622.

Al-Muḥarram

Al-Muḥarram is a forbidden month as battles were prohibited (*ḥarām*). Strictly speaking, there is no religious significance in celebrating the ushering in of the Muslim New Year. However, the whole month, and especially the tenth day known as the *Day of 'Āshūrā'*, is significant. Fasting on this day expiates (minor) sins of the previous year and is the best fast after Ramaḍān (Ibn Mājah, 3:1742). It so happened that when the Prophet (ﷺ) arrived in Madīnah in 622 CE, he witnessed the Jewish community fast on this day. He was informed that this was the blessed day when Allah had saved the Children of Israel from their enemy (in Egypt) and so Prophet Mūsā (Moses) fasted, giving thanks to Allah. To which the Prophet (ﷺ) commented, 'We are closer to Mūsā than you are.' So he fasted and encouraged Muslims to fast also (al-Bukhārī, 5:278). However, in general, Muslims add a day before or after it to make a distinction. It is a holy day and a time of additional prayer. It is considered virtuous to be more generous on this day. Thus, some parents and teachers are found to be more generous to their families and students on this day. Shī'a communities commemorate 'Āshūrā' for the martyrdom of Al-Ḥusaīn so for them the key concepts discernible at this time are martyrdom and redemptive suffering.

Rabī' al-Awwal

For Muslims, this is significant because the Prophet (ﷺ) was born in this month. The commonly accepted date is the twelfth and seventeenth for the Shī'a. In some communities, over the centuries, the celebration of the birthday of the Prophet Muḥammad (ﷺ) has become popular to the extent of becoming an official public holiday (***Mawlid al-Nabī***). There is no denial in the fact that his birth was of great significance. However, some Muslims argue that the Prophet (ﷺ) and his Companions did not mark it as 'a celebration', and, as such, it is a later addition without a religious basis. Others mark this day with local variations and might include frivolous and extravagant activities, such as fireworks, street parades, decorating homes and streets, feasting and public speeches. A middle ground is adopted by others who shun what could be termed as 'secular' and 'an innovation' (***Bid'ah***) activities and, instead use this day for education and reflection on his life by attending events in mosques and elsewhere which may include poetry, speeches and meals. In the UK and elsewhere, a couple of years ago, some Muslims distributed roses of friendship to the general public with pamphlets about the Prophet (ﷺ) to create a better awareness of his *Ṣīrah* (Krayem, 2016). Some Sufis perceive this to be the most significant day for humanity as it was on this day that the manifestation of God's most beloved Prophet (ﷺ) took place.

Rajab

This month, as a whole, is blessed and sacred. Importantly, it is a prelude to Ramaḍān. When the Prophet (ﷺ) sighted its crescent he supplicated for Ramaḍān, and so Muslims use Rajab and Sha'bān to think about and welcome Ramaḍān. Scholars have determined that there are no specific modes of worship prescribed for Rajab; in fact, all recognised modes of worship may be carried out.

In the tenth year of the Prophet's mission, an extraordinary event happened, generally accepted to be on the twenty-seventh of Rajab. *Al-Isrā'* and

Al-Miʿrāj refer to two parts of a miraculous journey (***Laylat al-Isrā' wa al-Miʿrāj***). It is an occasion celebrated in many parts of the Muslim world; in some places with a public holiday and optional prayers. Many mosques, minarets and streets are illuminated as a symbol of this single night journey. The narrative is a favourite in and by itself, but the story has been subjected to numerous artistic endeavours and it provides some sanction for the importance of Jerusalem in Muslim piety (Rippin and Bernheimer, 2019).

Muḥammad (ﷺ) was accompanied by angel Jibrīl from Makkah to Jerusalem at the site of the al-Aqsa Mosque; this is *Al-Isrā'*, mentioned in (17:1). In Jerusalem, it is believed that he led all the prophets in prayer, showing that he was the Prophet of all prophets. From there, according to *ḥadīth* reports, it is believed they ascended to the Heavens (*Al-Miʿrāj*). The purpose of this miraculous journey was to show him some of God's signs. He met several great prophets in different heavenly spheres including Adam, Yaḥyā, ʿIsā, Idrīs, Hārun, Mūsā and Ibrāhīm (peace be on them).

There are no established festivities, fasts or prayers from the Prophet (ﷺ) to commemorate *Al-Isrā'* and *Al-Miʿrāj*. However, some Muslims organise commemorative functions, where the event is narrated in poetry or lectures to remind them of the significance of the miracle in the life of the Prophet (ﷺ), the history of Islam and the importance of Jerusalem. Muslim scholarship has debated the nature of the *Al-Isrā'* and *Al-Miʿrāj*, whether it was undertaken in the physical sense or as a spiritual vision (Salahi, 2002).

Shaʿbān

The Prophet (ﷺ) tended to fast for most of this month (Mālik, 1:688). The fifteenth night is known as ***Laylat al-Barā'ah*** (the Night of Deliverance) and is marked by some. It is thought that Allah's mercy descends to the nearest heaven offering forgiveness, sustenance and safety abundantly (Ibn Mājah, 2:1388; 1389). Some pay no heed to the night on the basis that the chain of the reporter is weak.

Nevertheless, others mark the night with prayers and devotions and the following day with an optional fast. In some countries, it is a public holiday. Some Shīʿa occupy the night with supplications, worship, and the day in festivity, since it symbolises the birthday of the last Imām, Muḥammad al-Mahdī, who is believed to be the Mahdī (Momen, 2016).

Ramaḍān

Ramaḍān is the month of mercy, the Qur'ān and forgiveness, and is the most venerated. A detailed exposition was presented in the previous chapter. On the fifteenth, the Shī'a remember the birth of Ḥasan, the second Imām, and from the nineteenth to the twenty-first, the death of 'Ali through vigils and mourning.

Night of Power

Laylat al-Qadr (Night of Decree) is one of the major events of the year. God only knows its precise occurrence, although it is commonly marked on the twenty-seventh and odd nights of Ramaḍān (Abū Dāwūd, 1:1378). Some Muslims have reported to have experienced and sensed the night. This night was granted because the Prophet (ﷺ) often pondered over the longer lives that people of the past lived which meant people of his community would be surpassed in righteous acts. Therefore Allah, as a blessing, increased the reward of worship in this night to exceed worship of a thousand months (97:3). Consequently, Muslims spend a larger part or the whole night in extra worship and devotional activities; some sleep in the mosque in search of the blessings of this night. For the Shī'a, the days are either the nineteenth, twenty-first or twenty-third. In any case, the night surpasses in value 1000 months (97:3). This verse mentions the night as having peace and therefore the revelation, meaning, the Qur'ān is peace (Cole, 2018).

`I'tikāf

This is a spiritual retreat mainly in mosques, usually performed during the last ten days of Ramaḍān to acquire the blessings of the twenty-seventh night and draw closer to Allah through recitation, remembrance of Allah and other acts of devotion. Women tend to observe it at home. In an age of technological challenges, work and family demands, and materialistic impulsiveness, for some, this retreat is potentially transformative with an intense spiritual experience, achieved through serious devotion, reflection and dedication, and prioritising the Hereafter. The Prophet (ﷺ) practised it in the last ten days in search of the night of *qadr* (al-Bukhārī, 1:237).

'Īd al-Fitr - the festival of fast-breaking

The two major festivals of *'Īd* are not linked to a person or season, rather they are a response to the submission offered by Muslims. It is a universal festival observed to mark the end of Ramaḍān as soon as the crescent of the first Shawwāl appears. In many Muslim countries, *'Īd* days are national holidays. Muslim communities the world over, including in the UK, express immense joy and festivity in them. Many Muslims take a day off work to join the communal prayer and be with their extended families; for some it lasts three days

(Esposito, 2016). Therefore, on both days of *'Īd*, fasting is prohibited. The atmosphere is full of excitement and the greetings of *'Īd Mubārak* (May *'Īd* be blessed for you) or its local variants are exchanged and the Shī'a also recite the ***Du'ā Nudba*** supplication for the protection and assistance from Imām Al-Mahdi. Some attend organised events for Muslim families in community halls or private bookings of play centres (Scourfield et al., 2013).

For some, preparations begin a few days earlier as they think about the less fortunate. Consequently, they offer **Ṣadaqat al-fiṭr** (welfare due) to the poor. It is recommended that this reach the recipients as soon as possible, preferably before *'Īd* prayers. It is discharged by the head of the family on behalf of everyone in the household including a newborn. It is for the most needy to enable them to join in the happiness.

The day starts, after sunrise, with a light breakfast which may include something sweet, as was the custom of the Prophet (ﷺ), and as a reminder that one is not to fast on this day. On this extremely happy occasion, after a bath, there is a tendency to don new clothes although it is customary to wear the best of what one has. Most children will have a new outfit, haircuts, and fragrance is applied. *Ṣalāt al-'Īd* is offered in thanksgiving for the guidance which they have received from God in the form of the Qur'ān and the mercy and forgiveness derived through fasting. They express their gratitude for all the intense worship, the accomplishment of a great religious feat, other good deeds and the spiritual benefits they have accrued through these. All Muslims try to attend, even those who may lapse in offering their daily prayers.

Shawwāl

The first day of Shawwāl, as above, is *'Īd* day. In this month, some Muslims observe six days of voluntary fasts as the Prophet (ﷺ) likened the fasts of Ramaḍān to observing ten months of fasting and the six days of Shawwāl like observing two months. Together it is like fasting a lifetime (Abū Dāwūd, 2:2427).

Dhū al-Qa'dah

One of the sacred months when pilgrims begin to arrive in Makkah.

Dhū al-Ḥijjah

Ḥajj is performed in this sacred month the twelfth (last) month of the Islamic calendar. The first ten days have great virtue. During the first to ninth, Muslims try to fast, glorify, praise and remember God profusely. Some stand during the night in prayer, repent, read the Qur'ān and do more good deeds than normal. Many will fast on the auspicious day of *'Arafāt*, desiring to be with the pilgrims.

In mosques, and individually, there is a unique action only performed during this time of the year. It is known as **Takbīr al-Tashrīq**. It is a collective audible proclamation glorifying Allah by the entire congregation which commences from the morning prayer of the ninth until after late afternoon prayer on the thirteenth.

'Īd al-`Adhā is celebrated on the tenth. For both *'Īd* prayers, Muslims may gather in dedicated local prayer grounds, or local or main mosques after sunrise. In the UK, in some cities, local parks are used. Both prayers are identical in that they constitute a homily, two units of prayer followed by a *Khuṭbah*. After prayer, on *'Īd al-`Adhā*, some proceed to perform their own sacrifice (**'Uḍhiyyah**), which is preferable, though in the UK, this is sometimes a challenge; even then, some visit their nearest abattoir. It is customary that this meat or meal is the first food consumed after prayers. On the eighteenth, Shī'as celebrate 'Īd al-Ghadīr Khumm (Momen, 2016).

According to the Qur'ān, the philosophy behind this act is that: 'Their meat will not reach Allah, nor will their blood, but what reaches Him is piety from you. Thus have We subjected them to you that you may glorify Allah for that [to] which He has guided you; and give good tidings to the doers of good' (22:37). Hence, the meat is shared with the poor, friends and neighbours. It also reminds Muslims of Prophet Ibrāhim's sacrifice of Ismā'il as a symbol of obedience to God. Therefore, Muslims reflect on their commitment and love of God.

Additional matters

There are a few things which are prohibited for Muslims: the meat of carcases, blood, pork and animals dedicated to other than Allah (16:115). Also, strangled animals or those killed by a violent blow, by a head-long fall or by the goring of horns, those from which a wild animal has eaten, except when they are slaughtered before death, and those which are sacrificed on stone altars and seeking decisions through divining arrows (5:3). Wine, intoxicants and gambling are also disallowed (2:219; 5:90–91). Sexual intercourse outside marriage in all forms is rejected (17:32). Homosexuality is impermissible (7:80–83; 26:165–170) as well as zoophilia, zoosexuality and bestiality. Also, lying, stealing, cheating, murdering (4:93) and committing suicide are prohibited (4:29) (Adh-Dhahabī, 2012). The avoidance of major sin means lesser sins are forgiven and lead to paradise (4:31).

The many permissible animals must be slaughtered in the name of God. Otherwise, the meat is considered prohibited. There is disagreement among scholars regarding the food of Christians and Jews, even though the Qur'ān permits this. This is because many jurists view that contemporary Jews and Christians have drifted away from following their true teachings. Some, however, rule kosher food as being permissible, when necessary. Yet, based on a literal reading of the verse (5:5) some will permit both so long as some conditions are met. Gold and silver utensils as food containers and service are forbidden as they are akin to hoarding wealth.

Case study 7.1 'Id al-Fiṭr

Jonathan was completing his final school-based teaching practice. In his class he had a few Muslim pupils, children from other religious traditions and some from secular backgrounds in a large school. In addition, there were a few children with special education needs and disabilities. He was enthusiastic to provide religious education which would be most appropriate to all these children and to appeal to their senses. He was also keen to promote conversations and had thought about offering pupils the experience of studying Islam as he felt it was much needed in the context of his school. Professionally, he was mindful that this was his final practice and so he wanted to teach religious education, which he had done before and teaching Islam would be a first. He believed that pupils should be taught many religions and felt that they were entitled to a multi-faith curriculum. At university, he had learnt that the autumn term offered many opportunities to teach about festivals. However, when he examined his school mid-term plan he found that 'Id al-Fiṭr was planned for a different term. So he consulted the subject leader who agreed to shift the teaching to allow him the opportunity to teach. This enabled him to plan, teach, assess and evaluate the impact of his teaching of a major festival. He decided to provide a variety of opportunities which included practical work such as:

- making a crescent covered in foil which he hung on a string across the class
- writing 'Id greetings and messages on pages with decorated borders

(Continued)

- designing geometrical patterns using chalk and ICT
- eating some Asian sweetmeats in a circle with the class at the end of the lesson
- viewing a video and listening to the song '*Eid-un Sa'eed*' by Zain Bhikha (2010)
- a group saw images from across the world on how Muslims celebrate 'Id al-Fiṭr
- a group creating a display of key words related to Ramaḍān
- displaying deliberately chosen artefacts used for devotion and worship by Muslims

Jonathan was content that there was a wide range of activities provided for the pupils in his classroom. To finish the lesson, he sent three pupils to each class in his school with a paper plate containing sweets. This helped them experience giving and to learn about the significance of sharing which is particularly important for Muslims during Ramaḍān and 'Id al-Fiṭr.

Jonathan appears to have given particular thought to making provisions for SEND. Based on this case study:

- What would you say were the values which informed the type of religious education he wished to deliver in future?
- How was Jonathan ensuring that the complex learning needs of the pupils were being met as he taught them 'Id al-fiṭr?
- Which of his activities appeals to you most?
- If you were to work with a group of children with dyslexia, what provisions would you make when teaching them about 'Id al-fiṭr?

Summary

In this chapter, you have learnt that families in Islam are considered the cornerstone of a community. Marriage is the means for the establishment of a family and an important source for achieving emotional contentment, sensual pleasure, spiritual rectitude and moral development. Islam takes a realistic view of marriages and recognises that some will falter; hence, it makes a provision for divorce. You have recognised the rituals that are performed to welcome newborns into the wider Muslim community. Parents have a responsibility for nurturing their children and in turn, children are expected to honour and serve them. You have also identified some of the key months in the Islamic calendar and significant annual events which help Muslims to enjoy their life, be happy and remember Allah.

Reflection tasks

- Critically evaluate the Islamic attitude to marriage and divorce.
- Describe the significance attached to children by Islam.
- Why is Friday (*Jumu'ah*) spiritually important in the life of Muslims?
- How do Muslims mark *'Īd al-Fiṭr* and *'Īd al-`Adhā*?
- How would you teach children about the birth rituals observed by Muslims?
- How do some of the events during the year assist Muslims to pursue their own salvation?

Further reading

Kheri, A.A. (2008) *A Comprehensive Guide Book of Islam*. Delhi: Adam Publishers.

This is a complete guide on all aspects of Islam. It has rich details written in response to the resurgence for accurate information from both new Muslims and a younger generation of Muslims.

Siddiqi, M.I. (2010) *The Family Laws of Islam*, revised edn. Delhi: Adam Publishers.

This book covers the status of women in different civilisations, Islam and women, necessity and benefits of marriage, equality, divorce, children, duties, conjugal relations, polygyny and veiling.

PART 2

CONTEMPORARY ISSUES

8

THE ETHICAL DIMENSION

In this chapter you will:

- know and understand the significance of morals in Islam for the well-being of society
- reflect on the key ethical ideas, principles and frameworks for Muslims
- develop a critical awareness of the range of ethical codes arising from the teachings of the Qur'ān and ḥadīth in various contexts
- recognise how Muslims are expected to organise their everyday conduct.

Overview

In Chapters 2 and 3, you discovered that Islam is a comprehensive way of life, and morality is one of the foundations of its teachings. Ethics and morality are the fundamental sources of a community's strength and survival, just as immorality can be a cause of decline. This chapter outlines some of the norms and regulations extracted from a branch of the teachings of Islam, which is concerned with characters, morals and ethics so that the interconnected nature of Islam becomes apparent. As part of this, you will become familiar with answers to several key social issues and the Islamic perspective on what constitutes a good life and how happiness is to be achieved. The content particularises some right and wrong actions to illustrate how Allah is both requiring and forbidding, and in doing so, you will understand the status of morality. Importantly, you will recognise how Muslims are expected to organise their everyday behaviours, their ideals of how to live life and what morality is required from them (Raudvere, 2015: 185). This will be achieved by introducing you directly to the Qur'ān and ***ḥadīth*** literature. By the end of the chapter, you will have understood the significance that moral teachings have in guiding the life of a Muslim in relation to the nature of morality and moral obligations in personal matters, social dealings, economical activities and environmental matters.

Globalisation is probably the single most influential phenomenon that is affecting humanity, the animal kingdom and the natural world, whose impact is evident through pop culture, films, television shows, numerous social media outlets, music and consumerism. It may be added to this the shifting ideas about modernity, rapid and widespread urbanisation and the dominance of western cultural hegemony that is cutting across the globe and permeating the everyday life of ordinary people. Contemporary Muslims share these experiences with everyone else and, simultaneously, they are a generation challenged by different influences in the diverse contexts of various moral compasses, some of which are rooted in cultural traditions, religious beliefs and secular philosophies. All of this is intensified with the rising tide of Islamophobia.

Prior to the advent of uncontrolled social media and the prevalence of mass communication, it was easier for Muslims and others to imbue, teach and nurture children with the ideologies and values that they wanted their children to acquire. However, as globalisation intensified, and the world became a 'village', this changed dramatically. Muslim youth and their counterparts have become exposed to the rest of the world. Today, for some Muslims, their thoughts and ideals, whilst resonating with what they hear in mosques, are influenced by Vloggers, Snapchatters, Instagrammers and activists who are instant and constant influencers.

The content of this chapter is significant, as often this is a subject area which many people are less aware of and the negative publicity by some experts and media outlets tends to focus less on this branch of Islam. There is no lack of information which depicts Muslims as liars, cheaters and criminals or that the Qur'ān instructs the killing of non-Muslims and that Muḥammad (ﷺ) was a villain drowned in his own ambitions and sensuality (Hathout, 2008). Thus, it is important to transcend the presentation of Islam as being a list of things to do and not do. Islam aims to develop a personality that understands and accepts the role of humans as vicegerents on earth, allowing a person to manage the nature within and the nature outside of themself in harmony with the Owner's (God's) manual (Hathout, 2008).

Islam and morality

Islamic ethics, like other sciences, chiefly originate from the Qur'ān, which lays down the basis of a religious system solely on ethical principles; hence, there is very little to distinguish between Islam and Islamic ethics. The moral, civil, canonical and criminal codes of Islam are not separate systems or sciences ('Umaruddīn, 1996: 64). Muslims began the study of ethics along with the study of the Qur'ān, the ethical character of which is illustrated by verses in this chapter.

Morality and ethical living are both inculcated and felt and they exist for the benefit of individuals and the entire creation. A pious and virtuous Muslim is expected to embody these qualities. Thus, Islam acknowledges the importance of a moral life and considers it inseparable from the life of faith (Gywnne, 2018). In fact, a Muslim's whole existence is infused with ethical demands since, like worship, morality is a significant part of the teachings of Islam. In one sense, perhaps, it is more important than other aspects of its teachings because it is within this domain that Muslims have the opportunity to operate as God's vicegerents (Nomānī, 1982). For the proper functioning of society and its survival, the Qur'ānic worldview sees the need for rules (***aḥkām***) to exist. Equally, it recognises the role of rewarding beneficial deeds and disciplining those that it considers harmful. The Prophet (ﷺ) emphasised moral virtues when he declared that he had been sent to perfect good morals (Mālik, 2:1677). Moreover, like the Qur'ān, to motivate Muslims, the Prophet (ﷺ) strongly censured moral vices and contrasted these by assuring great rewards for those behaving ethically. In fact, ethical behaviour is a form of greater ***jihād*** carried out by the hand and tongue as an everyday struggle against temptations, which is an essential part of being a Muslim (Gywnne, 2018).

Revelation and ethics

Muslims are convinced that natural knowledge of good and evil is unreliable and that only by special enlightenment or revelation can the human mind clearly and fully obtain truth including moral truth. Islam holds that God has revealed His eternal Will via a special line of prophets, thus rendering the content of moral law more detailed and reliable. Moral duty is not just about establishing a society of justice and peace on earth. It is also about fulfilling the divine plan that destines humans for eternal communion with God. Given that morality stems from the overarching divine plan for the world and its human inhabitants, the primary source of moral teaching for Muslims is the sacred book in which the divine plan for subsequent generations is stored (Gywnne, 2018: 91). One of the chapters of the Qur'ān is aptly named '*Al-Furqān*' (The Criterion, 25:1) making it the definitive standard of good and evil and a decisive statement (86:13). The second source of moral teachings is the Prophet (ﷺ) himself. His life complements and comments on the truths and teachings of the Qur'ān; this includes not just the wisdom and insight of his teachings but the practical example of his actions. Muḥammad (ﷺ) was a living commentary on the Qur'ān (Gywnne, 2018: 92), some of which was illustrated in Chapter 3.

The content of this chapter focusses on some key verses from the Qur'ān and selected *ahādīth*. However, you need to be aware that the moral codes and norms are detailed in the **Sharī'ah** – the Islamic path, as a whole. Contrary to popular perception, Sharī'ah includes, in addition to ritual, economic, civil, social and criminal rules, the moral teachings and social dealings as well. Since for the Muslim everyday ethical behaviour is an integral part of one's religious life that is defined and shaped by religious law (Gywnne, 2018: 92).

Voice of a Muslimah

Working in the NHS makes my work liable to ethical standards. Sometimes I look at my professional body's Code of Professional Conduct from the viewpoint of the teachings of Islam. I feel satisfied that both of these help me in providing a better service for my patients. For example, the Code expects integrity, accountability and avoidance of illegal and immoral activities outside of work. I find all of these in the Qur'ān too. I am very pleased with this fusion as I can then rethink my services to my patients in religious terms. This gives me a sense of wholeness in my being, work and faith. (Ā'ishah, British–Indian, radiographer, female)

Ethical branch of Islam

In Islam, there is unity of body and spirit; religion is not considered to be separate from the worldly challenges faced by humans. Muslims believe that the spiritual life and worldly life are complementary. For instance, honesty is required as part of spiritual progress as well as in politics, economics and family matters to live in a psychologically and socially peaceful manner.

To understand the relationship between the different branches of the teachings of Islam, a classification of groups of actions performed by Muslims has been created. First, acts of worship (*'Ibādāt*) which express the divinity of God, like prayer and pilgrimage. Second, actions performed for personal needs – these fall into monetary affairs (*mu'āmalāt*) and social conduct (*mu'āsharāt*). Third, functions like propagation, teaching, forbidding evil and promoting good, and serving the cause of Islam (*da'wah* and ***tablīgh***). Fourth, actions associated with the stewardship of God. This encompasses moral virtues. For example, mercy is a virtue which is a Divine attribute; it is because of this God wants His servants to cultivate this noble quality within them to behave mercifully towards His creation (Nomānī, 1982).

Islamic ethics have a universal character. These are considered to be eternal and, as such, permanent. As noted above, they do not make a distinction between religious and civil regulations (Raudvere, 2015: 185). The concept of ethics refers to a coherent system of right and wrong. These are affected by contemporary living circumstances, which influence lifestyles and social patterns, and by advances and innovation in technology, sciences and medicine. This means the understanding and implementation of non-categorical ethical teachings is subject to the methods of interpretation developed in the legal schools derived from the Qur'ān and *ḥadīth* literature.

Classical Muslim scholars have discussed ethics from various standpoints. The likes of Al-Farābī (257–339AH/870–950) and Ibn Sīnā (370–429AH/980–1037CE) chose philosophy to discuss ethics emphasising that the rationale based on which people recognised good and evil, and perform good and avoid evil, determines moral quality. However, those concerned with inner piety and purity, the Sufis in particular, constantly sought ethical admonitions and approvals for the internalisation of the teachings of Islam in pursuit of higher ethical standards of living. These groups of people produced the most extensive and influential works on Islamic ethics. Some of them like Al-Ghazālī (450–505AH/1058–1111CE) blended theology and philosophy to pave a way for moral and spiritual perfection. On the other hand, the historian Ibn Miskawayh (320–421AH/932–1030CE) read Islamic ethics as a discipline. His most influential work on ethics is *The Refinement of Character and the Purification of Disposition*, which is positioned by many Muslims within the New Platonic philosophical school. Mu'tazilah theologians emphasised objective and absolute ethics arguing that humans have to face the consequences of the freedom of the human will. They also assign a vital role to reason in knowing moral truths (Raudvere, 2015: 186). In contrast, Ash'arī theology takes the view that what is right and wrong depends on the commands of God.

Principles and models

The central individual principle is to observe all matters which are ***ḥalāl*** and avoid ***ḥarām***. Another significant communal principle which stands out from the teachings of Islam is that it places a responsibility on everyone to better society as a whole by taking a balanced stratagem of enjoining good and preventing evil (3:104). Moreover, in pursuit of an ethical life, on several occasions, the Qur'ān provides an ideal character profile for Muslims to be true servants of God:

> And the servants of the Most Merciful are those who walk upon the earth easily, and when the ignorant address them [harshly], they say [words of] peace. And those who spend [part of] the night to their Lord prostrating and standing [in prayer]. And those who say, 'Our Lord, avert from us the punishment

of Hell. Indeed, its punishment is ever adhering. Indeed, it is evil as a settlement and residence.' And [they are] those who, when they spend, do so not excessively or sparingly but are ever, between that, [justly] moderate. And those who do not invoke with Allah another deity or kill the soul which Allah has forbidden [to be killed], except by right, and do not commit unlawful sexual intercourse. And whoever should do that will meet a penalty. Multiplied for him is the punishment on the Day of Resurrection, and he will abide therein humiliated – Except for those who repent, believe and do righteous work. For them, Allah will replace their evil deeds with good. And ever is Allah Forgiving and Merciful. And he who repents and does righteousness does indeed turn to Allah with [accepted] repentance. And [they are] those who do not testify to falsehood, and when they pass near ill speech, they pass by with dignity. And those who, when reminded of the verses of their Lord, do not fall upon them deaf and blind. And those who say, 'Lord, grant us from among our wives and offspring comfort to our eyes and make us an example for the righteous.' Those will be awarded the Chamber for what they patiently endured, and they will be received therein with greetings and [words of] peace. (25:63–75)

Values and ethics taught by the Qur'ān

The section below illustrates some of the key values and ethics from verses of the Qur'ān.

Chastity

> But let them who find not [the means for] marriage abstain [from sexual relations] until Allah enriches them from His bounty. (24:33)

For the spiritual and moral well-being of individuals, involvement in sexual relations outside marriage is prohibited. The verse above concerns those who are unable to afford a married life, either due to financial or personal reasons, and are encouraged to exercise patience, be disciplined and to find ways to refrain from indulging in illegal sex. For some, this is a challenging test. Thus, rather than violating their chastity, they are asked to continue seeking the bounties of God after which they may marry when appropriate.

Compassion

> Say, 'O My servants who have transgressed against themselves [by sinning], do not despair of the mercy of Allah. Indeed, Allah forgives all sins. Indeed, it is He who is the Forgiving, the Merciful'. (39:53)

Exegetes of the Qur'ān have established this as being addressed to all sinners, both Muslim and others (Ibn Kathīr, 2000). The key message is that Allah forgives all sins with repentance and obedience, which makes this a message of immense hope for grave sinners like murderers, adulterers and robbers. Some polytheists who had committed such acts came to ask Muḥammad (ﷺ) whether there was any atonement for them; subsequently this verse was revealed informing them not to despair of Allah's mercy. Whatever their past, turning to God sincerely with obedience, would have their sins forgiven. Likewise, it is the same today. Therefore, Muslims frequently use the names *The Forgiving* and *The Merciful* when they repent (Muslim, 1:221).

Consequences

> If you do good, you do good for yourselves; and if you do evil, [you do it] to yourselves. (17:7)

Here you can see that God is dignifying each person as an individual who shoulders his or her own responsibility. In other words, it means everyone matters to Allah as an individual. That is why Muslims consider guidance from their religion, parents and religious leaders to be significant as it assists them in making good choices and to improve themselves. Ultimately, blaming others will not help. Anything evil that a person does is actually self-harm, in this world or in the Afterlife. People will be responsible for taking the guidance or not, and will face the consequences of that choice, good or bad.

Courtesy

> And when you are greeted with a greeting, greet [in return] with one better than it or [at least] return it [in a like manner] . (4:86)

You may have heard many Muslims, including children, exchange greetings of *Al-salāmu 'alaykum* meaning 'peace be upon you'. There are many benefits of greetings. To be the first to do so is a means of overcoming self-pride. In addition, *Al-Salām* (Peace) is an attributive name of God which God made manifest on earth. Therefore, Muslims are urged to spread it among themselves as well. Nevertheless, this verse encourages Muslims to be polite with non-Muslims, especially when relations are strained. In fact, not only does it suggest Muslims should avoid harshness, it asks them to go a step further by returning something better than good manners.

Desires

> But if they do not respond to you – then know that they only follow their [own] desires. And who is more astray than one who follows his desire without guidance from Allah? Indeed, Allah does not guide the wrongdoing people. (28:50)

In the sight of God, faith, good actions, glorification and remembrance of His name matter rather than materialism and wealth. One day Muḥammad (ﷺ) was with his poor and weak Companions. The nobility of Quraysh asked Muḥammad (ﷺ) to sit with them without his Companions. God forbade him from doing so. Therefore, Muslims learn not to shun the lowly for the powerful. In addition, by being obedient to Allah, Muslims try not to follow their desires and lust since these distract them from the remembrance of God. They also think that it is important to be in good and pious company to develop good qualities and be God conscious.

Diet

> Eat from the good things with which We have provided you and do not transgress [or oppress others] therein, lest My anger should descend upon you. (20:81; 2:168)

Muslims believe that God is the Provider and everything that has been created is for the service of humankind. However, there are certain limits that have been set for them, for many reasons, when they use these wonderful blessings. Therefore, rather than submitting to their appetites and cravings, they try to control themselves and consume only what is pure and good. Muslims believe that the consumption of ***ḥarām*** has an impact on their quality of worship and supplications. In addition, since these are gifts from God they are mindful about wastage and being extravagant; simultaneously, they are grateful and generous to the less fortunate.

Diversity

> And of His signs is the creation of the heavens and the earth and the diversity of your languages and your colours. Indeed in that are signs for those of knowledge. (30:22)

Many Muslims are inspired by this verse to reflect on and celebrate the concept of 'unity within diversity'. It is also an important principle to challenge racism and to consider languages as a strength of individuals and communities. Often it is used to argue for plurality and co-existence. By referring to knowledge, this subtly challenges bigotry, which tends to be based on ignorance.

Khimār

> Tell the believing men to reduce [some] of their vision and guard their private parts. That is purer for them. Indeed, Allah is Acquainted with what they do. (24:30)
>
> And tell the believing women to reduce [some] of their vision and guard their private parts and not expose their adornment except that which [necessarily] appears thereof and to wrap [a portion of] their 'headcovers' (***khimār***) over their chests and not expose their adornment except to their husbands, their fathers, their husbands' fathers, their sons, their husbands' sons, their brothers, their brothers' sons, their sisters' sons, their women, that which their right hands possess, or those male attendants having no physical desire, or children who are not yet aware of the private aspects of women. And let them not stamp their feet to make known what they conceal of their adornment. And turn to Allah in repentance, all of you, O believers, that you might succeed. (24:31)

This verse uses the word *khimār*, taken to be the niqāb (face veil and/or head cover).

Taking both verses together, the primary address is to men. Nevertheless, the overall aim is to prevent lewdness and fortify chastity by instructing all, men and women, to discipline themselves by lowering their gazes and safeguarding their private parts. There is consensus on the practice of using the *khimār* as being obligatory. Scholars differ in their view about the covering by females of their hands and face but not the whole body. The avoidance of peeking into someone's personal matters and peeping into people's houses to divulge their secrets is extrapolated from this. In addition, the protection of private parts encompasses all restricted sexual acts. As with many verses, the Qur'ān identifies the initial cause, which might be detrimental to individual and social well-being. Thus, interestingly, it mentions the precursor (the eyes) and the final act (sexual encounter). By implication, all other actions, which mediate between the two, would be included. Disciplining the eyes and visual stimuli is paramount. It then lists categories of men with whom covering is not necessary. In a general sense, these are the *maḥārim,* with whom marriage is not allowed. In addition to the eyes, a *ḥadīth* mentions the misuse of all sensory organs as preliminaries for the sexual organ to act. Thus, all these need to be guarded against illicit sexual gratification. On a personal note, ***ḥijāb*** includes staring at all indecent images. Moreover, all are also required not to expose their ***'awrah*** even to their respective *maḥārim*, except to one's spouse. The chance glance, rather than lusting, is excusable. Hence, the final counsel for all is that if someone should err, they ought to feel repentant and beg pardon of Allah.

Jilbāb/Hijāb

> O Prophet, tell your wives and your daughters and the women of the believers to bring down over themselves [part] of their outer garments (*jilbāb*). That is more suitable that they will be known and not be abused. And ever is Allah Forgiving and Merciful. (33:59)

This verse uses the word *jilbāb* showing that veiling (***niqāb***) was applicable not only to the wives and daughters of Muḥammad (ﷺ) but to all other Muslim women. This was a preventative measure against the pain caused to the Prophet (ﷺ) and molestation of women. As a mark of distinction, free women should hide part of their face by drawing their covering cloak over their head to screen it except the eyes; although others see it as referring to *ḥijāb*, as the long and enveloping dress. Hence, *niqāb* is an established practice; the primary motivation is obedience to God. Of the many reasons for lowering of the gaze there is the acknowledgment of women as humans. Moreover, the hair and the body are considered private and many do not desire to show these in public, which are to be respected as a matter of choice.

> And women of post-menstrual age who have no desire for marriage – there is no blame upon them for putting aside their outer garments (*thiyāb*) [but] not displaying adornment. But to modestly refrain [from that] is better for them. And Allah is Hearing and Knowing. (24:60)

The outer garment (*thiyāb*) was also in vogue. However this part of the verse refers to 'the seated women' (lit.) meaning those incapable of bearing children, who do not relish sexual desire or excite men. As an exemption, they may put aside in their homes their outer clothes used to conceal their adornments as instructed in (33:59). This refers to those parts which can be exposed and not to nudity. Nevertheless, it is better for them to avoid doing do so altogether. *Tabarruj* is exhibitionism, so those old women whose sexual desires and want for personal beautification are absent but do possess a hidden desire in their hearts and have an urge for embellishment to display cannot avail themselves of this permission. When believers asked for something they needed from the Prophet (ﷺ), they were instructed to ask from behind a partition (*hijāb*) (33:53) so Muslims discuss the restricted nature of this command or its generality in that all females are expected to follow in the example of the wives.

Mocking

> O you who have believed, let not a people ridicule [another] people; perhaps they may be better than them; nor let women ridicule [other] women; perhaps they may be better than them. And do not insult one another and do not call each other by [offensive] nicknames. (49:11)

Physical, verbal and online bullying is a reality in many schools and in society. There are many reasons for bullying, some of which manifest in name-calling, defamation, intimidation and humiliation. As a preventative measure, for Muslims, this is a mandate not to ignore bullying and create a safe environment and a community-wide strategy. In addition, it persuades Muslims to look beyond the apparent and physical attributes of people and give respect to values and morality, as they are unaware of the inner thoughts and characters of people.

Modesty (*ḥayā'*)

> O children of Adam, We have bestowed upon you clothing to conceal your private parts and as adornment. But the clothing of righteousness – that is best. That is from the signs of Allah that perhaps they will remember. (7:26)

Modesty is a broader concept encompassing both external and internal matters and commonly related to being shy, bashful and self-dignity. It is not only a catalyst for the lowering of gazes and the covering of the 'awrah and adorning the *niqāb, jilbāb, khimār* and *ḥijāb*, but it is also to be mirrored, in different contexts, in speech, character, achievement, deed, thought, wealth and personality. Spiritually, modesty manifests in being mindful of God (*taqwā*) at all times and places. However, everyone is to embody it in their attire, albeit with differentials in terms of how, where and to whom it is shared. The purity in the external matters is psychological, emotional and physiological. Within the personal elements of self-respect and shyness, nakedness other than for one's wife is to be minimised to respect angels and God, since God has a greater right to feel shy of (Ibn Mājah, 3:1920). Overall, positive *ḥayā'* is to be ashamed to do something wrong and negative ***ḥayā'*** is to be ashamed of doing something required by God and His Messenger (ﷺ).

Parents

> And your Lord has decreed that you not worship except Him, and to parents, good treatment. Whether one or both of them reach old age [while] with you, say not to them [so much as], 'uff,' and do not repel them but speak to them a noble

> word. And lower to them the wing of humility out of mercy and say, 'My Lord, have mercy upon them as they brought me up [when I was] small'. (17:23–24)

In Islam, parents come immediately after God. The happiness of God lies in the happiness of parents. The expression of displeasure or exasperation is meant by '*uff*' and it implies the need to be very patient with them. This is also a protection against verbal abuse. Moreover, this verse establishes, with other verses, their right to be respected, obeyed and to be looked after. Importantly, they have a duty to protect their children physically, intellectually, morally, religiously and spiritually. In the long-term interests of their children, parents, to correct their behaviour, may take recourse to advice, rebuke and scolding. Children are expected to supplicate regularly for their parents.

Pride

> And do not turn your cheek [in contempt] toward people and do not walk through the earth exultantly. Indeed, Allah does not like everyone self-deluded and boastful. And be moderate in your pace and lower your voice; indeed, the most disagreeable of sounds is the voice of donkeys. (31:18–19)

This rejects pride, considered to be the most blameworthy characteristic disliked by Allah. It was first exhibited by Satan in relation to Adam which led to his downfall. Pride is an inner negative quality, which can make one see others as inferior and which may develop animosity, envy, anger, backbiting and scorn. It may prevent the acceptance of good counsel. In relation to God, it is the antithesis to humility. In short, it is the seed of immorality.

Reality

> And they say, 'There is not but our worldly life; we die and live, and nothing destroys us except time.' And they have of that no knowledge; they are only assuming. (45:24)

This is a refutation of the idea that there is nothing after life on earth. The method of argumentation is interesting, for the verse maintains that deniers of resurrection do so not based on knowledge but on speculation, whereas revelation offers logical arguments on the possibility of the Afterlife and that justice requires for there to be a judgement day to make life on earth meaningful. Second, they claim that the passage of time ends their existence. In other words, they deny the role of God in ending their life, and with God's role in resurrecting and judging.

Sex

> Your wives are a place of sowing of seed for you, so come to your place of cultivation however you wish and put forth [righteousness] for yourselves. And fear Allah and know that you will meet Him. And give good tidings to the believers. (2:223)

This has many themes. Sexuality is a balance between spirituality and fulfilling one's emotional desires and physical needs. However, for Muslims this needs to happen within legitimate relationships of marriage for its approval and avoidance of guilt. It implies procreation as a purpose of intercourse. In addition, sex in marriage is a form of worship and *ṣadaqah* (charity) (Muslim, 2:2198). Importantly, deprivation of sexual fulfilment for both is prohibited. Thus, they can be creative in their lovemaking positions but must avoid anal sex at all times and vaginal sex during menstruation, although association is allowed (Abū Dāwūd, 2:2157; 2162; Ibn Mājah, 3:1923).

Suffering

> And We will surely test you with something of fear and hunger and a loss of wealth and lives and fruits, but give good tidings to the patient. (2:155)

Life is a test. Suffering is part of the test. Some humans suffer in many different ways as explained in this verse. Patience as a response to suffering is promoted. This means that some Muslims accept and expect that at some point in their life something may become unfavourable and therefore they recognise that there is some wisdom based on which the All-Wise God has caused it to happen. Consequently, rather than asking questions about 'why it happened', some will ask 'what can I do?' and 'how can I respond?'.

Temptation

> O children of Adam, let not Satan tempt you as he removed your parents from Paradise, stripping them of their clothing to show them their private parts. Indeed, he sees you, he and his tribe, from where you do not see them. Indeed, We have made the devils allies to those who do not believe. (7:27)

God is warning the children of Adam against Satan and his allies by reminding them of his earliest enmity for the father of humanity. Satan connived to have Adam and Hawwa (Eve) evicted from Paradise and expose their nudity. Being a self-confessed enemy of humankind, he uses temptations to lure people away from God and good actions. This means that Muslims recognise the existence and enmity of Satan, but importantly they learn about his temptations and find solutions to assist them from succumbing to his temptations, which can be very challenging.

Tolerance

For you is your religion, and for me is my religion. (109:6)

One-day, some noble Qurayshī idolaters and pagans proposed to Muḥammad (ﷺ), as a compromise, that he should worship their gods and in return, they would worship his God. Consequently, this *Sūrah* was revealed disassociating both from each other's religion and actions. This means that Muḥammad (ﷺ) declined to worship their idols and compromise his beliefs, which means each would face the consequences of their actions. In so doing, the verse establishes the uncompromising principle of worshipping God alone.

Voice of a Muslim

I am a local barber who interacts with people from all backgrounds. People come and share their thoughts and feelings of whatever kind. We live in a community where they are mainly working-class people and not affluent so there is plenty of gossip. Sometimes this is about drugs, theft or crimes. People talk about kidnap and torture. So you get to hear about it. You hear about youngsters not looking after their mother. There are issues of gangs. So we become part of this. But in Islam there is a principle about rumours and advising. So we don't get embroiled but try to be peacekeepers and counsel them. We try to advise them before something silly happens. Once someone came, had a shave and cut and expressed the intention of suicide. So I talk with him and ask him what will happen to his family, etc. So he went home. He changed his mind. He came the following day, hugged me and said he had changed his decision. (Ḥasan, Pakistani, hairdresser, male)

The Prophet (ﷺ) teaches

The ample unambiguous instructions of the Qur'ān to obey and follow the Prophet (ﷺ), as discussed above and in Chapter 3, have consequences for the adoption of correct beliefs and rejection of heresies and polytheism. In addition, it also has consequences on moral behaviours and ethical thinking. In Chapter 1, you learnt that the Qur'ān and Prophet Muḥammad (ﷺ) emphasised three concepts: oneness of God; Day of Resurrection; obedience to Allah and His messengers. The ethical teachings of the Prophet (ﷺ) need to be considered in light of these. As a source of Islam, the utterances, practices and silent approvals of the Prophet (ﷺ) have directly influenced the classifications of the rules of Sharīʿah and have also determined matters of religious, spiritual, legal and ethical import. Moreover, the verses above have demonstrated that the Qur'ān is not a systemic ethics book only. Likewise, the Prophet (ﷺ) offers more than an ethical lifestyle; his integration of faith and good conduct is akin to the combination of morality and religiousness, which are central to Islamic ethics and spirituality. Following faith, he placed utmost emphasis on the cultivation of noble qualities of mind and character, and avoidance of nasty habits and cruel behaviour. His role was not only to recite and teach the Holy Book and wisdom, but also to purify the community (2:129).

The *ḥadīth* text cited below embraces the concepts and pedagogies of correcting manners (***ādāb***) and deeds in a narrative form all too familiar to Muslims the world over. Similarly, there exists a broad range of legislative, motivational and deterrent literature in many genres which offers advice cultivating *ādāb* and ***akhlāq*** (conduct) and to live a pious and virtuous life. These didactic texts dispensing ethics and virtues include stated rules of moralities, pious narratives, poetry, songs and entire treatises on a single subject or compendiums on all topics to exemplify moralities and characters to be remembered and acted upon. Guides in Islamic ethics have a long history that cross several genres of various lengths and sophistication, but they all build on the principle to reach answers to issues of immediate concern (Raudvere, 2015: 191). Let us now have a look at some selected instructions and statements from the Prophet (ﷺ).

Altruism

> There is no Muslim who plants a tree or sows seeds and then a bird, or a person, or an animal eats from it except that it is regarded as a charitable gift for him. (al-Bukhārī, 3:513)

The important role that trees have in the universe is well-known. Muslims have a responsibility to act as stewards of the earth. Trees are not to be burnt during war nor to be unnecessarily destroyed. This *ḥadīth* encourages the planting of trees. In return, the planter receives blessings from all those who benefit from it. This is also an encouragement for Muslims to be involved in planting, preserving and protecting trees.

Bribery

> Cursed be the briber and the taker of bribes. (Abū Dāwūd, 3:3573)

It is noteworthy that both the giving and receiving of bribes are prohibited so both will be accountable for any unfairness resulting thereof. The giver will have some decision made to his or her advantage, which, consequently, might infringe on another person's right. The receiver is making a personal gain by the misuse of power or decision entrusted to them. Bribery is thus wrong as it sows the seeds of corruption in society.

Consultation

> The consultant is placed in a position of trust. (Ibn Mājah, 5:3745)

Those who are consulted are therefore duty-bound to provide the most reliable, most beneficial and honest advice to their clients so that the trust placed on them is not betrayed. They have to serve the interest of their clients, unless it contravenes the teachings of Sharī'ah.

Employees

> Pay the labourer his due before his sweat dries. (Ibn Mājah, 3:2443)

This relates to the employer–employee hiring relationship. It is a metaphor instructing the prompt payment of what is due, regardless of whether the job produces sweat or not. The delay of the payment without a legitimate reason is unjust. It also implies that there should be agreement on the pay, duration and type of work in advance and employees, in turn, must satisfy their conditions.

Golden rule

> A believer is a personification of love, there is no virtue in one who does not love others and the others do not love them. (Tabrīzī, 4:4995)

To achieve unity, Muslims are invited to embody love and affection among themselves, otherwise divisions might take over. With the rest of creation, a Muslim should not only be a place where others find warmth, but they should be dispensers of affection as well.

Goodness

> One who guides to something good has a reward similar to that of its doer. (Muslim, 3:4665)

Taken as a principle, a person who motivates and guides others to do good will get a reward for the good deed carried out by the other person. This will not reduce the reward of the doer of the act; they too will get their own blessings. Conversely, a person is rewarded for deterring others from carrying out bad actions, regardless of whether the person heeds or ignores the advice.

Jihād

> The best *jihād* is (saying) a word of truth before an oppressive ruler. (Abū Dāwūd, 3:4330)

First, this reveals a spectrum of types of *jihād* and their respective religious, moral and socio-political duties meant by it. Second, it specifies the non-combatant application of the concept. Third, though it uses a superlative 'best', it does not preclude armed *jihād*. Fourth, it asserts a duty upon Muslims to speak up for the oppressed and stand up against transgressors. Fifth, it also denounces collusion or tacit approval of tyrannical rulers.

Judge

> A judge should not pass judgement between two people when angry. (al-Bukhārī, 9:272)

This ḥadīth is alerting to the dangers of anger, especially when speaking. It relates to making any judgement in the heat of anger, specifically for judges, since a judge holds a responsible position to administer justice and is bound by the law and evidence. They are not to be swayed by emotions and personal matters, lest they decide in an inequitable and impartial manner. This discourages them from making decisions in anger.

Love

> Your love for something blinds and deafens (you). (Abū Dāwūd, 3:5111)

This is akin to saying love is blind. In the pursuit of wealth, success, status, power, love and families, a person should not be unmindful of their duties to

God and His Messenger (ﷺ). Conversely, they should be blind and deaf to everything else when matters concern the love of God and His Messenger (ﷺ). In terms of humans and dealings with them, the love of someone or something should not cloud Muslims from justice and truth. In relation to God, a person should seek a state where they neither see nor hear anything and become intoxicated with love, taking them into another realm where only the radiance (*nūr*) and nearness (*qurb*) of the Beloved (God) is sensed.

Oppression

> Oppression will be a cause of many darknesses on Judgement Day. (al-Bukhārī, 3:627)

Good deeds will be a source of light in the Hereafter, which is what people will want. However, for the oppressors, instead, there will be layers of darkness. Based on this statement, oppression, which can take many forms, is a sin. The darkness might refer to adversities in the Afterlife.

Piety

> Allah does not look at your appearance or wealth but looks at your heart and actions. (Muslim, 4:6221)

God is interested in the quality of sincerity and actions rather than the physical appearances and material possessions of an individual. In another tradition, the degree of piety is mentioned as the determiner of the rank of excellence rather than the colour of their skin.

Repentance

> The Messenger (ﷺ) once told a story of a man who killed ninety-nine people. Later, he began to enquire whether he could repent. He came to a monk and asked him. He was told: 'There is no chance for repentance for you.' So he killed the monk also. He went further moving from one village to another to where there lived pious persons. He had covered some distance but was getting close to death. So he crawled upon his chest (to get nearer to the place where the pious men lived) but died. There then occurred a dispute between the angels of mercy and the angels of punishment. They decided to measure. The man was found to be nearer to the village where pious persons were living by about a span length. He was thus included among them. (Muslim, 4:6663)

The Prophet (ﷺ) used stories for teaching. This one illustrates the importance of seeking repentance and the existence of the abundance of mercy and forgiveness with God. Thus, it gives hope and promotes a search for clemency.

Righteousness

> Righteousness is good character, and sin is what causes uneasiness in your heart and you dislike others to become aware of it. (Muslim, 4:6195)

This relates to some uncertain matters which may be decided by conscience rather than those where the teachings of Islam have made clear rulings. A God-conscious person feels uneasiness in their heart or dislikes committing a doubtful act in public; these would indicate that the act is best avoided. In contrast, a transgressor would ignore these inner senses and continue to follow their desires and flout the rules.

Silence

> He who keeps silent saves themselves. (al-Tirmidhī, 4:2501)

There should be space and time for silence in the life of a Muslim. Sometimes, the use of silence becomes particularly significant during arguments to avert escalating the situation. This also implies being an active listener. However, another narrative mentions that speaking good is better than silence and silence is better than saying something bad. In other words, the principle is to be mindful of where, how and why the tongue is used, and what for.

Case study 8.1 Ethics and morals

Susan had recently attended a course on promoting classroom strategies which developed talk. Over the years, she had noticed that the use of talk partners to an extent was 'restricting' her pupils' perspectives and interactions as they tended to talk with the same partners most of the time in most of the subjects. In her inner city school, located in a deprived catchment area, she decided to remind herself of Spencer Kagan's structures and implemented a collaborative strategy. She very quickly noticed significant improvements not only in her teaching but also in her pupils' oracy and learning. She discovered that Kagan structures tended to be content free which allowed her to use them for thematic teaching purposes. It was also effective when teaching about values, morals and characters and assisted her to change the group dynamics of her class to build stronger collaborative work. She found that organising children into groups of four enhanced the quality and quantity of talk and, importantly, extended their perspectives. The strategy involved pupils talking to their *shoulder partners* (children next to each other) and *face partners* (children opposite).

Sometimes the way pupils are seated and organised in the classroom determines the dynamics of the lesson. Often making simple changes in the seating pattern can make a difference to the depth of learning, cohesion and satisfaction of pupils. There are many topics in this chapter which lend themselves to a different way of organising your teaching. Choose a few topics and consider for each topic:

- how you would organise the pupils in your classroom in a different way
- what your rationale would be for each style of organisation
- what you would intend to achieve through such organisation
- the challenges, if any, that you would anticipate in making such organisation

Summary

You have learnt what moral attributes are pleasing to God from the perspective of the Qur'ān and *ḥadīth* literature and which of them Muslims try to uphold and shun to gain the pleasure of God. You have also learnt how they are expected to conduct themselves in various walks of life. This chapter has demonstrated to you that the concept of *ḥalāl* and *ḥarām* is an all-encompassing one, which is beyond dietary requirements. Thus, Islamic ethics, as a theological and philosophical concept, is closely connected to the principles of *Sharī'ah* and ***fiqh***, as well as to conventions (***'urf***) and local rules of good behaviour (Raudvere, 2005: 191). Most importantly, you will have surmised that ethics in Islam is a corpus of guidelines laid down in the Qur'ān for the practical conduct of life and exemplified in the practice of the Prophet (ﷺ). These are used by Muslims in modern times in new situations and to critique existing socio-political systems and respond to the challenges of modernity in medicine, economics and technology.

Reflection tasks

- What would you consider to be the ten most important moral norms for Muslims?
- How does the existence of a moral code assist a Muslim to prepare and be accountable for their actions?
- What similarities and differences do you notice between these ethical codes and those in other religious and non-religious traditions?
- What are the implications of placing moral duty within a religious context and given religious interpretation?

Further reading

Abū Rīda, M.A. (1998) 'Norms and values', in A. Bouhdiba (ed.), *The Different Aspects of Islamic Culture*. Paris: UNESCO Publications.

This chapter is relevant as it examines ethics and philosophy in detail based on the Qur'ān and how it responded to morals that existed in the then Arabian Peninsula.

Denny, F. (2016) *An Introduction to Islam*, 4th edn. Abingdon: Routledge.

This book covers a wider range of topics including early civilisations and the origins of Judaism and Christianity, pre-Islamic Arabia beliefs, values and life, the broad topics in Islam and Islam in the modern world.

9

EDUCATION IN MUSLIM COMMUNITIES

In this chapter you will:

- understand the aims and objectives of Islamic education
- reflect on the key educational principles and concepts from the Qur'ān
- critically examine the educational institutes within Muslim communities
- evaluate the programmes of study offered to Muslim children in the UK
- consider the relationship between faith and intellectual endeavour.

Overview

In the story of the revelation of the Qur'ān, you will recall that the first word to be revealed was 'Read'. Muslims interpret this as an emphasis on reading and learning, making both a religious activity deserving merit. In seeking knowledge, the barriers of time and space are to be traversed, for the Prophet (ﷺ) is reported to have encouraged the search for knowledge from the cradle to the grave and to seek it even if it were in China (Al Zeera, 2001). Simultaneously, Allah is All-Knowing, therefore, though there is a limit to what humans can know, they are to continue to know, understand and explore the universe using God-given intelligence and spiritual capacities. This knowledge is both temporal and spiritual. In the Islamic tradition, acquiring knowledge is not conceived as an end in itself or a means purely for material and utilitarian goals. The aim is to know and understand the Will of Allah and to live one's life accordingly. To this end, Muslims petition Allah to help them with that which He has taught them, and to teach them that which will help them, and increase their knowledge. Condensing into a single chapter a review of the rich educational literature is beyond the purpose of this book, therefore selected features are discussed to illustrate educational philosophies, theories, institutions and practices from diverse settings.

Education and the Qur'ān

Pedagogically, the Qur'ān applies repetition to warrant its readers' attention and to impress upon their consciousness the centrality of some key concepts.

The derivations from the root *'i-l-m* (knowledge, to know) occur some 750 times, ranking it third in numerical tabulation and significance (Wan Daud, 1989: 32). This would be only one indication that the concept of knowledge as a whole is important in the grand scheme of the universe.

There are other ways through which the significance of this concept has been conveyed, for example, the occurrence of synonyms such as ***f-k-r*** (to ponder), ***f-q-h*** (to comprehend), ***d-b-r*** (to reflect), ***a-q-l*** (to think), ***f-h-m*** (to understand) and, coupled with this, there exists the negation of these synonyms (***la yafqahūn***, ***la ya'qilūn***, ***la-yubṣirūn***) and in addition, antonyms feature like ***j-h-l*** (ignorance). Over 600 verses urge its reader to ponder on the mysteries of nature, to reflect on God's creation and to use their reason (Sikand, 2005: 3). Moreover, the Qur'ān brings forth terms and objects employed for teaching and learning including pen (***qalam***), writer (***kātib***), scrolls (*suḥuf*), parchment (***qirṭās***) and others.

Beyond concepts, processes and artefacts, the necessity to secure constancy in the process of education features in a verse related to the command of *jihād*, wherein it states that:

> it is not for the believers to go forth [to battle] all at once. For there should separate from every division of them a group [remaining] to obtain understanding in the religion and warn their people when they return to them that they might be cautious. (9:122)

Thus, a section of the community is always required to be engaged in educational activities.

The prominence of education can also be established in view of the eminent status conferred on scholars (***'Ulamā'***) where the equality between those who know and those who do not is dismissed (39:9). Knowledge is also given prestige by attributing its possessors with the attainment of God-consciousness (35:28). The seeker of knowledge is like the one who walks the path leading to paradise (Ibn Jamā'ah, 1991). The search for knowledge is not only for reaching God but also a means for enhancing the quality of life of humanity.

Education and the Messenger (ﷺ)

The Qur'ān refers to Muḥammad (ﷺ) with the title 'unlettered Prophet' (***al-nabī al-ummī***) as he was not formally schooled in previous scriptures, denoting that he was unable to create a masterpiece that the Qur'ān is (7:157). However, when you study his life you will discover that it abounds with sayings and actions that elevate the significance of gaining and spreading knowledge which became inspirational for subsequent intellectual activities and the development of educational structures. First, he asserted that he had only been sent as a teacher (Ibn Mājah, 1:229). Thus in contemporary Muslim representation, the prophet is presented as Prophet–Teacher (*ar-Rasul al-Mua'llim*) (Abu Ghuddah, 2017). Then he declared that it was compulsory for everyone to seek knowledge, perhaps to promote utilitarian purposes and egalitarian aims (Ibn Mājah, 1:224). This does not mean everyone should become a scholar but to acquire functional knowledge in the practices of daily life and rituals. To promote higher ideals he confirmed that scholars were heirs of the prophets and that God would facilitate the path to paradise for the seekers of knowledge (Al-Hassan, 2001). Moreover, guardians were promised perpetual reward for educating their offspring. Though some of these ḥadīth have had their reliability scrutinised, they continue to positively influence Muslim attitudes and practices towards education. Then, practically, he took measures for the mass dissemination of education. As a teacher, he was accessible and made himself available to all sections of the community. He appointed teachers to teach reading, writing and arithmetic. On one occasion he bargained the freedom of prisoners of war in exchange for Muslims to be taught to read and write. The Veranda (*al-Ṣuffāh*) outside his mosque accommodated destitute and 'foreign' students (***Aṣḥāb al-Ṣuffāh***), some of whom later became prominent and leading experts in the Qur'ān, ḥadīth, ***fiqh*** and other sciences. In addition, history notes that at least nine mosques in Madīnah served as schools as well (Hamidullah, 1939).

Classification of knowledge

Early Muslim scholars were concerned with the acquisition and dissemination of all kinds of knowledge and, for this, prepared introductory books to assist teachers and students. These books included the classification of sciences which are many (Al-Muḥaqqiq, 2001; Ibn Khaldūn, 1989). For brevity that of Ibn Khaldūn is presented in Table 9.1.

Table 9.1 Classification of knowledge

Sciences of religious law	Rational sciences
Qur'ānic science	Arithmetic
Ḥadīth	Geometry
Jurisprudence	Astronomy

Sciences of religious law	Rational sciences
Religious obligations	Logic
Principles of jurisprudence	Natural sciences
Polemic and dialectic	Medicine
Speculative theology	Agriculture
Islamic mysticism	Metaphysics
Interpretation of dreams	Magic and talismans
Sciences of the Arabic language	Alchemy
Grammar	
Lexicography	
Rhetoric	
Literature	

Muslim educational thought and practice

In this section, you will learn about educational theory and practice as reflected in the works of classical scholars. This is significant not only in demonstrating that Muslim scholarship problematised and attended to theoretical and pedagogy issues of education, but also that there existed and continue to exist multiple conceptions of Islamic education which engender different actions (Waghid, 2011; Bano, 2017; Hardaker and Sabki, 2019) which, in turn, guide practice in a variety of ways.

Al-Zarnūjī (d. 620AH/1223CE):

- earliest contributor to the theory and practice of education
- emphasised that there is a moral need for learning
- supported holistic education rather than simply academic achievements
- favoured the discussion method for important problems
- advised on abstaining from shouting as it diverts from the real purpose of discussions
- censured debate with the express objective of defeating the adversary but advocated it in the spirit of learning (Al-Zarnūjī, 2001)

Ibn Jamā'ah (639–733AH/1241–1333CE) encouraged teachers to question students to ensure comprehension, clarify misconception and encourage those reluctant to admit to the need for further explanation. He stressed that teachers maintain equal treatment of their students and avoid favouritism of any kind as that would create resentment among them (Ibn Jamā'ah, 1991).

Ibn Khaldūn (733–808AH/1332–406CE):

- thought to be the founder of historiography and sociology (Ibn Khaldūn, 1989)
- attached significance to the role of talk rather than memorising
- believed that the easiest method of attaining the scientific habit is through acquiring the ability to express oneself clearly in discussing and disputing scientific problems
- suggested that poetry and Arabic philology should be taught first to minimise the existing corruption of language (Bano, 2017)

Ibn Miskawaīh (320–421AH/932–1030CE):

- interested in history, psychology, philosophy, chemistry, ethics, a librarian
- considered knowledge as the basis of good character and the foundation of all virtue
- believed that human perfection rested on acquiring knowledge (Alavi, 1988)
- maintained that character is acquired rather than being natural and that changes are achieved gradually
- learning good habits depended on thinking and willing, a quality produced at a particular stage in a person's life
- argued that children possess modesty and self-respect and so, avoid undesirable acts
- placed the duty of training children on parents using different methods of discipline
- advised that some methods of discipline may lead to the opposite effect whereby students become ill-mannered and unresponsive (Günther, 2016)

Imām Al-Ghazālī (450–505AH/1058–1111CE):

- emphasised lesson preparation and thorough knowledge of the subject
- highlighted the development of lessons with pupils to facilitate their understanding
- teachers should have full knowledge of their children and plan accordingly
- new knowledge should be related to previous learning
- cautioned teachers against presenting complex and difficult subject matters at the beginning lest the child becomes confused or loses interest (Alavi, 1988)

The common link between these educational theories is the significance attached to ethics in all aspects of teaching and learning. It seems to be a central and defining component in the search of classical Muslims for human perfection and happiness in both worlds (Günther, 2016: 90). However, projecting the conceptions of Islamic learning in the context of the post-apartheid political, cultural and economic South African context, Waghid (2011: 126) suggests that Islamic learning has to connect with the achievement of justice for all. Only then can learning be of value in leading human flourishing. According to him, one way of attending to the world's moral problems it to connect learning with cosmopolitan virtues, which includes engendering in people a willingness to deliberate in an iterative fashion, an attentiveness to connect hospitality with others and to act responsibly with the aim of changing a bad situation.

The challenges facing Muslims globally are manifold and their responses are equally varied. One of the key arenas where there is considerable innovation and creativity, especially in the western hemisphere, is education (Tan, 2014). In post-colonial legacies, there continues to be anxiety not only about the dichotomy of educational philosophy as 'secular' and 'religious' but also, importantly, about the impact of culture in some contexts over the ethos of schooling where the accumulation of facts, standardisation, a target driven environment, corporate models, and supposedly value-free philosophies are being questioned both within Muslim majority and minority contexts. Based in the USA, for El-Moslimany (2018: 1) this involves challenging the status quo and approaching the customary with scepticism. It is about scrutinising the history of why and how the prevailing methodology common to the vast majority of schools of all kinds came to be and the 'factory'- like education. In part inspired by ideas of Montessori and others, El-Moslimany (2018) models her school on the principles of *Tawḥīd* (Oneness of God, humanity, knowledge); ***fiṭrah*** (human nature); and the role of humans as vicegerents (responsibility and stewardship) to create a holistic philosophy of education.

The home

There is a profound statement issued by Muḥammad (ﷺ) which places a huge responsibility on parents regarding the nurture and safety of their children. He stated that everyone was a guardian and every guardian shall be questioned with regard to their trust (Muslim, 4:4496). In addition to placing this responsibility on the *Khalīfah* as a 'shepherd' of the community, he included a man and woman being responsible for their household and family. Therefore parents are like shepherds under divine obligation to nurture a wholesome Muslim personality. In educational terms, this means they are duty-bound to ensure their religious, spiritual, personal and physical development is catered for. The home is meant to be the primary institute where this is carried out whereby children observe and embody faith and cultural expressions. Thus, many Muslims believe that learning to live with family rules is the first step toward learning to live within society's laws (Altalib et al., 2013: 18).

However, like many communities, Muslims are facing multifaceted challenges and issues. There are various factors which influence the way in which children develop including genetics, family dynamics, socio-cultural beliefs, community support, economic circumstances and political leadership (Ebrahim, 2017). They impact on who and what children become. Family values have experienced a downward trend over the years. Muslim families have not been spared from this phenomenon in addition to their own particular problems and weaknesses. There is a rise in divorce rates, prison population, single parent families, crime, drugs and domestic abuse (Altalib et al., 2013: 43). For some, a climate of hostility towards Muslims and their faith is not only contributing to a crisis of identity which is affecting their self-esteem and dignity, but is also creating doubts about their faith leading some to abandon it altogether.

Muslim education in the UK

The experiences of the Muslim community in a pluralistic cultural environment are intrinsically linked to the phenomenon of postcolonial migration where their presence is considerably debated in the context of citizenship, identity, and integration of ethnic and religious minorities. It has been noted that national educational systems and curricula play a key role in the making of citizens, and, therefore, the issue of Islamic education has been a vital part of debates surrounding what it means to be a British Muslim and an important terrain in the negotiation of identity and co-existence (Mandaville, 2007: 224). The representation of Islam in educational systems is of concern to the community and to educationalists. Revell (2012) evaluated the dominant approaches to the teaching of Islam and argued that the pedagogy and curriculum challenge historical misrepresentation of Islam and Islamophobia. Institutionally, there are several ways in which Muslims have responded to educational matters.

Maktab education: Nurturing Muslim personality

The underlying philosophy of Islamic education is the holistic development of a child – the physical, intellectual and spiritual dimensions. In one conception, there are three frequently used words in Arabic for education (Boyle, 2004: 43). *Tarbiyyah* refers to education in the broadest sense and it implies the development of the human personality and includes nurturing and rearing aspects of education (emotional and social health). ***Ta'līm*** denotes instruction involving mental activity through which reasoning and training of the mind (intellectual health) takes place. ***Ta'dīb*** represents the training of the mind and the soul in relation to proper behaviour or ethical conduct (spiritual and moral health). In addition, Al-Azem (2016) notes that ***Tadrīs*** came to be used exclusively for teaching law. ***Mudarris*** (one who delivers the '***dars***' or lesson) and ***faqīh*** (jurist) served as interchangeable terms for the professor of law. Underpinning all these lies the consideration of *ikhlās*, often translated as sincerity, which is related to the concept of authenticity. Personal authenticity, as an educational aim, involves a process of coming to self-integrity and an awareness of personal choice and responsibility (Trevathan, 2016: 63).

To achieve the above, one of the ways in which parents fulfil their parental responsibility is to send their children to Islamic education classes. In their study of Muslim families, whilst Scourfield et al. (2013) found the existence of 'outliners' which they describe as families without any teachings of Islam, it was almost universal in the rest. Some children attend these classes from the age of five. The younger ones attended for an hour and the older ones for up to two hours ranging from three to five days a week with most attending between 5–7pm. Some families send their children at weekends. For those memorising the Qur'ān, their sessions tend to be longer.

Often the maktab/**madrasah** is referred to as a Qur'ānic school; this does not imply that Muslim children are exclusively taught the Qur'ān. The reasons for sending children to these settings are many and the provisions are diverse (Scourfield et al., 2013: 80; Gent, 2018). Suffice to say that the general pattern among those delivering a comprehensive age-related syllabus covers 'subjects' such as beliefs (*aqāid*), jurisprudence (*fiqh*), history (*tārīkh*), morals (*akhlāq*), (supplication) (***duā'***), aḥādīth and art of recitation (*tajwīd*). Some include the child's basic mother language and Arabic input, whereas others offer tuition to support mainstream school learning and Arabic with some Islamic studies.

The level of understanding and experience is affected by the effectiveness of the teaching pedagogies and curriculum. In some of these settings a disconnection is highlighted between the religious leadership and the linguistic and intellectual capabilities, and culture of the young people that they intend to educate (Hamid, 2016). Nevertheless, there is considerable innovation taking place. Some of the syllabi developed in the UK, for example, provide course books for each subject with differentiated activities and use an engaging child-friendly approach to make learning easy and enjoyable with the inclusion of colourful illustrations and inspiring stories. Some use age-relevant content as workbooks with tasks set using Bloom's taxonomy and are dyslexia-friendly. The content is referenced from authentic Islamic sources. Over the years, there has been a growth in the range of teaching methods used with some reflecting the practices of mainstream schools. In some cities, there are provisions for blind and deaf children, and others are beginning to cater specifically for special educational needs and disability by establishing dedicated madrasahs for SEND.

To cater for the specific needs of the visually impaired Muslim community in the UK, organisations exist to support and promote their well-being by catering for their religious needs. Material is available and produced in Braille and audio. Qur'ānic Arabic is taught in Braille by a number of qualified teachers. In some supplementary madrasahs, workshops on the introduction of Braille and British Sign Language (BSL) have been organised. Organisations exist to support deaf Muslims to cater for their faith, spiritual and cultural development. As part of their services, they organise indoor and outdoor activities including seminars, workshops, trips, Eid parties, translations and distribution of learning resources in BSL. They produce parts of the Qur'ān, ḥadīth, Islamic stories, interpretation of the Friday *khuṭbah* and monthly and weekly gatherings.

Post-maktab education: Dīn for Teens

There is a tendency for many Muslim children to complete their *maktab* education at the ages of 13–15 for a variety of reasons including preparing for their GCSEs (Scourfield et al., 2013; Gent, 2018). However, in some places, initiatives have begun to extend this provision by catering for the 14–19 age group which reflect several changes as demonstrated in Table 9.2.

Voice of a Muslim

This syllabus is used with 14 to 19 year olds, with parental consent due to the in-depth nature of some of the topics. It was developed to offer young Muslims a safe space in which they are able to express their thoughts and opinions on contemporary issues without judgement as minorities. Within the Madrasa setting, they are amongst their peers and are well challenged and supported by their teacher, who ensures they leave the setting with the most accurate representation of the topics. The aim of the syllabus is to provide a holistic picture of the topics from an Islamic and non-Islamic perspective and answer any queries or questions the young persons have. For too long the Madrasa system has neglected the contemporary needs of our children and has involved simple rote-learning without focusing on the true spirit and essence of Islam, making it relevant to a young person living in twenty-first century Britain. The impact of it has been that those who remain quiet in settings in which they are minorities are able to express themselves in a setting better suited to their needs. They have grown to love their faith and its teachings and know how it fits into the life of a twenty-first century Muslim. ('Abdul-Salām, British–Indian, madrasah teacher, male)

Table 9.2 Syllabus for Muslim 14–19 year olds

Week	Day	First 30 mins	Second session	Last 30 mins
1	Mon	Qur'ān. Tajwīd	Sīrat (Al Nabi al-Khātam and PPT)	Q&A. **Naṣīha. Ta'līm (Faḍāil e A'mal).** Plenary.
	Tues		Ḥadīth (**Provisions for Seekers**)	
	Wed		Fiqh (Ta'leemul Haq)	
	Thur	Surats syllabus	**Duā's** (Child's Gift)	
2	Mon	Qur'ān. Tajwīd	40 lessons (Imam Ghazali)	Q&A. Naṣīha. Ta'līm (Faḍāil e A'mal). Plenary.
	Tues		Contemporary issues (list below) and 'Aqīdah Taḥawiyyah	
	Wed		Tafsīr of last 12 Surats and Fātihah (personal notes)	
	Thurs	Surats syllabus	Duā's (Child's Gift)	

Class requirements	Teaching materials
Water, pen	Laptop – PPT presentations for Sīrat/Ḥajj/ Ramaḍān
Ring-binder pad	Kutub and An-Naṣīha: The World of Teens
Ṣalāh diary	Surats and Duā' record sheet
All books – everyday	Record keeping of every lesson – attendance and topic

(Continued)

Table 9.2 (Continued)

Contemporary issues		
Sexuality	Music	History
Identity	Hip hop culture	Islam and the environment
Integration	Drugs	Muslim contribution to the world
Gender interaction	Substance abuse	Muslims today
Parents	Halal income	Allah and His qualities
Family	Gambling	Different sects
British values	Peer pressure	Extremism
Haram relationships	University/school/college	War on terror
Pornography	Self-harm	Islamophobia
Social media	Suicide	Racism
Cyber safety	Netflix and chill	Islam and slavery
Islam and women		Atheism
		Problem of evil
In addition to this, every term, they must read an Islamic-themed book and write a subsequent book		

These chapters of the Qur'ān (Surats syllabus)	**Volunteering/ enrichment opportunities**	**Other**
From Al-Duhā (87) to the end of Al-A'la (93)	Partnership with police force, six weeks' knife crime awareness	Careers sessions – writing CVs, personal statements, advice etc.
Verse of al-Kursī	Sessions at Crown Court. SkillZone etc	Class party every term, plus BBQ in summer (ex-students invited)
Aaman ar-Rasulu (last two verses of al-Baqarah (2)	Volunteering with FairShares – hour for an hour	**Jamā't** every termly holiday for three days – ten days in summer
Surah (18) Kahf (first ten and last ten verses)	Free first-aid training	Salah Diary – (compensate missed prayers)
Surah (36) Yāsīn	Class discussions, debates and projects	Enrichment week
Surah (67) Tabārak	Organising events – football tournaments etc.	
Surah (32) Sajda		
Parents evening will take place twice a year, and parents are able to communicate with me anytime regarding any concerns or queries. Dates and times will be set mutually.		

National educational landscape

The vast majority of Muslim children attend their local school. This would suggest that most parents adopt an integrationist path of sending their children to 'state' schools (Mandaville, 2007). Some send their children to schools run by Christians and other faith groups; perhaps they see matters of faith taken more seriously within an approach to education which proffers greater attention to spiritual development or for convenience. Others enrol their children in independent Muslim faith schools and nurseries. For some parents, this is mainly prompted by concerns over identity, belonging, perceived discrimination, values and attitudes, and where Islamic studies with another major religion is offered. In addition, in response to changes in educational policy by governments, Muslims have also participated in establishing Free Schools with an Islamic ethos. This is an illustration of the multifarious ways in which Muslims think education should be provided to their children. It is also indicative of the disparate perspectives that underpin their philosophy of education. Research shows a need for better communication, trust, engagement and understanding from school in regard to several issues identified by Muslim mothers (Din, 2017).

One of the criticisms levied against faith schools in general and particularly towards Muslim faith schools is that they are isolationist and contribute to segregation. Even though many faith communities have established their own schools, the brunt of the charge tends to fall on Muslim communities. It is important, as educators, to recall that separate schooling is not a Muslim initiation. The English education system, since its inception in 1870, has been based on the concept of separation which manifests itself in terms of class (independent/private schools), gender (boys/girls schools), religion (faith and religious denominational schools), ability (grammar), comprehensive schools (non-selective) and home education. Therefore, in addition to viewing their contribution to education along faith lines, they should also be seen in their socio-political and economic contexts.

Dārul 'Ulūm

During the period of the Prophet (ﷺ), education was imparted mainly in the mosque but also in homes and other locations. Deputations and delegations were also used as a means to disperse the revelation and practices. The Prophet (ﷺ) himself was a mobile teacher and taught wherever he happened to be. As Islam spread beyond the Arabian peninsula, the need for a more complex educational system to meet the educational needs of the population and for the administrative activities of the *Khilāfah* led to the inception of the *madrasah* as a separate educational institute. Eventually, the *madrasah* became the foremost institution for formal higher education even though religious education continued to be 'delivered in mosques, Sufi quarters (***khānqāhs***, ***ribāt***), literary salons, books shops, libraries, homes of scholars, makeshift caves and under trees' (Sikand, 2005: 25). However, the **Dārul 'Ulūm** was seen as having the primary role in transmitting the knowledge revealed to the Prophet (ﷺ) and passed down from one generation to the next by qualified 'Ulamā' (Sikand, 2005: 2; Hardaker and Sabki, 2019).

Over the centuries, these *Dārul 'Ulūm* (lit. House of Knowledge) also known as *madāris* (sing. *madrasah*), ***Hawza***, ***Zāwiya***, ***Turba*** and *Jāmiah al-Islāmiyah* (Islamic University), became a feature of Muslim societies (Hussain, 2013). In the UK, the first *Dārul 'Ulūm* was established in 1973 and since then several have been established. They play a significant role in the training of faith leaders, both male and female. Alongside the delivery of the traditional Islamic programme usually of six years, they also offer secondary education and A-levels. Some offer a foundation year for languages such as Urdu. Many have boarding facilities whereas others accommodate day-students from local areas. Most of them also offer Qur'ān memorisation classes for those who choose to do so as a precursor to the main programme. After completing the programme which is usually based on the ***Dars-i-Niẓāmi*** curriculum, students are ready to take the role of being faith leaders to serve Muslim communities in various ways. Some continue with their studies for a year or two to specialise in areas such as jurisprudence to qualify as a **Muftī.** Gifted jurists might become Muftī issuing formal legal opinions in response to questions from the public at large. Some exceptional *Muftī* have their ruling complied as a ready resource (Lowry, 2010). In the UK, some Muftīs have established their own *Dār ul-Iftās.* Others specialise in ḥadīth, *tafsīr* and *qirā'ah* by enrolling in universities outside the UK whereas some join British universities either to continue an aspect of Islamic studies or read a new discipline altogether (Scott-Baumann and Cheruvallil-Contractor, 2015; Hardaker and Sabki, 2019).

Imāms and faith leaders have a difficult task as they are called upon not only to fulfil their role as prayer leaders and pastoral mentors within their respective communities, but, as mediators in a hostile world, they also lead them from the margins to the centre of society. Across Europe, there are signs of an emerging Islamic education which is celebrating intercultural and interreligious learning while being committed to its own theological development. In Europe, as a community of shared values, Muslim leaders are making diverse and important contributions to this end (Aslan, 2012).

In the context of madrasah education, Hardaker and Sabki (2019) provide deeper insights of Islamic pedagogy from a spiritual perspective based on the premise of the inseparable nature of knowledge and the sacred. They used four broad claims concerning sensory orders, identity, embodiment and spirituality to structure their study of higher education institutions in different countries and show how these feature in the UK and USA, for example.

The mosque

Initially serving a predominantly migrant community from terraced housing, many contemporary mosques in the UK have matured and transformed themselves significantly and continue to do so in order to serve the changing needs of the community. The hub of the community remains the mosque for their religious and spiritual betterment. Beyond the services which you have become aware of thus far, some mosques have taken on the role of advocacy of national issues, inter-faith alliances, and campaigns of mutual concern with religious and secular groups. Nevertheless, many continue to serve from smaller premises.

Table 9.3 reflects the development of a model in which a *masjid* is attempting to follow what they perceive to be an example of the mosque set up by the Prophet (ﷺ) as a centre of love, warmth, openness and excellence and which brings communities together. It caters for the academic, social and spiritual needs of the entire community regardless of race, religion and ethnicity. Since its inception three years ago, it acts as a nurturing environment by providing emotional, physical and spiritual support through many educational and outreach projects.

Table 9.3 Services at Madīnah Institute, UK

Primary areas	Strands	Audience and activities
Masjid and Community Hub	*Safety in the Community*	Police, fire services and some local Mosques
Daily prayers		
Friday lecture		
Friday sermon		
Nikah (marriage)		
Funeral services		
Weekly dhikr		
Calendar events		

(Continued)

Table 9.3 (Continued)

Primary areas	Strands	Audience and activities
	Open days	Schools and public service institutions
	Back to basics initiatives	Monthly *Sīrah* classes, etc.
	Planet Mercy	Free legal advice
		Relaxation and meditation class
		Stress management workshops
		Monthly food kitchen
		Weekly sister circle (*ḥalaqah*)
	Youth zone	Youth club for boys
		Youth club for girls
		Boxing academy for boys
		Martial arts for girls
		Indoor sports and games zone
		Recreational classes
Adult education	Seminars	On various topics, contemporary issues and religious sciences
	Three-tier Islamic scholarship programme	Part-time study (weekly online or onsite) opportunity for students and professionals to study Arabic and the Islamic sciences at advanced level
	Standalone courses	Arabic, Fiqh, Aqīdah, Tajwīd, etc. weekly for adults
Child education	Qur'ān academy: three core subjects: *Qā'idah/du'ās* with *sūrahs* and Islamic Studies	Children from six onwards, four days a week, mostly hourly sessions
	Sunday school: nurturing Prophetic Character in a child-centred and structured learning environment	Small groups, ages 6–10, uses storytelling, hands-on activities, *nashīd* singing, analytical reasoning supplemented with books and worksheets

The earlier generations established mosques in houses and those after them built purposeful impressive ones. However, one of the current tasks facing the community is to make the current generation feel at home therein. This is a question Muslims across Europe are grappling with in different ways. Even though advances have been made in meeting linguistic needs, some youngsters feel the need for their religious figures to come to terms with their local context and embrace further contemporary local and global challenges. This will make those spaces more welcoming for their youth and culturally relevant. Consequently, some younger religious leaders have founded alternative spaces to teach and worship in more meaningful and germane ways.

The use of study circles (*ḥalaqah*)

The Companions sat in the formation of a circle (***ḥalaqah***) in the presence of the Messenger (ﷺ) as he dispensed knowledge, wisdom and the Qur'ān inside and outside the mosque. Later, these were also held in private houses, bookshops and libraries and were usually supervised by teachers, scholars, ***shaykhs*** and judges (***ḥākims***), according to the accomplishment and needs of teachers and pupils (Hardaker and Sabki, 2019: 18). The religious sciences were usually the main subject taught in these, although subjects like language, literature, poetry and history were included. Interestingly, often teachers in such study circles would select their own topics relevant to the moment. Other related institutions include the library, ***dār 'ilm*** (House of knowledge) and ***majlis*** (gathering) which catered to the mystical–theoretical approaches (Hardaker and Sabki, 2019).

The use of the *ḥalaqah* as a dialogic pedagogy within a primary school with Muslim children in the twenty-first century is used to promote *Shakhsiyah Islāmiyyah*, which is defined as developing an individual, who, through autonomous and critical thought, chooses to follow an Islamic worldview and identity which they can exercise in a Western secular–liberal society. ***Tarbiyyah*** in a Ḥalaqah approach in the UK is theorised as a process of developing social and political awareness by following the pedagogy of hope from Paulo Freire, which for them builds on the Prophetic model to challenge injustice (Ahmed and Lawson, 2016). It also incorporates Alexander's dialogic teaching and Mercer's 'Exploratory Talk' as useful pedagogical models. Naturally, since their approaches are informed by a Muslim worldview, there are some contentions with some issues within secular critical pedagogies, yet they are able to draw on critical pedagogy for a more transformative education. In applying the early

Islamic tradition of question and answer, they find resonance with contemporary pedagogy. In theorising ***ta'līm*** in this way, a parallel is seen in the social cultural theory informed by the Vygotskian purview where interaction occurs between the teacher and learner or between pupils. The *Ḥalaqah Curriculum* nurtures children to become thinking and reflective committed Muslims who consciously choose to embrace the Islamic way of life and embody 'Islamic Personality'. It incorporates elements of citizenship, PSHE, history and religious education in which child-centred and child-led processes operate to learn about Islam in the context of living as Muslims in British society, contributing positively to society and facing the challenges of the contemporary world. The practice is oral, reflective, dialogic and transformative, and children interact with the revelation on a personal level, reflecting on their own knowledge and character. Beyond the confines of formal settings, the *ḥalaqah* operates online and in mosques and other venues for faith matters and contemporary issues.

Voice of a Muslim

The Qur'ān occupies an important place amongst my people. Learning how to read and interpret the Qur'ān is seen as an obligation for all our children. When a child or young person completes the Qur'ān, this occasion is often celebrated by all family members proudly coming together to appreciate this achievement. Completing the Qur'ān simply means that the child now knows how to read the entire text. Knowing how to read and interpret the Qur'ān puts you in a higher and well-respected social position amongst our people. As a graduate, you are expected to become the Imām of your town and hold a leadership position among your people. It is a core believe amongst our people that learning the Qur'ān makes the child more respectful to their parents and promotes their social and religious values. (Yūsuf, Liberian, carer, male)

Scholars, scientists and philosophers

You have learnt from previous chapters that the Qur'ān has a universal characteristic whereby many people from different walks of life can relate to it and understand it to inform their personal, spiritual, ethical and socio-political activities. However, simultaneously, it is so sophisticated that over the centuries it has perplexed the minds of philosophers, scientists, linguists and theologians. In it, they have found their theories and produced encyclopaedic works on metaphysics, philosophy, the unseen world, medicine, astronomy, mathematics, the psyche, and the nature of plants, animals and minerals (Al Zeera, 2001: 81). With this, Muslim scholars acknowledge the influence of Greek, Indian and Persian civilisations. Al Zeera (2001) also notes that almost all of the great Muslim philosophers and scientists were strong believers in God. A characteristic which distinguished Muslim scholars was their multifaceted scholarship as they wanted to discover and experience the truth from different angles and from different dimensions. The main reason behind their perseverance was that God asked them to do so and challenged them to discover the consistency of God's words (Al Zeera, 2001: 82). Unlike some Europeans of the time, they were not constrained by superstition and anti-intellectualism (Morgan, 2007: 185). The verses of the Qur'ān instruct Muslims to glimpse the Divine in the 'signs' of nature and to view the world as a continuous epiphany. It imbued a healthy attitude to both intellectual endeavour and curiosity (Wallace-Murphy, 2006: 87). A few scholars are mentioned below which have implications for your teaching and your familiarity with their contributions. Coles (2008) has offered useful practical ideas for their inclusion especially in the science curriculum.

Mathematics and philosophy

Al-Khuwārizmī (d.c.249AH/863 CE):

- a most distinguished mathematician of the Middle Ages
- worked in astronomy, geography and trigonometry, versed in Greek
- known as the 'Father of Algebra' for his innovative work on solving equations using the *al-jabr* method, meaning 'combination of broken parts' or 'restoring'
- his name became westernised to Algoritmi and the mathematical term 'algorithm' was developed from this. Triggered by the Hindu dot representing nothingness, he identified the missing link to unlocking all the planes of the universe – the zero (Morgan, 2007; Alkhateeb, 2017).

Al-Kindī (c.185–260AH/801–873CE):

- Father of Arab philosophy who mastered the works of Aristotle
- attempted to harmonise Greek philosophy with Islamic teachings

- also studied mathematics, music and medicine
- penned over 360 works in many fields including on perfumes
- trusted reason as a source of truth and believed that revelation was a guide to the same end (Alavi, 1988)
- his most profound thought came regarding relativity and the relationship between matter, space and time. He said it was not absolute nor good fortune (Morgan, 2007).

Al-Rāzī (c.251–313AH/865–925CE):

- recorded many of his medical observations in several books; some were later used as textbooks in western medical schools
- based on observations, he discovered how to distinguish different diseases
- was the first to describe smallpox and measles, showing that they were separate afflictions (Morgan, 2007)
- believed that diseases had specific scientifically-based physical causes and were not punishments by God; rejected superstition and primitive dogma not based on observable physical reality
- the theory that fever is the body's natural defensive mechanism emerged from his work; this made Al-Rāzī (Latin Rhazes) an influential doctor.

Ibn Al-Haītham (c.354–430AH/965–1039CE):

- known as Alhazen, one of the first theoretical physicists who made contributions to astronomy and mathematics
- first scholar to absolutely apply the principle of empiricism with mercy, unlike the intellectual theorising of the Greeks (Morgan, 2007); he did not take any scientific statement on faith
- argued light was composed of rays, proved it travels in a straight line (Alkhateeb, 2017)
- assisted in developing the scientific method and performing of experiments
- his *Book of Optics* merged his interest in empirical science, optics, lights and the skies to produce the most scientific and accurate view of the physical universe
- Sitt al-Mulk, reportedly the richest woman in history, patronised his research (Morgan, 2007)
- The scholar, Ibn Rushd (520–595AH/1126–1198CE) (Latin Averroës) of Spanish origin, was most famous as a philosopher and expert in Islamic law, rather than astronomy. He followed the Greek philosopher Aristotle and insisted that the natural world followed scientific laws that God created. As a freethinking rationalist, he defended philosophy against the criticisms of theologians (Morgan, 2007; Alavi, 1988) and advocated a concentric model of planetary orbits around the Earth.

Medicine

There is no disease that Allah has created, except that He also has created its treatment, said the Prophet (ﷺ) (al-Bukhārī, 7:582). Muslims took a keen interest in medicine and studied ideas from various geographical areas (Wallace-Murphy, 2006: 123). Muslim scholars advanced these works and introduced new medical theories and practices. Ibn Sīnā, the Prince of Physicians, was revered by Europe for 400 years as the greatest thinker of all time (Morgan, 2007). At 10, he memorised the Qur'ān and, at 13, commenced studying medicine. He began treating patients at 16. He had read Aristotle's Metaphysics several times, which initially he did not understand so he memorised it. Eventually, he bought Al-Fārābī's (c. 258–339AH/870–950CE) commentary on Aristotle which unlocked his understanding, for which he thanked God (Morgan, 2007: 191). Ibn Sīnā (Avicenna) stated that there existed 700 drugs, diseases spread through soil and water, and that tuberculosis was infectious. He described the causes of rabies, breast cancer and other tumours and offered information about toxins and antidotes. *The Canon of Medicine* by Ibn Sīnā (370–428AH/980–1037CE) became a standard textbook in medical schools with a lasting influence in Europe and Islamic lands. He had a rational outlook on eschatology.

Astronomy

Beyond the human body and its intellectual domain, astronomy was an important part of Islamic sciences. It was prompted by the Qur'ān to reflect over the universe and natural phenomena. The allusions to the mathematical nature of the heavens could not be ignored (Alkhateeb, 2017). Astronomy was used for navigation, to determine the calendar, and for religious purposes such as locating the direction of Makkah and prayer times. Muslim astronomers built large observatories for viewing the stars. They also designed detailed celestial globes showing the positions of the stars and planets in relation to the Earth. New tools were developed including the quadrant and the astrolabe. Many stars have names originating from the Arabic language (Morgan, 2007).

Muslims and the natural world

As teachers, it is useful to know about the interest in beautifying the physical world. There is useful information about the arts in Islam and suggestions for curriculum (see Coles, 2008). The architectural style included arches, domes, minarets, courtyards and their rectangular portals and the ***muqarnas*** in mosques, palaces, fortresses, towers and tombs.

Gardens and courtyards are an important part of Islamic architecture. Arabesques use intricate patterns depicting plants, leaves and flowers. Some artists abstained from using figures of animals and people lest it results in idolatry. Other patterns use geometric shapes to create colourful tessellations, symmetrical and repetitive designs.

Muslim artists created a range of ceramic glazes and styles, some influenced by Chinese porcelain, which resulted in beautiful pottery and tiles. Decorated carpets are used as floor coverings, prayer mats, wall hangings and cushions. Carving is popularly used for ceilings, doors, gates and floors. Qur'ān stands were often carved from wood.

Miniature painting was most popular, sometimes used in illuminated manuscripts. These paintings were distinguished from other art and often contained pictures of animals and people such as in medical books. Calligraphy is popular decorative writing sometimes used to create designs using verses from the Qur'ān.

Case study 9.1 Mosque visit

Visiting places of worship was an established practice across several year groups in a school situated near the peripheral of a large city; every pupil in Year 4 visited a mosque. As usual the class teacher sent letters home to inform parents and guardians about the educational purpose of the visit and other necessary details. The next day, to the surprise of the teacher, a few parents declared that they would not permit their children to visit the mosque. The teacher tried to allay their concerns about safety. They insisted on withdrawing their children and said the visit ought to be cancelled altogether. The teacher then referred them to the Headteacher so they could speak about their concerns. After listening to the parents, they reached a consensus and the Headteacher decided that the visit would go ahead. In class, before the visit, the pupils were asked what a place of worship was. Their responses were recorded using a thought shower. They were invited to make closer observations of an image showing the outside of a mosque. The teacher then asked them to list the sources where they could find information about it. These were recorded and displayed for future use. A virtual tour was shown. At intervals the pupils were asked to identify some questions to ask at the mosque. They also thought about what they expected to see, hear, feel and smell. This built up a sense of anticipation in the pupils. They then discussed the concept of 'sacred places' and why people visit them. Following this, they talked about the idea of respect. Then preparations for the visit were discussed including dress codes and removal of shoes. The teacher explained the religious, aesthetic and practical reasons for this. Pupils then had an opportunity to ask questions. At the mosque pupils were first given time to absorb the atmosphere. They were then given a 'free' walk to experience the open space and examine closely the structures within the mosque, directed by their own curiosity and not to hinder their mystery, awe and wonder. Following this, they had an opportunity to talk with the Shaykh who took them on a guided tour. Finally, the Shaykh offered a hot seating session and answered their pre-prepared and spontaneous questions. The teacher took many photographs and literature, and everyone returned to school.

You have been delegated the responsibility of organising a visit to a different place of worship. Considering some of the information in this case study:

- What would your aims and outcomes be of taking pupils on a visit?
- How would you assess the learning of your pupils?
- How would you deal with some parents opting out of the visit?
- What preparations would you make prior to the visit?
- What activities would you involve the pupils in at the place of worship?
- What would be your follow-up activities in school?
- How would you celebrate and share this experience with others?

Summary

In this chapter you have considered the impact of the first revelation on the attitudes and practices of Muslims towards learning, teaching and education. You have learnt that the Qur'ān is replete with concepts related to intellectual endeavours just as it has matters of faith and spirituality. You discovered that the Prophet (ﷺ) is depicted as a teacher who made great efforts to disseminate knowledge to the masses. The chapter has attempted to convey to you the inner plurality in which education is conceived and the multifarious ways in which the aims and objectives are being pursued by different communities in various parts of the globe. The chapter has indicated briefly the religious nurture provided to children and adults. You became aware of the institutes of higher education which train scholars and faith leaders in the UK. There are many challenges facing the different communities in the UK. To this end, you have studied two case studies which have demonstrated to you some of the current services provided by mosques and a programme to cater for the UK youth. You have briefly explored biographical sketches of some scientists and philosophers who influenced and contributed to different fields of knowledge.

Reflection tasks

- Analyse the status of knowledge in Islam.
- Describe the role played by Muḥammad (ﷺ) in disseminating knowledge.
- Identify the ways education is provided by Muslims to their children.
- Evaluate the role of a mosque in the Muslim community.
- Compare and contrast your educational ideas with those of Muslim educators.
- Imagine you were teaching about Muslim scientists and philosophers. How would you do this? Who would you highlight?
- Imagine you were teaching about Muslim arts and craft. How would you design your curriculum?

Further reading

Davids, N. and Waghid, Y. (2018) *Ethical Dimensions of Muslim Education*. Switzerland: Palgrave Macmillan.

This interesting text looks at ethical dimensions of Muslim education to address social and societal conflicts. It focusses on Qur'ānic conceptions of being Muslim, education and individual autonomy.

Morgan, M.H. (2007) *Lost History: The Enduring Legacy of Muslim Scientists, Thinkers, and Artists*. Washington: National Geographic.

This book reveals why Muslim intellectual achievement was once an envy of the world. The author affords the credit and respect due to Muslim pioneers in many fields of learning. It is a history which is lost both to Muslim and non-Muslims alike and written for popular readers.

10

THE SHĪ‘A TRADITIONS

In this chapter you will:

- know the historical events which led to the emergence of the Shī'a faith
- learn the key principles in Shī'ism
- understand the practical manifestations of the Shī'i five pillars
- discern some distinctive features within Shī'ism.

Overview

This chapter presents the historical development of Shī'ism from the Muslim community by tracing its roots to the earliest period. In Chapter 5 you learnt about the foundations of faith and in Chapter 6 you encountered the five pillars ostensibly as conceptualised by Islam. In this chapter, specific focus is given to the main sources of law, the five foundations and ten obligations in Shī'ism. To this, some doctrinal statements and rituals have been added to allow you to gain a deeper understanding by analysing the similarities and differences with those presented earlier. The role of the Imāms, the status of ***Karbalā'*** and other related key features are elucidated to establish Shī'a theology. Thereafter, a discussion of the three major branches of Shī'ism is presented to show you the spectrum within it.

The community

In Chapter 2 you read that Muḥammad (ﷺ) passed away in the year 10AH/632CE. Following his demise, Abū Bakr was appointed, by the process of community consensus ***(ijmā')***, as the ***Khalīfah*** ('Deputy') of the Prophet and led between 11–13AH/632–634CE. It has been suggested that the selection happened through open debate as more than one contender existed (Hathout, 2008). Abū Bakr remained in this role for about two years. During the discussions of leadership, 'Alī was occupied with matters of death and, being the son-in-law of the Prophet, with family members. Nevertheless, less than a dozen men thought 'Alī should be the leader (Glassé, 2013). However, after six months, he explained to the public that he withheld his allegiance as he thought he should have been consulted about the matter. Thereafter, he accepted Abū Bakr as his *Khalīfah* and supported him (Muslim, 3:4352; Daftary, 2013). This coincided with the death of his wife Fāṭimah, daughter of the Prophet (ﷺ) (Daftary, 2013).

Before his death, Abū Bakr appointed 'Umar (13–23AH/634–644CE) as his successor who guided the community for another ten years. 'Alī accepted the selection of 'Umar and had even given one of his daughters, Umm Kulthūm, to him in marriage (al-Bukhārī, 4:132). Before his death, 'Umar convened a committee to elect a leader and an arbitrator to oversee the process. 'Uthmān (23–35AH/644–656CE) was selected as the third *Khalīfah*. Then, 'Alī (35–40AH/656–661CE) was chosen and accepted the position about twenty-four years after the death of the Prophet. These four were later designated as the '*four rightly guided deputies*' (*Khulafā' ar-rāshidūn*, 632–661) as they lived and followed the life of Muḥammad (ﷺ) and were selected by the community. Consequently, their example, in addition to that of Muḥammad (ﷺ), is authoritative practice (Sunna), which future generations have continued to follow. Since the Qur'ān had perfected the religion, finalised the revelation and declared Muḥammad as the 'Seal of the Prophets' (33:40), this pattern of deputyship was adopted because no one could succeed Muḥammad (ﷺ) in his nature and quality as a prophet (Kerr, 2018a). Moreover, these four were accountable directly to the community. They did not have authority in and of themselves, but only insofar as they implemented the Qur'ān and Sunnah and all four were elected in some form or another (Saud, 2013a). In other words, the office of the *Khalīfate* was secularised by empowering the community (Saud, 2013a). Nevertheless, they were and still are guides in understanding faith and its expressions, as per the instruction of the Prophet (ﷺ) himself (Muslim, 4:6150).

Khārijis

'Alī inherited a problematic situation when he became the *Khalīfah*. On the one hand, the governor of Syria, Mu'āwiyah, demanded from 'Alī that he brought to justice the murderers of 'Uthmān. 'Ali was not involved in the assassination but some of his supporters were. 'Ali's priority was to stabilise the situation first. However, this impasse led to the Battle of the Camel (656AH) which 'Ali won. Subsequently, Mu'āwiyah and 'Ali faced each other at the Battle of Ṣiffīn (37AH/657CE), where 'Alī is said to have accepted arbitration. Some people considered this to be a sign of disloyalty to the religion, as they believed that only God could arbitrate about such matters. They also believed that 'Alī should have continued to fight (Crotty and Lovat, 2016). However, since he did not, they deemed the decision by 'Alī to be synonymous as not accepting the position of being the rightful *Khalīfah*, and, consequently, broke rank (Maqsood, 2010).

These dissatisfied people seceded from his army and later, as a grievance, one of them assassinated 'Alī (Daftary, 2013). This tiny group were termed *Khārijis* (separatists) as they had seceded. After the declaration of the arbitration, they took their authority from the Qur'ān and deemed those who held different views as infidels worthy of death, and over the centuries, continued to oppose the *Khalīfahs* (Silverstein, 2010; Esposito, 2016). They were deemed puritans and absolutists for they consider grave sinners to be out of Islam (Saud, 2013a). They opposed both 'Alī and Mu'āwiyah and selected their own leaders (Brown, 2017).

After 'Alī, in the year 661–662CE, his son Al-Ḥasan (03–50AH/625–670CE), preferred to cede the *Khilāfah* to Mu'āwiyah who ruled from Syria (d.60AH/660–680CE) rather than confront him. His brother Al-Ḥusaīn, however, set out to challenge him. He was initially promised support from Kūfah but was betrayed and eventually martyred at Karbalā' on the tenth al-Muḥarram (see below).

Shī'ism

After the death of 'Alī, the community split into two (La'Porte, 2001). The majority accepted the rule of Mu'āwiyah. To them, their leader Muḥammad (ﷺ) was the final prophet. They honoured the four leaders after him as the community had appointed them. They considered those after them 'temporal' figures not carrying the authority similar to that of the Prophet (ﷺ) and the *Khulafā'* (Crotty and Lovat, 2016). They later became known as the *Ahl al-Sunnah wal-Jamā'at* (Sunnī in short).

However, another group felt that a *Khalīfah* must be a direct descendant of Muḥammad (ﷺ), which would be 'Alī and, after his death, his sons Al-Ḥasan and Al-Ḥusaīn. They claimed that 'Alī should have been the true and legitimate successor of the Prophet (ﷺ) because of his family connection, being his son-in-law and cousin and that leadership must be hereditary (Hibbard, 2013). In other words, 'Alī had a Divine right to be the *Khalīfah* (Glassé, 2013). They called themselves *Shī'at 'Alī* (the party of 'Alī ['Alīds, Shī'ites and Shī'a]). They also claimed that 'Alī was side-lined when the first three were chosen, and hence they rejected them. This includes their tradition (Momen, 2016). In passing, it is important to note that all four were related to the Prophet (ﷺ). Therefore, the movement began as an expression of political dissidence, but where politics could not be separated from religion as striving for justice is a religious mandate. However, over time Shī'ism took the form of an Islamic sect which focussed on the belief that 'Alī and his progeny were eligible (Hathout, 2008: 61). The origin of the succession reverts to the death of the Prophet (ﷺ). However, Shī'a identity, it should be noted, did not take a definitive shape until the first decades of the Abbasid Empire (750–1258CE) (Delong-Bas, 2018). The Sunnī–Shī'a fissure tends to be conceptualised as a dispute over the successor to the Prophet (ﷺ). Using critical analysis of legal texts, Haider (2011) shows that this fracture materialised a century later. The early Shī'a used specific ritual practices to develop independent religious and social identities.

The Shī'a take recourse to an event at Ghadīr Khumm, where Muḥammad (ﷺ) publicised a key statement about 'Alī (Brown, 2017: 156). The pool (*ghadīr*), in the valley of Khumm, is located some three miles from al-Juhfa on the way from Makkah to Madīnah. On return from the farewell pilgrimage amid a large gathering, Muḥammad (ﷺ) gathered the people for prayer and then announced the famous statement '*man kuntu mawlāhu fa 'Alī mawlāhu*' (he whose *mawlā* [master] I am, 'Alī is his *mawlā*). Over the centuries, this has had a far-reaching impact on Muslim communities. Muslims have an agreement on the historicity of this event, but the interpretation of the statement is contested. For the Shī'a, this was a *nass* – an explicit appointment for 'Alī to lead Muslims after Muḥammad (ﷺ) (Brown, 2017). However, many members of the community of the faithful had turned away from 'Ali, ignoring the Prophet's *nass* (Daftary, 2013). The Sunnī community maintains that it called for 'Alī to be held in high esteem and that it was a statement of his virtue (*faḍīlat*) just as the Prophet (ﷺ) made for many other Companions. The Shī'a also use the verse (33:33) to present the case of infallibility. The cause of the split was political rivalry which later took the form of a theological movement. The central figure through whom the Shī'a actually became a religious movement is said to be Ja'far al-Sādiq (Rippin and Bernheimer, 2019).

Key sources

The Qur'ān and the Traditions are the key sources determining legal and ritual matters. However, for the Shī'a, reason is a primary source in relation to basic theological principles, as discussed below.

The Qur'ān

In Shī'ism the Qur'ān is accepted as the Word of God revealed to Muḥammad (ﷺ) for the guidance of humanity. The text in the recension composed under the supervision of the third *Khalīfah*, 'Uthmān, is accepted by both communities. There is consensus that nothing had been added to the Qur'ān. Nevertheless, early Shī'a did not accept the standard text of the Qur'ān in terms of what was specifically omitted from it regarding the extolling of 'Alī which was indicated to his Imāmat. Over time, however, most Shī'a were of the view that nothing had been added or omitted from the Qur'ān (Momen, 1985). Still, a small minority has attempted to have some portions accepted as being missing from the Qur'ān. They also believe that the hidden meaning within the Qur'ān was 'given' to 'Alī by the Prophet (ﷺ) (La'Porte, 2001).

Ḥadīth

The Imāms in Shī'ism are considered sinless and infallible; therefore, their words and actions are a guide to follow. These were written down over time after initially being transmitted orally. To the Shī'a, the *ḥadīth* constitute the *Sunna* (practice) of the Prophet (ﷺ) and Imāms. The latter is known as *khabar* (pl. *akhbār*, lit. information).

You will learn in Chapter 11 that among the Sunnī there are six main collections of the Traditions of the Prophet (ﷺ) which were transmitted through his Companions and, as such, are accepted as canonical. However, in Shī'ism, since the majority of the Companions had accepted the *Khilāfah* of Abū Bakr, 'Umar and 'Uthmān in preference to 'Alī, they are deemed to have erred and, therefore, cannot be regarded as reliable transmitters of traditions (Momen, 2016). Thus, the Shī'i traditions tend to rely on the deeds and words of their Imāms and even those that reach the Prophet (ﷺ) are usually conveyed through one of the Imāms. In any case, special significance is given to the *ḥadīth* corpus affirming the authority and status of 'Alī (La'Porte, 2001).

The four early collections regarded as canonical are:

1. *Al-Kāfī fī 'Ilm al-Dīn* (The Sufficient in the Science of Religion) by Muḥammad al-Kulaynī (d. 328AH/939CE).
2. *Man la yaḥduruhu al-Faqīh* (He Who Has No Jurist Present) by Muḥammad ibn Bābūya (d.381AH/991CE).
3. *Tahdhīb al-Aḥkām* (The Rectification of Judgements) by Muḥammad aṭ-Ṭusī (d. 460AH/1067CE).
4. *Al-Istibsār* (The Perspicacious) by the author above.

In addition to these four, there are three other books highly regarded in this field: *Al-Wāfī* (The Complete), *Wasāi'l al-Shī'a* (The Means of the Shī'a) and *Bihār al-Anwār* (Oceans of Lights). A modern collection is *Mustadrak al-Wasā'il* by Ḥusayn an-Nūri aṭ-Ṭabarsi (d.1320/1902) (Momen, 1985: 173–174). The *Nahj al-Balāgha* is a collection of the prayers, teachings and sayings of 'Alī which are held in high esteem. The *Al-Ṣaḥīfat Al-Kāmilat Al-Sajjādiyya* by Imām Zayn ul-'Ābidīn, the great grandson of the Prophet (ﷺ), is also popular for prayers.

Independent search

Some verses of the Qur'ān are interpreted as prohibiting blind imitation of others in matters of religion (5:104–105; 17:36; 21:52–54). This proscription is taken to refer to the fundamentals of faith (*Uṣūl ad-dīn*). However, in matters related to the details of law and ritual practices, individuals are expected to search a person known to them as the most learned in religious law and to follow that person. This following of the ***mujtahid*** is called *taqlīd* (imitation) and the follower is called *muqallid,* while the *mujtahid* becomes the *marja' at-taqlīd* (reference point of imitation) (Momen, 1985).

Thus, in Shī'ism, belief in the fundamentals of the religion (*Ūṣūl ad-dīn*) must be the result of each individual's own independent investigation and must not be the result of merely following one's parents or religious leaders. However, with respect to the subsidiary elements of the religion (*Furū 'ad-dīn*), religious law and rituals, these can only be learnt through extensive study and anyone who has not carried out this study follows the guidance of those who have (Momen, 1985: 176).

The five foundations (*Ūṣūl*) of faith

Chapter 5 detailed the foundations of faith as seen by Islam. In Shī'ism, there are five roots (*Ūṣūl ad-dīn*). *Tawhīd* (unity of God), *Nubūwwah* (prophethood) and *Ma'ād* (the resurrection) are common to both in terms of foundations of faith, but in Shī'ism the fundamentals of *Imāmah* (the Imāmate) and *'Adl* (Justice of God) are added.

Divine unity (*Tawḥīd*)

This is reflected in the first part of the *Shahādah,* which states: 'There is no god but Allah.' In the theological dispute that took place between the Mu'tazilī and Ash'arī theological positions, Shī'ism took the Mu'tazilī standpoint, and a consequence of this was that they maintained that names and attributes of Allah do not have independent existence from the Being and Essence of God; separating these entails polytheism. Likewise, holding the view that the Qur'ān is the uncreated Word of God is considered as setting up two eternal entities (God and the Qur'ān) which they hold to be polytheism. For the Shī'a, the Qur'ān has been created in time. Moreover, again related to the Mu'tazilī viewpoint, Shī'ism asserts that God does not have a physical form and that the verses, which appear to attribute physical organs like a face and hands to God, must be interpreted metaphorically rather than literally (Momen, 1985). To the *Shahādah,* the Shīʿa add the phrase 'and I bear witness that 'Alī was the friend of God.'

Prophethood (Nubuwwah)

In Shīʿism all prophets are believed to be intermediaries between God and humankind. Their mission was to bring Allah's unadulterated revelation to people. These prophets lead and interpret the word of Allah. To assist them with carrying out this mission, God endows them with sinlessness and infallibility (Momen, 1985). Muḥammad (ﷺ) is believed to be the Seal of the Prophets sent to all humanity.

Resurrection (Maʿād)

In line with the numerous verses discussed in Chapter 5 regarding the Day of Resurrection, the occurrence of resurrection is considered to be a logical necessity of divine justice since only after resurrection can each human's full reward and punishment be given (Momen, 1985).

The Imāmate (*Imāmah*)

Imāmate as a requirement of faith only exists in Shīʿism. Therefore, it is a distinguishing feature for them. The overwhelming majority of contemporary Shīʿa refer to themselves as *Twelver Shīʿa* (Ithnā-ʿAsharīyyah) since they believe that between 632 CE and 873 CE, there existed 12 Imāms, who directly descended from 'Alī and Fātimah, the daughter of Prophet Muḥammad (ﷺ).

In Shīʿism, the succession to the Prophet (ﷺ) is a matter which is designated by the Prophet of an individual ('Alī) as Imām, and as such, each Imām was specifically assigned by the previous Imām (Momen, 1985). This belief has far-reaching political consequences for the Shīʿa as Imāms have both religious and political authority (Hibbard, 2013). Importantly, they can make *ijtihād*, meaning that they make independent legal decisions based on their interpretations (La'Porte, 2001). The Imāms possess a significant mandate as they can define the meaning of the Qur'ān and decide what the laws should be.

Shīʿism considers several attributes as being necessary for their Imāms which they maintain are proved by tradition and logical necessity. Scholars have established several attributes to substantiate their Imāmate, some of which include:

- *Manṣūṣ* (designated) – meaning the Imāmate can only be passed on from one Imām to the next by divinely inspired designation (*naṣṣ*).

- *Ma'sūm* (sinless or infallible) – this immunity (*'Isma*) is established since the Imāms command obedience, thus, he can only order what is right.
- *Afdhal an-nās* (best of men) – since they are immune from sin.
- They also possess general and religious knowledge; for the latter they have an exoteric and esoteric, including allegorical, interpretation of the Qur'ān and mystical knowledge.
- *Wilāyah* – Imāms are a spiritual friend, guide and religious authority.
- *Hujjat* (proof) and *Ayat* (sign) of God's existence (Momen, 1985: 150–157).

Among the Sunnī, the *Khalīfah* is equal among people and is elected, ideally, by consensus. However, historically, hereditary succession did take place. The title of Imām has wider application including the leader of prayers and for experts in theology, jurisprudence, exegesis and *ḥadīth* literature denoting their excellence in these disciplines.

As the Shī'a movement crystallised over time, the theory of the Imāmate became more significant and elaborate. The figurehead of the Imām is that of a semi-divine figure who, as a successor to Muḥammad (ﷺ), must be a descendent of him and an intermediary between humans and God. There could only be one Imām at one time.

However, there is a difference of opinion regarding the number of Imāms as depicted in Table 10.1 (Momen, 1985; Daftary, 2013). All Shī'a accept the same first four, thereafter, they factionalised. This is a reflection of which Imām is considered as living and how descent is traced. The Twelvers maintain that there were twelve descendants of Muḥammad (ﷺ) who were granted the divine light by God. The twelfth Imām (Muḥammad al-Mahdī) went into hiding and will return as the Imām Al-Mahdī (the Chosen One) to usher in the end of the world. It is important for you to note, however, that all Shī'a agree that Muḥammad (ﷺ) appointed 'Alī as his successor and granted him the divine light so that 'Alī had the power of Allah to decide what Muslims could do and not do. In turn, this power was passed on from 'Alī to his sons and from them further down.

In the absence of the Al-Mahdī, religious authority is vested in learned scholars (***mujtahids***) (La'Porte, 2001; Hibbard, 2013). The Shī'a believe that divine guidance is open and can be available through the descendants of Muḥammad (ﷺ), through Imāms. Thus, rather than the books, they emphasise sacred people (Crotty and Lovat, 2016). Every generation has an Imām who is charged with declaring the meaning of the Qur'ān and its ramifications in current circumstances. The Imām can make contemporary decisions about belief and practice.

Table 10.1 The Twelver Imāms

Fiver	Sevener	Twelver	Title	Birth–Death AH/CE
ʻAlī	ʻAlī	ʻAlī ibn b. Tālib	Imām	d.40/600–661
Al-Ḥasan	Al-Ḥasan	Al-Ḥasan b. ʻAlī	Al-Mujtabā (the chosen)	03–49/625–669
Al-Ḥusaīn	Al-Ḥusaīn	Al-Ḥusaīn b. ʻAlī	Sayyid al-shuhadā (leader of martyrs)	04–61/626–680
ʻAlī	ʻAlī	ʻAlī	Zayn al-ʻĀbidīn (the pearl of worshippers)	38–94/658–712
Zayd b ʻAlī	Muḥammad (brother of Zayd)	Muḥammad (brother of Zayd)	Al-Bāqir (opener of knowledge)	57–114/676–732
Zaydi Shīʻism	Jaʻfar	Jaʻfar	As-Ṣādiq (the truthful)	83–148/702–765
	Ismāʻīl s/o Jaʻfar	Mūsā (not Ismāʻīl) s/o Jaʻfar	Mūsā Al-Kāẓim (Master of himself)	128–183/745–799
	Ismaʻili Shīʻism	ʻAlī b. Mūsā	Al-Riḍā (the approved)	148–203/765–818
	Maḥammad al-Maktum (the awaited) (d.809 or occulted) s/o Ismāʻīl	Muḥammad al-Jawwād (the generous) s/o ʻAlī	Al-Taqī (the God-conscious)	195–220/810–835
		ʻAlī b. Muḥammad	Al-Hādi (the guided)/Al-Naqī (the distinguished)	212–254/827–868
		Al-Ḥasan s/o ʻAlī	Al-ʻAskarī (the detained)	232–260/846–874
		Muḥammad al-Mahdi	Al-Qāim (the one who will arise); al-Muntaẓar (the awaited); al-Mahdī	869 (in major occultation)
		Imāmi /Ithnā ʻAsharis Shīʻism		

Divine Justice (*'Adl*)

You became familiar with the names and attributes of Allah in Chapter 1, so it would seem obvious to ask why a single attribute of God has been selected by the Shī'a to be part of their fundamentals of faith (*'Ūṣūl ad-dīn*). This is also a historical legacy from the Mu'tazilī–Ash'arī debate when Shī'a doctrine was being crystallised in the fourth–fifth AH/tenth–eleventh CE centuries (Momen, 1985). The Mu'tazilī stance was adopted by Shī'ism, which emphasised that individuals are responsible for their actions and God's subsequent judgements of these actions will accord with God's justice (Saud, 2013c: 94). On the other hand, the Ash'arīs stressed that God created humans' actions and, consequently, there is little room for an individual's own volition. It was due to these fierce debates that the Mu'tazilī concept of divine justice became enshrined as one of the fundamental principles of the Shī'a (Momen, 1985: 177–178).

Voice of a Muslim

Imām Zayn al-'Abidīn [38–94AH/658–712CE]

O God, bless Muḥammad and his Household, spare me the concerns which distract me, employ me in that about which Thou wilt ask me tomorrow,

and let me pass my days in that for which Thou hast created me,

Free me from need, expand Thy provision toward me,

and tempt not with ingratitude!

Exalt me and afflict me not with pride!

Make me worship Thee and corrupt not my worship with self-admiration! (Al-'Abidīn, 1988)

The ten obligations

The Shī'a have ten obligatory acts to fulfil; five (Shahādah, Ṣalāh, Ṣawm, Zakāt and Ḥajj) are common, with some distinctions in details. They also have Jihād, commanding the good and forbidding evil. However, the *Khums* are exclusive to Shī'ism, whereas love for the Family of the Prophet (*Tawalla*) and turning away from those who are unjust to his family (*Tabarra*) is another feature.

Chapter 6 analysed the five pillars in detail, therefore in this section some of the differences are highlighted.

Ṣalāh or Namāz (obligatory prayer)

Muslims believe that there are five obligatory prayers in a day. However, in Shīʿism, it is permissible to combine together the noon and afternoon, and the evening and night prayers so that there are three separate occasions of five prayers during the day (Saud, 2013a).

As regards the call to prayer, there are three differences. In the Shīʿa *adhān*, the phrase 'Come to the best of actions' is added, and, similarly, for the dawn prayer the phrase 'prayer is better than sleep' is omitted. Then, after the declaration Muḥammad is the Messenger of God, among Shīʿa, it is commendable to add the phrase 'I bear witness that 'Alī is the *Walī Allah*' (here it means the guardian of the religion) and acknowledge the appointed of their Imāms as rightful successors.

The exclusive Shīʿa feature is that of insisting, though not obligatory, that the forehead is placed on dust or earth, so on a prayer mat, a tablet of baked mud (*turbah/mohr*) from the earth of Karbalā' is used during the prostration phase of the prayers. This allows the person to connect with the site of the events of martyrdom. Short texts or symbols are engraved on them (Raudvere, 2015).

Ṣawm

Fasting is similar except that among the Shīʿa it ends after the sun has completely set. In addition, they also spend three days in Ramaḍān mourning the death of 'Alī who was martyred on the twentieth.

Zakāt

The main difference with regard to Zakāt is that in the Sunnī communities it is meant to be given to the state where such governance exists and the state disburses it according to the Qur'ān (9:60). In the absence of this, like in the UK, Muslims send it directly to the poor, or give it to their local mosque or a registered charity, which discharge it on their behalf to the appropriate recipient as discussed in Chapter 6. However, in Shīʿism it is paid to their *marjaʿ at-taqlīd* or *mujtahid* for distribution. From gold, silver, cash and profits through business transactions, they give 2.5 per cent after household and commercial expenses have been deducted. In the case of livestock and grain, the formula for ascertaining how much to levy is complicated (Momen, 1985).

Khums (one-fifth)

Unlike Zakāt, there is an annual tax of one-fifth (*khums*) on the net excess income (Saud, 2013a). It is levied because of a different verse which states: 'And know that anything you obtain of war booty – then indeed, for Allah is one fifth of it and for the Messenger and for [his] near relatives and the orphans, the needy, and the [stranded] traveller, ...' (8:41). Thus, one-half of this money is distributed to the Prophet (ﷺ), his family through his daughter Fātimah and the remaining half (a tithe) is the share of the Imāms (*sahm al-Imām*) as they inherit from the Prophet (ﷺ) for being Imāms. This is paid to their *marja' at-taqlīd* in his capacity as the representative (*nā'ib al-'āmm*) of the hidden Imām (Momen, 2016: 190) who utilises it for welfare projects (Saud, 2013a). Among the Sunnī, the application of this verse was abolished with the death of the Prophet (ﷺ).

Ḥajj

The details of pilgrimage are more or less the same. However, it is highly recommended for the Shī'a to complete their pilgrimage by travelling to Madīnah to visit the tomb of the Prophet (ﷺ), Fātimah and the Second, Fourth, Fifth, and Sixth Imāms at the ***al-Baqī'*** cemetery (Momen, 1985). They also go to Karbalā', Najaf and other places where they believe they receive grace (*barakah*) from visiting the tombs and mausoleums of their saints (Raudvere, 2015).

Jihad

In Shī'ism, it is an obligation for all able-bodied Muslim males to participate in *jihād*. However, this obligation has rescinded, with the occultation of the Imām since only an Imām can announce an offensive *jihād* against the non-Muslim world. Nevertheless, *jihād* in its metaphorical meaning – the war against one's own corrupt desires – is a continuous battle. Some forms of missionary efforts in the non-Muslim world are classified as *jihād* (Momen, 1985).

Enjoining good (*Amr bil-ma'ruf*)

For the Shī'a, it is a commandment for everyone to lead a virtuous life, perform all the religious obligations and act in accordance with the religious law (Sharī'ah). In addition, they should individually encourage all other Muslims to do the same (16:125). For some Sunnīs, it is a general recommended instruction rather than an obligation.

Exhortation to desist from evil (*nahy 'an il-munkar*)

For the Shī'a, it is obligatory on each of them to avoid all evil actions prohibited in religious law. It is also obligatory to enjoin this on others and to act to prevent evil being committed (3:103; 3:109). For the Sunnī, it also obligatory to avoid all evil. However, commanding against it, according to some scholars, is a recommended act.

Tawalla

All Muslims respect the *Ahl al-Bayt*. However, the Shī'a interpretation includes the 14 pure ones among these (Momen, 2016). *Tawalla* is therefore to associate with good people who follow the *Ahl al-Bayt* and to live according to their example. The term *Ahl al-Kisā* (People of the Cloak) is also applied to Muḥammad (ﷺ), 'Alī, Fātimah, Al-Ḥasan and Al-Ḥusaīn following the event related to the verse (3:61–63).

Tabarrah

In contrast to the above, *tabarrah* means that the Shī'a stay aloof from those who they consider to be the enemies of *Ahl al-Bayt*. This includes a rejection of those who do not accept the Imāmate of the *Ahl al-Bayt*. In essence this would be Sunnīs, although it may include disassociating with evil people in general.

Voice of a Muslim

Imām Mūsā al-Kāẓim [128–183 AH/745–799 CE]

> The metaphor of this world is that of a snake which has a soft body, while it conceals deadly poison. Wisemen avoid it, but immature persons (literally children) are drawn to it. (Imani, 1998)

Ritual and doctrines in Shī'ism

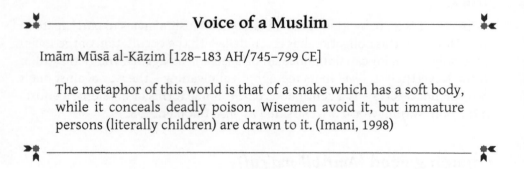

In terms of doctrines, the Shī'a have positioned doctrines specific to themselves in parallel with those accepted by Sunnīs. In jurisprudence, there are ritual observances (*'ibādāt*) and social transactions (*mu'āmalāt*). In the former, Shī'ism does not differ considerably from the four schools of jurisprudence among the Sunnī. However, in relation to social transactions, such as marriage and inheritance, there are clear differences. The Shī'a have a tendency to highlight these differences from the Sunnī, even in ritual observances by emphasising parallel rituals that are specific to Shī'ism (Momen, 1985).

Doctrines

In matters of doctrine, God's justice is placed alongside the unity of God and they define that justice in a way which differs from the Sunnī concept. The Imāmate is positioned in parallel to the doctrine of prophethood and even the highly significant belief in the Day of Resurrection is displaced by attributing more significance to the Return of the Twelfth Imām and focussing the attention of the Shī'a on this event (Momen, 1985: 181).

Rituals: Friday and other prayers

In Shī'ism the true leader for the Friday prayer is the Imām. However, since the Twelfth Imām has occulted, the prayer has never held the same importance for them as it has for the Sunnī. Nevertheless, in many Shī'a centres, where it is offered, it does not attract large numbers. In addition to the obligatory prayers, the Imāms within Shī'ism have revealed a large number of prayers for special occasions like Ramaḍān or for other devotional purposes. These are known as *du'ā* or *munājāt* (Momen, 1985: 181).

Visiting Shī'a shrines

The custom of visiting the shrines of the Imāms *(ziyārat)* developed as an alternative parallel activity to the extent that to the ordinary person this might appear to exceed the significance of *Ḥajj* itself. Najaf, Karbalā', Kufā, Mashhad, Qum and other places are important activities in Shī'a religious life where anyone could participate. Detailed rituals were written to assist in the performance of these visitations, again in parallel to the rituals of pilgrimage in Makkah. Moreover, visitations to the shrines of minor Shī'a saints and especially the descendants of the Imāms, called *Imāmzādas*, have also become important activities with each shrine having its own prayer of visitation (Momen, 1985: 182). Sometimes the pilgrim addresses Imām 'Alī's tomb as though it is present as a living person (Momen, 2016). In Shī'ism, intermediaries between humans and God are 'vital' for salvation (La'Porte, 2001: 341). Thus, visitations to tombs and shrines and their belief in their intercession are an integral part of the divine plan for salvation. The principal personalities are the Fourteen Pure Ones: the Twelve Imāms, Fātimah and the Prophet (ﷺ) (Esposito, 2016).

Religious dissimulation (Taqiyya)

Concealment of faith (religious dissimulation) while maintaining mental reservation is considered lawful in Shī'ism. It is to conceal one's Shī'ism and is practised in sophisticated situations where there is overwhelming danger of loss of life or property and where no danger to religion would occur thereby (Raudvere, 2015). Shī'a believe that touching non-Muslims renders them ritually impure for ritual prayer (Momen, 2016).

Temporary marriage (*Mut'ah*)

This type of marriage is for a fixed term and usually for a predetermined financial arrangement. It is considered permissible by Shī'a (La'Porte, 2001). The marriage could be for any length of time, even for a matter of hours. A husband has no obligation to provide any form of support to a wife and it does not involve inheritance between the two. Children born out of such as union would be legitimate. Shī'a themselves consider it inferior to permanent marriage (Amir-Moezzi and Jambet, 2018). There is also a period of time after the marriage during which the woman is not supposed to marry again. Sunnīs do not hold temporary marriage to be permissible and indeed consider it to be mere prostitution (Maqsood, 2010: 222). Shī'ism maintains that it was a practice that was allowed during the Prophet's lifetime and was abolished by 'Umar. In Persian it is called *sīgheh/sigha* or in Arabic *nikāḥ al-muwaqqat* (temporary marriage). Shī'a maintained that the Qur'ān refers to this practice in (4:24). Iranian feminists object to it as being exploitative (Momen, 2016). However, not all Shī'a permit this.

Divorce (Ṭalāq)

Generally, divorce is more difficult within Shī'a law than in Sunnī law. Only the stricter divorce, which is given according to the Sunnah, is allowed, meaning the ***ṭalāq al-sunna***. As distinct from the Sunnī schools, the Shīʿa law holds that the statement of the divorce formula must be made explicitly, in the presence of two witnesses, and is not allowable if made in a state of intoxication or rage. However, both agree that if a man divorces his wife three times, he cannot marry her again unless she is first married to another. The irregular divorce (***ṭalāq al-bidʿah***) is impermissible. Shīʿa do not allow the three statements of divorce to be made on one occasion (Momen, 1985: 183). In Shīʿa a man may not divorce a wife during confinement after childbirth, during her menstrual period or if sexual intercourse has occurred since menstruation. Moreover, declarations of divorce made indirectly by oath, wager or swearing are forbidden among Shīʿa (Amir-Moezzi and Jambet, 2018).

Inheritance

In Shīʿa law the presence of male heirs does not exclude the female, although the share of the male is in accordance with a Qur'ānic rule, double that of the female.

The important position held by Fātimah amongst the Shīʿa contributed to the favourable attitude toward women in divorce and inheritance (Momen, 2016).

The Qur'ān

Shīʿa do not believe in the eternal nature of the Qur'ān and consider it to be created by God and everything in it; they believe it has a hidden meaning, which requires interpretation by religious leaders. Some of them also believe that it is not final and that the Sunnīs have removed the reference to the Twelve Imāms. Many of them also believe that accepting the atoning death of Al-Ḥusaīn brings them salvation from their sins and with it heaven on the Day of Judgement (Momen, 1985: 172–173).

Festivals

There are two main festivals among the Shīʿa. The *Ghadīr al-Khumm* marks the designation of ʿAlī by the Prophet (ﷺ) as the Imām at the pool of Khumm on eighteenth Dhul-Hijjah when they are encouraged to fast. Poetry is recited and sermons are delivered. It is considered the greatest ʿId. *ʿĀshūrā* marks the death of Al-Ḥusaīn at the field of Karbalā'. Hence the shrine ground in Karbalā' is regarded as sacred ground (Crotty and Lovat, 2016: 64). This is an event which is deeply rooted in the consciousness of the Shī'ite. During these occasions, annual processions are held where passion plays (*ta'ziya*) and theatrical performances take place and some display self-flagellation, called ***zanjīr*** (Gwynne, 2018). A horse is draped with bloodstained sheets and arrows are fixed in its harness. Often its models are also processed in streets. Shī'a also celebrate the death and birth anniversaries of the Imāms.

Sub-groups

As each Imām died his following divided into sects (Momen, 2016); thus disagreements regarding the identity of the legitimate spiritual leaders occurred resulting in sub-divisions (Daftray, 2013). The Shī'a are divided into many groups with contrasting beliefs as shown in Table 10.2. The differences between the five Shī'a mainly focus on historical figures and claims to inspiration.

Table 10.2 The main groups within Shī'ism

Twelvers (Ithnā 'Ashariyyah)	The largest Shī'a group who believe that the Twelfth Imām in the line of 'Alī is currently hidden.
Fivers (Zaydis)	The most conservative among the Shī'a, taking their name from the fifth Shī'a Imām Zayd, who was deposed. Community can choose leader from the descendants of 'Alī. Of the others, these are closest to Sunnī.
Seveners (Ismā'īlīyah)	The Aga Khan heads this group. They maintain that Ismā'īl, the son of the sixth Imām Ja'far, who died before his father, was the seventh Imām and after Ismā'īl the line terminated. The Seveners further group into Nizāri (Khoja) and Musta'lis (Bohra).
Druze	They emerged in Syria and Lebanon in 1021, taking their name from their first leader, al-Dazaroi.
'Alawies	The Proclaimers of 'Alī who incorporate elements of Christianity in their faith, such as Jesus' resurrection.

The difference among the various Shī'a communities rests on the question of which of 'Alī's descendants inherited from him and upon the extent and nature of this inherited authority (Glassé, 2013). There are further groups and offshoots, which are beyond the scope of this book. Nevertheless, the Ibāḍiyyah emerged prior to the main Sunnī–Shī'a split whose origin is identified with the wife of Muḥammad (ﷺ), Khadījah. They claim to be preserving the pristine teachings of the Prophet (ﷺ). As for the Ithnā 'Ashariyyah it is the state religion of Iran, the largest of all. The Druze, considered outside of the fold of Islam, believe in reincarnation and do not observe the five pillars. They also believe that the Fātimid Khalīfah Al-Ḥākim was God. The Nizāri Khoja (led by the Aga Khan) believe that Imāmate continues from Ismā'il to the present day as there is no Hidden Imām (Khan, 2013). The Alevi of Turkey and 'Alawī (Nusayris) in Syria are not to be confused (Nielsen and Otterbeck, 2016: 167). The former revere 'Alī but do not call themselves Shī'ites; traditional Sunnī rites are 'hardly' practised by them and they use gathering houses instead of mosques.

Case study 10.1 What is good and bad?

A playground incident led Amarjit's Headteacher to discuss how to assist someone to be a good friend. After an assembly, Amarjit thought that she would extend her wonderful assembly by bringing the issues in to her religious education lesson which was on learning about some of the teachings of the Qur'ān on making people and the community better. She chose a verse which talks about the promotion of good and the prevention of bad. She felt this was something to which all her pupils could relate and it was important for them to understand that both of these are needed for a healthy community. Importantly, she knew some of the pupils in her Year 3 class would enjoy this as they loved philosophical questions which resulted in some real actions. Using a horseshoe shape to organise her class, she asked them whose responsibility it was to promote good. She recorded their answers on a scatter diagram. She then asked them whether pupils and adults should be preventing bad. The class had an open forum for this. She recorded these responses too. Thereafter, on one side of her flip chart paper, she recorded their reasons on why they thought good ought to be promoted and bad prevented. She then brought out two plants, one that had been looked after and the other which had not. She asked them to comment. She then explained that the one being looked after was watered regularly and cleaned to keep it good whereas to make the other bad, it did not require anything to be done to it. It dried and wilted by itself. She invited them to talk about the plants and what she had said. Finally, she

(Continued)

asked them to close their eyes and think about what was the most important thing they had taken from the lesson.

Amarjit appears to have taken an integrated approach to school experiences.

- Identify the features which suggest she thinks education should be holistic.
- Reflect on how Amarjit established cooperative learning to teach her pupils to take responsibility for their own work and behaviour.
- Her method reveals traces of philosophy. Consider how she involved her pupils to think about consequences, and individual and collective responsibility.
- To what extent would you say Amarjit empowered her pupils as learners?

Summary

You have learnt that Shī'ism emerged many years after the demise of the Prophet (ﷺ), initially as a dissident political movement and later it took on a theological perspective. The main contention of the Shī'a is that 'Alī should have inherited the leadership of the community; since this did not happen they repudiate the first leaders. Sunnīs regard all of these leaders with reverence and worthy of emulation. You have examined the foundations and obligations from the perspective of Shī'ism and have understood where some of the similarities and differences exist. You have also become familiar with the concept of Imāmate and have recognised the existence of sub-groups within Shī'ism.

Reflection tasks

- Analyse the factors which led to the emergence of Shī'ism.
- Evaluate the role of the ten obligations for contemporary Shī'a.
- Describe the importance of 'Āshūrā' for both Sunnīs and Shī'a.
- Discuss the significance of visitations for Shī'a.
- Reflect on the ways you would teach the concept of Imāmate.

Further reading

Hugo, J. (2019) *A Concise History of Sunnīs and Shi'is*. London: Saqi Publishers.

This text, by a lawyer, counters the simplistic narrative of Sunnīs and Shi'is logged in religious war showing also their cross-fertilisation and harmonious times and draws attention to this sectarian politics against the reaction to the West and the spread of nationalism.

Pierce, M. (2016) *Twelve Infallible Men: The Imams and the Making of Shiism*. Cambridge: Harvard University Press.

In this text the author conceptualises the relationship between history, author, text and audience. This is an examination of several collective biographies of the twelve Imams.

11

MUSLIM HERITAGE AND INTELLECTUAL CONTRIBUTIONS

In this chapter you will:

- understand the meaning of Sharīʿah and its implications for Muslim conscience
- learn about the sources of law in Islam
- know the main canonical schools of jurisprudence (*Fiqh*)
- consider the influence of *ʿIlm ḥadīth* in preserving the Sunnah lifestyle
- reflect on the main theological strands (*Kalām*) and the key issues they raise
- understand the spiritual pathways (*Taṣawwūf*) and their role in Muslim piety.

Overview

Presenting Islam as a religion is a partial projection of what its reality entails. This is because Islam is actually the 'water' which nourished the civilisations and cultures that stretch from Alaska to Australia, Chile to China and Sweden to South Africa, enveloping the beliefs and lifestyles of diverse ethnic communities. Over the centuries, it has produced a myriad of spiritual pathways, philosophical perspectives, juristic schools, theological strands, arts and sciences. To understand fully the impact of Islam in these domains of human activity and the role of the Qur'ān and the Sunnah in informing these endeavours, it is important for you to briefly consider some of these as they continue to sustain the thoughts and practices of Muslims across the world. This chapter will enable you to explore the religion in a wider sense and further deepen your understanding of Muslims.

Sharīʿah

For a long time, in the discourses on Islam mainly in the western hemisphere, but recently on a global scale, the term *Sharīʿah* has been presented notoriously and viewed, in some quarters, with considerable disdain and suspicion. As educators, it becomes paramount for you to gain a nuanced appreciation of what it is, its objectives (***maqāṣid***) and scope.

Literally, it means the path to be followed or pathway in the desert that leads to a watering place. In Islam, it means 'the Law', and as such, the phrase 'Sharī'ah Law' becomes redundant. Sharī'ah refers to the law set up by God as guidance for the regulation of life in the interest of humans. It encompasses more than the obligations on a Muslim (Abdulla and Keshavjee, 2018). Its objective is to show people the 'best' way and to provide them with the most 'successful' and most 'beneficial' way of life. The violation of this law has consequences of various kinds including actions classified as sins as well as legal crimes and capital punishment. Therefore, the scope of *Sharī'ah* is much broader than is commonly thought as it comprises religious, social, political, domestic, private and moral matters for those who accept Islam and those living within the jurisdiction of Islam. For Muslims, therefore, it is the knowledge of rights and duties owed to God, to fellow humans and the rest of creation and a light to traverse this worldly life as they prepare themselves for the Hereafter. In essence, it distinguishes the truth and falsehood and the approved and disapproved.

The *Sharī'ah* establishes several rights in relation to God:

- have faith in and acknowledge the existence of God
- accept the authority and unity of God
- worship God alone and none other than God
- love and obey God wholeheartedly and unreservedly

Muslims are expected to fulfil these obligations in a way that these take precedence over others and sometimes they have to give up rights owed to others including themselves. For example, in executing the obligation to fast for God, Muslims give up their personal rights of satiating their appetites and embrace hunger.

The *Sharī'ah* offers individuals many rights including safety of life, property, religion, inheritance and freedom of belief and what it views as lawful acts. Interestingly, it occurs only once in the Qur'ān (Wills, 2017) and there it does not mean law but a 'way' (18:45) and other variants (5:48; 42:13). Thus, it is more than a criminal code and its literal application as it is understood in different ways by jurists, principalists (***uṣūlliyyūn***), philosophers and mystics (Ramadan, 2017). Its objectives embrace the creation of an ideal society within which the welfare of all humanity is paramount. In addition to securing individual rights, it places duties and responsibilities on everyone for the well-being of communities, the state and humankind at large. Concurrently, it is expected from all individuals that they avoid infringing the rights of others. Therefore, the *Sharī'ah* prohibits theft, bribery, interest, forgery and cheating. The wisdom behind this is that whatever is obtained through these means is achieved by causing a loss to the other. Similarly, gambling, lottery, monopoly, hoarding, black-marketing and games of chance fall within this remit. Murder is prohibited since an individual has no right to take the life of another for personal benefit. Adultery, fornication, homosexuality, incest, and bestiality also fall under forbidden practices (Esposito and DeLong-Bas, 2018).

Four sources of Sharīʿah

Notwithstanding some disagreement at the peripheral regarding some secondary principles, overall, Muslim jurists from the ninth to the nineteenth century showed remarkable agreement on the basic source framework (Brown, 2017: 181). The theory itself became the subject matter of a branch of scholarship known as the study of the 'roots of jurisprudence' (***Uṣūl al-fiqh***).

All four main Sunnī schools of jurisprudence accept the Qur'ān and Sunnah as the primary sources of law and also consensus and analogical reasoning. The first source is the Qur'ān and, as you have learnt, it covers guidance on belief, morality, economics, politics, legal matters, spirituality and metaphysics. The Qur'ān offers the principles regarding life and the Prophet (ﷺ) demonstrated how these principles were to be practised. Therefore, the Sunnah is the second source. For this reason the Sunnah has been preserved through a continuous consensus (*tawātur*) since the period of the Prophet (ﷺ) as recorded in the collections of aḥadīth.

Qiyās (analogical reasoning)

The Qur'ān is not a legal text per se as a very large number of its verses are moral in nature. Simultaneously, there are matters and questions that are not answered by the Sunnah of the Prophet (ﷺ). The third source, *Qiyās*, analogical reasoning, is a legal term which refers to the use of reason and judgement to ascertain Sharīʿah rulings. It is exercised in the absence of a direct ruling from the primary sources on a particular issue. This method examines known cases and addresses new ones using the similarities between the two categories. To illustrate, the Qur'ān categorically prohibits the consumption of wine (*khamr*). The issue then arose about other intoxicants. Since the basis of the Qur'ānic prohibition is that wine intoxicates the mind and inhibits human faculties, most legal schools prohibit other intoxicants as well (Saud, 2013a:59).

There are several other legal principles and methods of deriving laws based on the guidance provided by the Qur'ān and Sunnah. *Istiṣlāh* is a principle whereby the strict application of a legal rule may be overruled on the basis of considerations of public good and interest (*maṣlaḥah*). There is also the religious law prior to Islam (*shar' man qablanā*) and custom (*'urf*) of Muslims when it does not contradict the hierarchically higher sources. *Istihsān* is juristic preference which allows the qualified jurist to apply a personal judgement by departing from the strict application of *Qiyās*. *Ẓarūra* is the principle based on which an established rule of law can be suspended in extreme circumstances.

Ijtihād (independent juristic reasoning) can only be undertaken by qualified and competent scholars (*mujtahids*) who arrive at their opinion (*ra'y*) by using various sources. It is a role which is contested in terms of who can fulfil it and when. *Ijtihād* provides a mechanism to derive guidance with regard to new issues faced by the community (Siddiqui, 2018). Jurists unqualified to exercise *ijtihād* must restrict themselves to applying established rulings. In other words, to adhere to authoritative precedent (*taqlīd*). In contemporary times, *taqlīd* has gained a 'bad' reputation, often interpreted as blind following, whereas it is better seen as an acknowledgement that not everyone is a genius (Brown, 2017:182). When such is the position regarding jurists, for the laity, some have argued that following a school is necessary (Furber, 2016; Usmani, 2001).

Ijmā'

The consensus or agreement reached on a specific issue through independent juristic reasoning during the period of the first four Rightly-guided *Khulafā'* and other Companions is known as *Ijmā' al-Ṣaḥābah* (the consensus of the Companions). As a fourth source this is accepted as binding (Siddiqui, 2018). For Imām Mālik the sources are hierarchically prioritised and include the practices of the people of Madīnah.

Subsequently, there was scholarly consensus by qualified Muslim jurists as well which is followed. However, this can be changed by other scholarly consensuses. Today, it so happens that jurists in one country may arrive at a consensus on a particular issue. However, this consensus will only be acceptable elsewhere, or globally, when it is endorsed by a committee of world renowned jurists. Thus, *Ijmā'* provides a mechanism for maintaining unity in changing situations and *Ijtihād* is a tool used to ensure the dynamism of the Sharī'ah and assists the Ummah to face changing challenges (Siddiqui, 2018). For Sunnīs the collective reason of the community is superior to the rational faculty of an individual, whereas for the Shī'a, the reason of the Imām supersedes that of the community at large (Saud, 2013c: 95). In the absence of the Imām and the rejection of analogy and consensus as legal sources, the interpreters of the law (*mujtahids*) serve as their representatives in Shi'ism (Esposito, 2016: 110).

The status of Sunnah

The above exposition of the objectives (*maqāsid*) and details of the sources of *Sharī'ah* raises questions about the status and role of Ḥadīth. In Chapter 2, you discovered that the Qur'ān is the ultimate source of law and guidance for Muslims and that the life of Muḥammad (ﷺ) is a model of these teachings. In this section, you will reflect on a few verses which establish categorically the legislative and interpretive nature of the Prophet's (ﷺ) authority, which is denied by a very small minority and has been refuted (Usmani, 1990; Azami, 2012; Brown, 2018). These verses (7:157; 33:36; 59:7; 24:47–52) invite Muslims to accept his authority, arbitration and verdicts. Equally, there are many verses which he demonstrated because the Qur'ān did not mention their practical implementation such as the method of prayer (*ṣalāh*), pilgrimage and alms giving. Thus, what he said and did, in his capacity as a Messenger (ﷺ) has been taken as binding for his followers. However, some matters outside *Sharī'ah* domains are left for human curiosity and their efforts to solve them (Usmani, 1990). Thus, in Islam, the Qur'ān and Sunnah are the primary sources of law and life practices for Muslims.

Voice of a Muslim

Servant leadership in society is necessary, and I believe it is critical in schools. It gives me an opportunity to develop a culture of respect, and empathy towards others, but more importantly leads to harmony across school. Servant leadership must be identified by others, they must recognise it in your actions and achievements. I know that the Prophet Muḥammad (ﷺ) and great Islamic leaders of the centuries have used this leadership style to deliver substantial societal reforms in many communities. Servant leadership is sometimes perceived as weak leadership because leadership is generally seen in terms of power and control, but servant leadership is a legacy leadership requiring real engagement with stakeholders, trust, respect, some form of spiritual connection. Once leadership is seen beyond power and control and leaders see authority and responsibility as going hand-in-hand and when they accept being challenged on decisions made, which sometimes may go wrong, then such leadership becomes part of a healthy society. (Thāqib, Pakistani, education leader, male)

Legal schools

The four main Sunnī schools of law (*madhāhib*) are Mālikī, Ḥanafī, Shafi'ī and Ḥanbalī. The Shī'a are Ja'fari, Ismāi'li and Zaydi. The Ibādi belong neither to the Sunnī nor Shī'a schools of law (Abdulla and Keshavjee, 2018). These eight schools of jurisprudential understanding (*fiqh*) represent the understanding of Sharī'ah as codified within a particular school.

Fiqh is the term used to denote Islamic jurisprudence. Literally it refers to 'intelligence', and 'understanding', and it implies the independent use of the intellect to arrive at a ruling based on the knowledge gained through the study of the Qur'ān, *ḥadīth* and other sources of law. The *Sharī'ah* is derived from God and his Prophet (ﷺ), whereas *fiqh* is the human effort to discover God's ideal law through intellectual methods (Saud, 2013b: 58). Among the Sunnī, four major schools of law (***madhhab***) have survived over the years, while remnants of others do exist.

Ḥanafī

The Ḥanafī school in contemporary times has the largest following. The school was founded by Imām Abū Ḥanīfah Numān ibn Thābit (80–150AH/699–767 CE). It is said he met Anas, a Companion of the Prophet (ﷺ), which makes him a Tābi'i (Successor), and elevates his status (Nu'mānī, 2004: 7). In theory, he is famous for permitting a higher degree of flexibility than his counterparts (Brown, 2017: 178). As part of his methodology, he used personal judgement (*ra'y*), juristic preferences (*istiḥsān*) and developed *qiyās*, which is to derive new legal positions on the basis of prior legal analogous positions (Saud, 2013b: 55). He was offered the first ever post of *Qāḍi* (Chief Judge) by an Abbāsid *Khalif* which he declined preferring to remain independent. Its followers are mostly found in central and Western Asia, especially in countries like Bangladesh, India, Pakistan, Syria, Tajikistan and Turkey (Abdulla and Keshavjee, 2018). Abū Ḥanīfah continues to be one of the most influential Muslims in history (Khan, 2010).

Māliki

The founder of this school is Imām Mālik ibn Anas (94–179AH/711–796CE). His school accepted the practice of the people of Madīnah as precedent and evidence of Sunnah as he had direct access to oral traditions and constant meetings with the *Tābi'un*. His jurisprudential work *Kitāb ul-Muwaṭṭa'* is the earliest surviving book on law, rituals and practices. He codified the common law and by doing so paved the way for further developments of juridical thought and system. He differed from Abū Ḥanīfah by excluding inferences and deductions, basing his system on traditions of the Prophet (ﷺ). His followers are mainly in Upper Egypt, North and West Africa, and especially in Algeria, Libya, Morocco, Tunisia and in Sub-Saharan countries like Mali, northern Nigeria and Senegal (Abdulla and Keshavjee, 2018).

Al-Shāfi'ī

Imām Muḥammad ibn Idrīs al-Shāfi'ī (150–204AH/769–822) was a student of Mālik ibn Anas and, as such, cognisant of the Mālikī system. He is considered the greatest systematiser of Islamic legal theory (Brown, 2017: 178). It is predominant in East Africa, Indonesia, Lower Egypt, Malaysia and South East Asia (Abdulla and Keshavjee, 2018). He reconciled the positions of the traditionalists and rationalists and anchored both in common sources by articulating the four sources of law discussed above; his methodology pervades all the legal schools (Saud, 2013b: 58).

Ḥanbalī

Imām Aḥmad ibn Ḥanbal (164–241AH/780–855CE) is characterised as being orthodox. He was a student of Imām Al-Shāfi'ī. Some of his stance on orthodoxy irritated the sovereign. Consequently, he was imprisoned by Khalīfah Mu'tasim. He regularly denounced the rationalist Mu'tazilah doctrines. He carried out a comprehensive study of the ḥadīth and his monumental work known as *Musnad Imām Aḥmad* contains nearly 30,000 narrations, which, rather than being ordered according to subject matter, are organised according to the names of the Companions of the Prophet (ﷺ). In his *fiqh*, he made the least use of reason and attempted to derive rulings from ḥadīth, and as such, some perceive it to be more 'rigid' than the others. It is predominant in Saudi Arabia and has followers in many Arabian Gulf states like Kuwait, Qatar and UAE. However, Oman follows the *Ibādi* school of law (Abdulla and Keshavjee, 2018) whereas the Ẓāhirī school, which is almost extinct, places emphasis on not going beyond the literal meaning of revelation for applying the law.

Shī'i schools

The most significant school of law among the Shī'a is based on the principles of Muḥammad al-Bāqir and Ja'far al-Sādiq, the sixth Imām, and is named Ja'fari.

He was a scholar of ḥadīth and *fiqh* and influenced both communities. Many prominent scholars were among his students including Imām Mālik and Abū Ḥanīfah who studied under him, which makes him the scholarly connection between Sunnī and Shī'a, and both have high regard for him. Ja'far was also a major spiritual guide who appears in all Sufi chains of genealogy (***silsilah***) (Esposito, 2016: 109). This school does not markedly differ from Sunnī schools on most points of substance, although there are significant exceptions in inheritance, temporary marriage, divorce, *ijmā'* and the teaching of the Imāms being part of the Sunnah (Brown, 2017: 183). It is mainly found in Iraq, Iran and Lebanon, as well as in India and East Africa. The Ismā'ilī school formulated as *Da'ā'im al-Islam* is the main legal code for the Tayyibi Musta'lian Ismā'ilī, including the Daudī Bohras of South Asia. The Nizāri, commonly known as Ismā'ilī, follow the guidance of their living Imāms, who are known as the Aga Khans, in their legal, normative and ritual practices. The Zaydi school is mostly found in Yemen and is followed by the Shī'a there (Abdulla and Keshavjee, 2018).

'Ilm al-ḥadīth – the science of ḥadīth

When the Prophet (ﷺ) was alive, people directly asked him questions which he answered and they verified matters with him personally. Likewise, after his demise, people relied on the Companions (*Ṣaḥābah*) to ascertain what they had heard and observed the Prophet (ﷺ) saying and doing. After the death of the Prophet (ﷺ), Islam spread to many lands and the constitution of the society diversified and raised sophisticated theological, legal and social issues. Hence the need to determine the authenticity of the sayings of the Messenger (ﷺ) arose. To this end, over time the *muḥaddithūn* (scholars of ḥadīth) developed a set of principles and methodologies known as *'ilm al-ḥadīth* (the science of ḥadīth).

There were several factors which led to ascertain the authenticity of these practices and reliability of these reporters. These matters had spiritual consequences; getting it right was very important (Saud, 2013b: 54). It became necessary to distinguish between the genres of ḥadīth and *Sīrah*, which developed simultaneously but had different statuses. The latter included biographical material. Controversy had also developed within the Muslim community, and some people within each group began attributing their own partisan statements to the Prophet (ﷺ). Others forged ḥadīth for chauvinism, storytelling or for pious motivations but not all were malicious acts (Brown, 2018). Thus, for a variety of reasons the science of determining the genuineness or otherwise of ḥadīth developed. Mālik ibn Anas was the first codifier of the *Sunnah* and belonged to the generation born after the death of the Messenger (ﷺ) known as Successors (Tābi'ūn). He employed a methodology of a verbal chain of transmission (*sanad*). Any narration was to be accompanied by a reference disclosing who had heard or seen a report (Saud, 2013b: 53).

Literally, the Arabic word ḥadīth means conversation and/or communication; be it secular, religious, historical or contemporary. However, according to the scholars of *ḥadīth* (m. *muhaddith*, f. *muḥadditha*), in the science of *ḥadīth*, it represents the types of transmissions regarding the Prophet Muḥammad (ﷺ), his actions (*fi'l*), sayings (*qawl*), tacit approvals of actions (*taqrīr*) or descriptions of his *ṣifāt* (characteristics) (Azami, 2012: 3). Sometimes the term encompasses narrations about the Companions. In general, *ḥadīth* tends to refer to Muḥammad's (ﷺ) sayings and Sunnah indicates his practice.

Orientalist Western scholarship ostensibly led by Goldziher and the most influential Western authority on Islamic law, Schacht, earnestly doubted the historicity and authenticity of the ḥadīth (Al-Azami, 1996), the main contention being that they were written much later and that the term 'Sunnah of the Prophet' developed for the first time in the eighth century around 722AH (Esposito, 2016). However, Esposito (2016: 105–106) argues that this stance creates an unnecessary vacuum in Islamic history and totally ignores the Muslim science of criticism and verification. It also neglects the deeply rooted tradition in Arab culture, which Muslims and non-Muslims acknowledge. It is significant to note that the reference to 'authentic' and 'forged' refers to Muslim standards for reliability, not Western historical ones (Brown, 2018).

Structurally, each *ḥadīth* has two constituents. The *sanad*, meaning 'support', and the *matn*, meaning 'substance'. The system of *isnād*, meaning the ability to verify prophetic traditions, roots Islam in some objectivity, and even empirical veracity (Saud, 2013b: 54). It evaluated the reliability of the transmitters in terms of their mental capacity, age, names, memory, character, occupation, and possibility of meeting their teacher or conveyer and other factors. The character of each narrator was analysed with specific reference to his or her truthfulness and veracity. For example, if a narrator had excellent character but was considered to have a weak memory, the narration would be questioned. Likewise, if a narrator was accused of crime, the tradition would be questioned or disapproved. They had to state either that they were present or had heard it directly from the Prophet (ﷺ) and must provide a complete chain of narrators from the final link to the Prophet (ﷺ). If it were contrary to historical evidence, a report was rejected. Narrators had to be learned for the correct understanding of a report and to convey it to others faithfully. Consequently, a specific genre known as *Asmā' ul rijāl* (lit. names of people) was developed wherein the biographical details of narrators were recorded which assisted in compiling aḥādīth (Azami, 2012). Moreover, as the chains lengthened and reporters became further distanced, the collectors used precise terms to define the mode of transmission.

In addition to examining the chain of narrators, compilers of *aḥādīth* were equally diligent regarding the text which they criticised to prove its genuineness. For example, for a report to be presented as faithful it had to be stipulated that something was said or done by Muḥammad (ﷺ). If a narration was contrary to reason, common sense or the doctrines of the Qur'ān and *ḥadīth*, it would be unacceptable. In judging the veracity of a report, the occasions and circumstances were also evaluated. However, the Qur'ān was the litmus test for judging the legitimacy of a *ḥadīth*; that which agreed with it was accepted, otherwise rejected (Azami, 2012).

These were not the only stringent criticisms applied for examining each *ḥadīth*. There were other criteria as well. For example, some would suspect, deal with caution or reject reports from a Khāriji or Shī'ite which supported their doctrines or forged their causes (Azami, 2012). As a result, this rigorous judging of the merits of each *ḥadīth*, among the *Ahl al-Sunnah*, resulted in many compilations, of which six emerged as the most authentic collections. It is important to recognise that this does not imply that other collections do not have authentic and reliable reports.

In brief, based on these investigations three main grades emerged: *Ṣaḥīḥ* (authentic), *Ḥasan* (agreeable) and *Ḍa'if* (weak), and based on the chain of narrators up to 23 categories were made including *Muttasil* (contiguous), *Mutawātir* (continuous), *Mu'allaq* (suspended), *Maudu'* (fabricated), *Matruk* (discarded) and others (Siddiqi, 1994). The divergent practices within the Muslim community in relation to their obligations can be explained as resulting from this. This also makes it necessary to know the chronology and other circumstances of the ḥadīth as an individual cannot merely take a single ḥadīth from a collection and reach a judgement on it. Moreover, it is important to note that the merit of a ḥadīth is not dependent on the prestige of the compiler since every ḥadīth is tested according to its own merit (Azami, 2012: 107). In Chapter 10 you read about the collections held in high esteem by the Shī'a. For them, not only are their Imām best sources for the sayings of the Prophet (ﷺ), but their infallibility also makes them sources of their own ḥadīth (Brown, 2018).

Naturally, since there are 'Fourteen Impeccable Ones', the traditions among the Twelver Shī'a are more voluminous. In these, the portions devoted to Ja'far al-Sādiq are much greater (Amir-Moezzi and Jambet, 2018).

Ṣaḥīḥ al-Bukhārī

The most authentic collection is one by Imām Muḥammad ibn Ismā'il (194–256AH/810–869CE), born in Bukhārā, Uzbekistan. His mother cared for him after his father died. He began the study of *ḥadīth* when he was less than ten years old (Azami, 2012: 87). By the age of 16, he had acquired a high reputation for his knowledge and had memorised several books of leading scholars. He had a prolific memory and so much so that his peers would correct their manuscripts by comparing what he read from memory. He was fond of history and travelled extensively to collect as many narrations as possible. Of his many books, his *al-Jāmi' al-Ṣaḥīḥ* with some 9082 reports with their biographical details is considered the most authoritative book after the Qur'ān as his criteria for selection were the most stringent. He led a strictly pious, simple life and supported students with stipends. He was an excellent marksman (Azami, 2012).

Ṣaḥīḥ Muslim

Abu al-Husaīn Muslim Al-Qushayrī (202–261AH/817–874CE) was born in Nisāpur and is known as Imām Muslim. His father was a traditionalist of great reputation giving him his early education. He began to study ḥadīth at the age of 15 (Azami, 2012: 94) travelling to Iraq, Syria, Egypt, Hijaz and Baghdad in pursuit of knowledge. He devoted his entire life in pursuit of traditions, learnt from al-Bukhārī, and, like his teacher, applied the severest textual criticism. From the point of classification, arrangement of subject matter, and authenticity his *Jāmi' al-Ṣahīh* is peerless. In his collection of 3033, he does not pay attention to legal extractions and records only those which were authenticated by scholars. He was a merchant of good fortune and reputation (Azami, 2012: 94).

Sunan Abū Dāud

Sulaīmān Al-Ash'ath (202–275AH/818–889CE) was born in Sistān and began travelling whilst under 20 to all the important centres of learning including Khurāsān, Iraq, Harāt, Egypt and Damascus to study and collect whatever he could find (Azami, 2012: 97). He was a contemporary of al-Bukhārī. He authored many books on Muslim law. However, his most important work is his *Sunan* containing 4800 narrations. Many scholars regard this as the third most authentic work. He was a lawyer, critic, collector and compiler who was famous for his honesty, trustworthiness and accuracy. It is one of the best and most comprehensive collections on the subject of legal ḥadīth. Interestingly, he points out some of his own weak ḥadīth as he felt it was better to do so than to use the opinion of the scholars (Azami, 2012: 101).

Sunan al-Tirmidhī

Muḥammad ʻIsā (209–279AH/831–892CE) was born in Tirmiz in Uzbekistan. He was one of the greatest traditionalists and went in his search for ḥadīth to Iraq, Hijāz and across Khurāsān. His collection, often known as *Jāmiʻ ul- Ṣahīh*, consists of 1600 narrations. He also wrote the famous *Kitāb ul-Shamā'il* on the habits and characteristics of the Prophet (ﷺ). He includes a discussion of the legal opinions of early Imāms of *fiqh* and analyses the quality of ***ahādīth*** with an explanation of any weaknesses therein. The book is divided into 50 sub-sections with 3956 ahādīth covering subjects like international law, social behaviour, exegesis of the Qur'ān, beliefs, biographies and other laws. Methodologically, he first gives a heading then presents a ḥadīth followed by a comment on the quality of the ḥadīth and opinions of jurists (Azami, 2012: 104).

Sunan al-Nasā'ī

Aḥmad Shuʻaib (215–303AH/831–915CE) was born in Khurāsān. At the age of 15 he began his extensive travels (*riḥla*) to all the important centres of learning and spared no pain in collecting authentic traditions, which numbered 5764. He belonged to the Shāfiʻī school of jurisprudence (Siddiqi, 1994). He was a great scholar and critic to the extent that some consider him higher than Imām Muslim. He was brave and participated in Jihād with the governor of Egypt whilst keeping aloof of the governor. His methods included the recording of weak ahādīth to show their defects. For each narration he has included different chains (*isnād*) (Azami, 2012: 97).

Sunan Ibn Mājah

Muḥammad Yazīd (209–273AH/824–886CE) was born in Qazwin in Iraq. He journeyed to Basra, Kufa, Syria, Egypt and Hijaz in search of aḥadīth. He gathered a huge number, which were compiled in his *Sunan*. He was a prolific writer and penned a commentary on the Holy Qur'ān and a book on history. Scholars unanimously accept his great scholarship and trustworthiness although some have censured him for including some weak and apocryphal narrations (Azami, 2012: 105). Unlike Abū Dāwūd and al-Tirmidhī, Ibn Mājah does not comment on the status of his aḥadīth nor does he explain his criteria and aims in compiling his 4341 narrations. However, there is minimum repetition and it is one of the best in the arrangement of chapters and sub-chapters.

In the earliest decades of Muslim history, female Companions (*Ṣaḥābiyāt*) diffused their first-hand knowledge of the Messenger (ﷺ). These included his wives such as 'Ā'ishah and Umm Salamah and many others who have reported hundreds of aḥādīth. Some narrate a single observation of something related to the Prophet (ﷺ) which has then been preserved by the collective memory of Muslims. As witnesses to the life of the Prophet (ﷺ), they were sought for their views on credal, ritual and legal matters. Thus their contributions lay in the very origination of some of these narratives, in contrast to those of later generations who were reproducers of actual ḥadīth (Sayeed, 2013: 5). Thus, these *muḥaddithāt* appear as part of the chains of many compilers of aḥādīth influencing Muslim lifestyles.

Voice of a Muslimah

In my experience Muslims are too restrictive with the resources/topics they're willing to expose themselves to. If it's not deemed an Islamic source or on the topic of Islam it can be diminished as not important. Within that there is also a limitation on the individuals we take our learning from. Of course it's important to be critical of who you learn from but it's too often done indiscriminately. It's important to be open-minded lest you end up harming yourself whilst assuming you're 'protecting' your faith. I think we would benefit from increasing education on personal development and all its different facets which would have a spiritual benefit also. Inculcating a love of reading from a young age so people become lifelong learners is also hugely important. (Batool, Somali, administrator, female)

'Ilm al-Kalām – theological schools

Muslims developed ways to defend the tenets of their faith against the criticisms of other religions. There emerged a major movement by the name of Mu'tazilah who systematised *Kalām* (scholastic theology). Unlike the schools of philosophy, *Kalām* restricted itself mainly to religious matters (Nasr, 1987: 305). It is reported that Wāṣil ibn 'Aṭā', the founder of this movement, was listening to his teacher Ḥasan Al-Basrī (21–110AH/642–728CE) when he differed with him regarding the point of Divine Decree. Wāşil stood and departed from the circle. Thereupon, Ḥasan remarked: *I'tazala Annā* (he isolated from us). The name Mu'tazilah, subsequently attributed to this group, was derived from this phrase. Others suggest that it was due to the ideological differences between Wāṣil ibn 'Aṭā' and 'Umar ibn 'Ubaid and the *Ahl al-Sunnah*. The former two opined that a person who commits major sins is neither a Muslim nor an unbeliever, but is in a state between the two.

The Mu'tazilah called themselves people of justice and *Tawḥīd*. To them, since God was Just, it meant that God had to punish evildoers and reward the pious. They also argued that God can only be Just when humans are free to act according to their will, meaning, when God does not intervene in human affairs. They were also disturbed by the belief that if God controls all human actions then it does not suit Him to punish people for their evil actions. If God does so, He would be committing tyranny (Siddiqi and Siddiqi, 1987: 170–182). Their doctrine of free will led them to declare belief in predestination as inappropriate (Smart, 1992: 286). They did not want to make God's attributes something apart from God. Therefore, to them, it was nonsensical to say that the Qur'ān was God's speech and eternal. In other words, Mu'tazilah argued that the Qur'ān was created by God and was not everlasting (Smart, 1992: 286). They defended their position on rational bases and were vehemently opposed to anthropomorphism. In other words, they regarded all verses in the Qur'ān referring to hands, sight, or sitting on the throne as metaphors (Smart, 1992: 286).

Reliance on reason led them to introduce new thoughts which appealed to reason and were apparently coherent to a degree, but often their basic ideology was opposed by the orthodoxy of *Ahl al-Sunnah* who argued that human intellect cannot necessarily fully comprehend all the beliefs. Consequently, the Mu'talizah ultimately denied beliefs in matters contrary to reason such as the night journey (*Mi'rāj*), the Bridge (*Sirāt*), the Fountain (*al-Kauthar*) and other such matters (Siddiqui and Siddiqui, 1987: 181). Like the Khawārij, a minority of the Mu'talizah deny the punishment of the grave. It has been suggested that they were influenced by Greek ideology and Aristotle, according to whom, every cause has its effect and so the universe is mechanical. They went as far as to suggest that those who believed in God having attributes negated *Tawḥīd*.

In response, the most decisive and coherent position was formulated by Imām Al-Ash'arī (260–324AH/873–935CE) and also Abu Manṣūr al-Māturīdī (d.333AH/944CE) among the *Ahl al-Sunnah wal-Jamā'at* who argued that anthropomorphist expressions are applied to God in a manner which humans cannot comprehend. This school eventually triumphed. Briefly, their preferred position being the affirmation of what Allah affirms and negating what has been negated such as determining any similitude between the Creator and created (42:11) and entrusting the exact meaning and precise details to Allah. The Ashā'irah regard the Qur'ān as eternal, being an attribute of God unlike the attributes of created beings. Thus, the Qur'ān is the uncreated Word of God. God is all-powerful and determines human actions, but individuals acquire responsibility for their actions (Smart, 1992: 286). Moreover, they establish the punishment of the grave through the Qur'ān; aḥadīth reported by multiple narrators and consensus.

The above categorisation lends itself to rationalists (Mu'tazilah) and the traditionalists (Ashā'irah). However, as this subject matter is intricate, some individual scholars are unlikely to be positioned neatly within all the viewpoints of an individual school. Some scholars adopted different standpoints in the course of their life.

The Khāwārij, those who 'went out' from 'Ali, as in their view, he disobeyed the Qur'ān, were pious believers who thought that actions were good or bad and that the Qur'ānic instruction to 'command good and prohibit evil' must be applied uncompromisingly. In addition, they interpret the Qur'ān and Sunnah literally and split the worldview between belief and unbelief. For them, any action opposing the law is tantamount to a grave sin which renders a person a non-Muslim, an apostate. In contemporary times, their stance has informed some radical groups. There is a moderate branch within them known as Ibādiyya (Esposito, 2016: 48–49).

The Murji'a postponed the judgement regarding the ultimate fate of major sinners, suspending the decision to God (Brown, 2017: 197). Qadariyyah, which should not be confused with the Qādiriyyah (a Sufi pathway), emphasise God's power over human freedom, whereas the Jabariyyah upheld a deterministic position arguing that humans had no choice or power to act on their own.

Tazkiyyah – Islamic spirituality

At the outset, it is important to emphasise that Islamic spirituality (*tazkiyyah*) is an essential process for the purification of the soul, heart, spirit, morals and ethics. One of the specific prophetic roles explicated by the Qur'ān for which Muḥammad (ﷺ) was sent, in addition to reciting the verses of God and teaching the Qur'ān and wisdom, was to perform the *tazkiyyah* of people, meaning to purify them (62:2). This involved correcting belief, rectifying behaviour and inner transformation. Despite the Qur'ān attributing the term *tazkiyyah* for this role, a related term, *taṣawwuf* (mysticism) – a term absent from the Qur'ān, from which Sufism has evolved – has gained popularity. The dimension of

Islam that is more concerned with the elevation of the inner relationship with God, over the centuries, came to be known as Sufism in English. Since it is a pathway to God (*al-Ṭarīq il-Allah*), the achievement of this objective is not confined to organised Sufi pathways (*ṭarīqah*, pl. *ṭuruq*). Spirituality is linked to the world of spirit, which in Islamic parlance is related to the word ***rūḥ***. Saritoprak (2018) finds spirituality more Qur'ānic than Sufi as it is more inclusive, concerning everyone.

To begin with, it is helpful to reflect on the term Sufi (feminine, Sufiyya) from which Sufism developed, as it affords many root meanings. The most common explanation is that it is derived from the Arabic *suf* (meaning 'wool'), based on the simple woollen tunic, which, according to some, was adorned by early Muslim ascetics. A second view suggests that it originates from the word *saf* ('row'), perhaps a reference to those Muslims who positioned themselves in the first row (*al-ṣaf al-awwal*) of prayer or Jihād unlike those lagging in matters of faith and spirituality (4:95). The name may have resulted from *suffah*, a term used to describe the veranda at the entrance of the Prophet's (ﷺ) mosque, where the *Ahl al-Suffah* (People of the Veranda) attached themselves (Hamid, 2016). These mostly underprivileged Muslims had given themselves to the Prophet (ﷺ), and were preoccupied with learning and worship and relying totally on God. The Qur'ān refers to such as *al-fuqarā'* (the poor), the singular of which is ***faqīr***, from which, in Persian, comes the word *darvish*, a term common in Sufi literature. Yet, another proposition is that Sufi stems from *safā* (purity), a quality typified in acts such as ritual ablution and Zakāt. Notwithstanding these, Hujwīrī offers the following explanation: 'He that is purified by love is pure, and he that is absorbed in the Beloved and has abandoned all else is a "Sufi"' (Baldock, 2004: 59–72; Hujwīrī, 2014: 30–34). In reality, a Sufi or Sufiyya should not describe themselves by this term but rather by *mutasawwif* or *mutasawwifa* (one who attempts to be a sufi) (Kerr, 2018a).

The objective is to fulfil the commitment made, as God loves those who are God-conscious (3:76). Often, *taqwa* is rendered as 'fearing' God. However, in reality it is the willing choice to allow one's conscience to be guided by God (Sonn, 2016). The essence of Islam is to gain God's pleasure in all spheres of life as encapsulated in the *Ḥadīth of Jibrīl* mentioned at the beginning of Chapter 5. You have read that the angel explained to Muḥammad (ﷺ) that *Iḥsān* is to worship in such a way that God is 'seeing', and if not, to know that God is 'looking'. Thus, in principle, Islamic spirituality is concerned with both the literal and inner meanings of the teaching of the Qur'ān and Sunnah to beautify the soul, develop beautiful virtue, and eliminate all vices. This makes Sufism a manifestation of *Iḥsān*, and as such, it would be misleading to conceive Sufism as another 'ism' in Islam (Kerr, 2018a). Simultaneously, it means that the *Ṭarīqah*

(Sufism) and *Sharīʻah (Law)* are interdependent. This implies that no Sufi is exempt from the obligation of obeying religious law (Hujwīrī, 2014). This is because this 'psycho-spiritual' aspect covers three levels of religions – *islam* (submission), *iman* (faith) and *ihsān* (spiritual excellence) (Hamid, 2016). Other related terms are ***maʻrifah*** and ***ʻirfān***.

Sufism is about seeking closeness with God through the adoption of a disciplinary pathway leading to spiritual elevation (Kerr, 2018a). The presence and company (*ṣuḥbat*) of the Prophet (ﷺ) transformed and purified the Companions. Some came to him with their personal inner struggles and he offered counsel. At times, he advised them collectively. Later, people gathered around individual figures who were distinguished for their knowledge, piety and scrupulousness in faith and practice and guided their immediate communities in matters spiritual. Gradually, these circles became formalised. Progressively, over the centuries, with the growth and spread of tutees from these circles, Sufi Pathways (*ṭuruq*) became crystallised and were named usually after their guide (Shaykh/***Pir***). Those affiliated to these guides came to be referred to by their Shaykh or order to which they associated themselves. Equally, it is important to recognise that some of them were masters in theology, *tafsir*, ḥadīth, *fiqh*, history and other disciplines.

Like other Islamic disciplines, here too, a spiritual guide is recommended. To create a formal bond, a seeker (***sālik/murīd***) would undergo a formal initiation (*bayʻah*) usually an oath consisting of repentance and intention to follow the teachings of Islam and to participate in certain practices (***wird/sulūk***). This establishes a *nisbah* (connection) through the spiritual mentor to the entire chain (*silsilah*) as far back as the Prophet (ﷺ) to transmit grace (*fayḍ*) and auspiciousness (*barakah*). The disciple maintains regular contact and follows the prescribed practices of the pathway. The major pathways discussed below have their own formulae. The 'progress' is 'monitored' by the mentor, often by gauging their inner state (*hāl*). Progress is acquired by way of spiritual exercises (*riyādat*), lengthy sacrifice, spiritual conditioning (*tarbiyyah*), constant *dhikr* and meditation (*murāqabah*) (Makki, 2010). It is important to acknowledge that, sometimes, these spiritual mentors proffer their grace to the public.

Once the Shaykh perceives that a disciple has attained a spiritual status (*hāl*) and stage (*maqām*), they are bestowed an authority (*khīlafah*) to initiate their own tutees and the system continues. Over the years, different sub-pathways and groups emerged within these numerous pathways. At the local level, some groups fell short and drifted away from the true teachings of the Qur'ān, Sunnah and normative beliefs, sometimes by fusing folk culture and customs, which are criticised. Often the synthesis of several faiths is deemed to be out of the fold of Islam or in need of reform. Thus, it is common among some of them to declare that 'there is no *Ṭarīqāh* without *Sharī'ah'*, meaning that following a Sufi path does not absolve one from the external and obligatory teachings and practices of Islam and the Sunnah.

The Sufi chain (*silsilah*) resembles *isnād*, discussed earlier, of the *muḥaddithūn*, whose lineage is traced to the Prophet (ﷺ) (Baldock, 2004: 63). In Islam, this *isnād* principle also applies to the transmission of Qur'ān recitation, the religious sciences (*tafsīr*, ḥadīth, *qirā'at*). As a general principle, the *isnād* mechanism is an Islamic knowledge-validation principle designed to guarantee connection to the Prophet (ﷺ) and his Companions.

The Pathways (sulūk)

The **Qādiriyyah** pathway has its roots in the teachings of Abd al-Qādir Gilānī, a Hanbalī (470–561AH/1077–1166CE) who has followers from Morocco to the Philippines. Prominent scholars like Al-Ghazāli, Aḥmad Sirhindi of India and Ibn Taymiyyah were Qādiris. Abu'l Ḥasan al-Shādhilī is said to be the founder of the Shādhiliyyah pathway whose influence is prominent in Morocco, Egypt and Syria. In West and North Africa, the Tijāniyyah and Qādiriyyah have a strong presence. In the Turkish region, the Mawlawiyya Order guided by Mawlānā Jalāl al-Din Rūmi has immense influence. The **Naqshbandiyyah** and **Chishtiyyah** are other major pathways and found in Central Asia, India and Pakistan as well as in Europe and the Americas (Nasr, 1993). In the UK, the Naqshbandiyyah is the most dominant Sufi order (Ansari, 2018).

Some of the great Sufi personalities were at the forefront to defend Islam intellectually as they had accessed higher metaphysical truths of Islam. Among these, Ibn Sinā and Al-Farābī are renowned. The Spaniards Ibn Bājjah, Ibn Ṭufayl and Ibn Masarrah also belonged to this category, whereas Ibn Bannā' al-Marrākushī and Nāṣīr ul-Dīn al-Ṭūsī were great scientists attached to Sufi pathways. In the arts, you will observe that they also contributed to calligraphy and poetry. In fact, most of them composed spiritual poetry. In polemical issues and in resisting the influence of other religions, secularism and materialism, Sufi Shaykhs offered rebuttals whilst bridging understanding at the same time. In other words, internally they preserved the light of faith and externally they spread and defended it. For example in resisting colonial subjugation of the French, British and Russian forces, the Amir al-Jazāiri of Algeria and others played key roles. The most popular order in Iran is the Ni'matullāhī (Nasr, 1993: 66–67).

From the above, within Sunnis, it would be questionable to attribute a sectarian label, 'Muslim Sufi community', to a single community on the basis that every Muslim is a 'sufi' as *Ihsān* is an individual aspiration and that Sufi pathways exist in most interpretations of Islam. This should also make it clear for you that an exclusive claim of being 'Sufi' by any Muslim community at the expense of another would be questionable. Neither is 'Sufism' a breakaway sect as suggested by Crotty and Lovat (2016: 65). That is not to suggest that some groups may not have taken on attributes of a 'sect'.

In addition, Ibn Taymiyyah (661–728AH/1262–1328CE), a great reformer, is generally known as a scholar of theology (*mutakallim*), a dialectic jurist (*faqih jadali*), a great scholar of ḥadīth and one thoroughly familiar with the exoteric sciences. However, Makki (2010), based on writings and contemporary testimonies, has demonstrated that Ibn al-Qayyim, al-Dhahabī, Ibn Kathīr and Ibn Rajab al-Ḥanbalī all regarded Sufism and the Sufis in a positive manner. Importantly, he has shown that Ibn Taymiyyah was a Shaykh of *Ṭarīqah* (spiritual mentor) and Imām of *Taṣawwuf* (spirituality) on the level of being a *qutub* (pole) in this field, in addition to being an Imām in various religious sciences and disciplines.

Moreover, you have learnt about some of the doctrinal and practical divergences between Sunnī and Shī'a. Here it is important to recognise that both are concerned with esoteric interpretations of the Qur'ān and Sharī'ah and with the outer life as well which means that 'the important mystical tradition of Sufism has seen a confluence of Shī'a and Sunnī consciousness' (Kerr, 2018a: 63).

You should also be aware that many academic institutes of learning (*madāris*) have Sufi 'lodges' (*khanqah)* and that many teachers within them are also seekers on the spiritual path. Some mosques incorporate activities of a *khānqah* within them. Over centuries, Sufis, rather than being passive, have played important roles in society and politics and have resisted regimes of various kinds. Many have also participated in armed Jihād (Nadwi, 2015). This means that Sufism is a global phenomenon.

Case study 11.1 Educational curriculum

Faduma's own educational experience was regrettably based on a narrow delivery of the humanities subject as the National Curriculum of her time was said to be Eurocentric. She had not really gained a basic understanding of other civilisations. She remembered learning about the Romans, Greeks and Egyptians and had enjoyed studying the Tudors and Victorians. In secondary school she had been introduced to the Dark Ages, the

Renaissance and the Enlightenment but barely about Muslim, or other non-Western, civilisations. At college, she learnt that what Europe called the Dark Ages was actually the peak of civilisation among Muslims and some eastern lands. Now, as a teacher, with some flexibility that the National Curriculum and academies offered, Faduma planned her history and geography lessons in such a way that they included Muslim heritage and other contributions. This provides her pupils a richer global perspective on human creativity.

Imagine you were made responsible for designing the curriculum of your school:

- ponder over the principles which would drive your curriculum
- deliberate on the extent to which your curriculum would prepare pupils for the twenty-first century
- importantly, in co-creating the curriculum, examine the way in which you would deal with any assumptions and biases.

Summary

In this chapter you have extended your understanding of the meaning, scope and aims of Sharīʿah. You have recognised it as a system of guidance covering all activities undertaken by Muslims so that they can follow the requirements of God and gain peace in this world and in the Hereafter. You have also discovered that the Sharīʿah has been codified using several sources. The chapter has also made the status and authority of the Sunnah clear which means you now know why some Muslims insist on following the model of Prophet Muḥammad (ﷺ). To determine the authentic practice of the Prophet (ﷺ), over time scholars of ḥadīth develop the science of ḥadīth. These aḥadīth have been compiled as books; you have become familiar with some of the most authentic collections. To understand and apply the Qur'ān and Sunnah, the legal jurists derived rules from these. Over time, several legal schools were established which most Muslims attach themselves to. You have also recognised the existence of some theological schools; it is here that questions about the faith of an individual become a matter of discussion. You have also seen that there are pathways followed by some Muslims to enhance their spiritual state and gain the pleasure of God.

Reflection tasks

- Describe the scope, aims and sources of Sharīʻah.
- Critically evaluate the status and authority of the Sunnah in Islam.
- Analyse the means through which Muslims have ensured the authenticity of aḥadīth.
- Examine the development of the schools of law (*fiqh*).
- What and how would you teach about *tazkiyyah* (spiritual development) in Islam?

Further reading

Rippin, A. (2008) *The Islamic World*. London: Routledge.

This is an excellent guide to the faith and culture of Muslims covering its geographical and historical diversity. It includes science and technology, philosophy, art, politics, film, law, Qur'ān, literature and the religious, intellectual and social dimensions.

Siddiqui, A.R. (2018) *Shariah: A Divine Code Of Life*. Markfield: The Islamic Foundation.

This concise text elucidates the meaning, scope and operation of Sharīʻah, assisting readers understand its importance for Muslims.

12

ISLAM AND CONTEMPORARY BRITAIN

In this chapter you will:

- learn about the historical settlement of Muslims in the British Isles
- reflect on the situation of Muslims in Europe
- discuss issues related to the Prevent strategy, Islamophobia and extremism
- analyse some of the different movements to which Muslims in the UK belong.

Overview

It is often assumed that the existence of Muslims in Britain is a direct result of the recent phenomena of migration. However, as teachers, you need to recognise that their history goes much further than this. Whilst it is true that the scale of their settlement has significantly increased post-Second World War, there is a long history of temporary and permanent settlements of Muslims in the British Isles (Gilliat-Ray, 2010).

History of Muslims in the UK

The first Muslims are said to have arrived in the late seventeenth-century as seamen ('*lascars*'), recruited in India for the East India Company. Initially, Muslims were transient settlers, usually unaccompanied single men with the intention of returning to their countries of origin. As temporary residents, Scourfield et al. (2013: 3–9) questioned whether they would have regarded themselves as British Muslims in any meaningful sense. In the past, there have been significant changes in the self-identification and description of Muslims. For example, terms such as 'Mohammadans', 'Moors' and 'Saracens' are now recognised as antiquated and disrespectful (Scourfield et al., 2013). Moreover, in recent decades, many Muslims in Britain have increasingly asserted their distinctive identity as Muslims whilst placing less emphasis on their ethnic origins.

Little is known about one of Britain's oldest Muslim communities. Yemeni Muslims arrived as imperial oriental sailors who have lived in Britain from the mid-nineteenth century. They married local British women, established networks of 'Arab-only' boarding houses and cafes, and founded the earliest mosques and religious communities. They encountered racism, discrimination and even deportation in the process (Seddon, 2014). Abdullah Quilliam (1856–1932), a Victorian gentleman and convert, opened what is argued to be the first mosque in Liverpool in 1887 by converting a terrace house (Geaves, 2017). Thereafter, came the purpose-built Shah Jahan Mosque in 1889 in Woking, Surrey, with substantial funds from Shah Jahan Begum (1838–1901CE) (Ansari, 2018).

Archival records also show that they initially arrived as traders, students, seafarers, and explorers from as early as the nineteenth century (Ansari, 2018). This is when a distinct Anglo–Muslim community started to emerge, ostensibly fuelled by Britain's colonial links with the Indian sub-continent. The port cities of South Shields, Cardiff and Liverpool played an important role at the turn of the twentieth century since Muslim seafarers from Yemen, Somalia and India were recruited to work on colonial shipping routes. After terminating their passage on ship, some would reside in dockland boarding houses and wait for the next outbound vessel. However, some adopted permanent residency, and consequently, the first embryonic British Muslim communities became established in or around port cities (Scourfield et al., 2013). Similarly, a number of Indian seamen were present in Scotland (Ansari, 2018).

In the centennial celebration of the First World War, some hitherto less known interesting information came to the attention of the public, which is useful for teaching. The Indian Army contributed about 1.5 million men and 173,000 animals to nearly all theatres of war across Europe, Africa and Asia. Importantly, one in every six soldiers of the British Empire was from the Indian sub-continent. This meant that its contribution was the equivalent of all the forces from the then dominions of the British Empire combined (namely Canada, Australia, New Zealand and South Africa). Of these around 400,000 were Muslims, which is about a third of the British Indian Army (see: ww1muslimsoldiers.org.uk/history/who-served-in-the-british-indian-army-during-the-first-world-war/).

The Second World War devastated the country. There was a need to rebuild towns and cities and with the expansion of manufacturing industries in the 1950s and 1960s, there was a requirement for unskilled and semi-skilled factory workers. To fill this shortage, Britain relied on countries with which it had colonial links to meet the labour shortages. Muslims also arrived because of a sense of loyalty to the British Empire after the wars (Scott-Baumann and Cheruvallil-Contractor, 2015: 18). Moreover, Muslim migration is linked to the British colonial past which facilitated the settlement of commonwealth citizens (Peuker and Akbarzadeh, 2014: 2).

Consequently, many relatively poor and uneducated migrant labourers arrived. Again these were mainly single men who looked forward to eventually returning home. Scourfield et al. (2013) suggest that at this time being a Muslim in Britain was a matter of belonging to a particular ethnic group. However, major legislative changes in the 1960s and 1970s had a huge impact on the composition of Muslim settlement in Britain. The law would restrict further large-scale immigration which meant that the possible reunification of families became a barrier. To avoid this, many South Asian men called over their wives and children from the sub-continent. This again became an inevitable consequence of families settling. Once their children were born and educated in Britain, they invested more time, energy and resources to develop community facilities, especially those that would support the religious identity, culture and spiritual well-being of the new British-born generation (Scourfield et al., 2013; Peuker and Akbarzadeh, 2014). The physical construction and appearance of institutions meant returning home was unlikely.

During the 1980s and 1990s, economic and political unrest in some parts of the world meant that Britain, mainly due to its old links, became an attractive destination for many educated and professional Iranians, Arabs, Kurds, Turks, and those escaping persecution in Bosnia, Somalia, Uganda and other African dictatorial states. More recently, the war in Afghanistan and Iraq has meant an increase of Muslims from these countries. In the past decade some Muslims from Syria have taken refuge as well. As a result, demographically, there was a significant change in the final decades of the twentieth century as Muslims in Britain further diversified. This pattern of migration continues to impact their internal diversity and social economic circumstances (Scourfield et al., 2013).

It is important not to lose sight of the growing community of reverts/converts to Islam. Conversion to Islam from many different ethnic backgrounds especially White British and African Caribbean is important because this can make the indigenisation of Islamic practice, thought and discourse in the West (Zebiri, 2008; cf. Scourfield et al., 2013). It is estimated that there are over 100,000 converts (Brice, 2010). This shows that the pattern of Muslim arrival is complex. Nevertheless, the periods of most intense movement coincided with the consolidation of Britain's position as a leading imperial and industrialised country at the end of the twentieth century (Ansari, 2018).

Voice of a Muslimah

I think education is vitally important (not just limiting it to secular education). It's what allows you to fully interact with the world you're living in. Education empowers you to make informed choices. An informed choice gives you the confidence to uphold your values and live up to your potential. Being Somali and Muslim I think education becomes even more important if you are a minority. If the educational gap is too wide the opportunity for inequality increases. (Batool, Somali, administrator, female)

The state and role of Muslims

In 2001, for the first time the question of religion was included in the census for the UK. As soon as the data were made public, it was evident that many Muslims in Britain were seriously affected by a range of social economic disadvantages, each compounding the other (Scourfield et al., 2013). In comparison to other faith communities, the vulnerable position of Muslims in relation to housing, education, employment and health became evident. The statistical information provided policymakers with evidence to provide strategies for alleviating this urban poverty in the longer term (Scourfield et al., 2013). The relative youthfulness of the Muslim communities is significant here. Approximately half of all Muslims in Britain are under the age of 25 and about half have been born in the UK itself (Scourfield et al., 2013).

It is also important to recognise that many families actively pursue educational success to enhance their socio-economic status. Nevertheless, it is the case that not all families have the knowledge or resources to enable this process to happen effectively (Scourfield et al., 2013). Therefore educational achievement remains a key challenge. As previously stated, Islam attributes a key role to mothers to nurture their future generation. This does not, therefore, mean that all women who are mothers are confined to this role, as Muslim communities in Britain are producing female doctors, teachers and professionals in varied fields whilst simultaneously fulfilling their other domestic responsibilities of motherhood.

This overview of Muslim history, demographics, patterns of settlement and relative success makes it difficult to speak about a 'Muslim community' for there is considerable diversity within these communities with regard to language, culture, ethnicity, race, geographical location, religious persuasion and economic characteristics. Nevertheless, many do retain strong transnational kinship links across the globe, as well as an over-riding identification with the worldwide Muslim population (the Ummah) (Scourfield et al., 2013).

This diversity and the relative proximity within which they live is seen as unparalleled in the UK. The Pakistani Barelwī co-exist with the Turkish Sufī, the Iranian Shīʿa and the Saudi Arabian **Wahhābī**. These groups tend to be aware of how different they are, and, as minority communities, they are equally aware of how similar they are. Some of these differences are manifested in their different languages, cuisines and dress codes. When these cultural differences are expressed in religion, shades of Islam emerge. For example, the language of the Friday speech may be different, women will adorn the *hijāb* in culturally unique ways and there is a preference for attending study circles and attachment to scholars. Some of these differences will run deeper to include different interpretations of history, rites and rituals, ḥadīth and aspects of belief (Scott-Baumann and Cheruvallil-Contractor, 2015: 161). Even then, rigid demarcations are not the norm in some communal events, such as funerals, weddings and charity, and in personal activities that take place in a fluid and hybrid way. There is also a strand of Muslim 'feminism' that features within this matrix, some of whom challenge patriarchy and with others finding complex ways of defining and expressing themselves in Islam.

As discussed above, demographically the Muslim population is young with 68.75 per cent being under the age of 35. Many were born and educated in Britain and have imbued the values and ethos of their environment: unlike previous generations, they are not only aware of, but also exercise, the British civil system and social practices. Some are educated, culturally savvy and confident (Scott-Baumann and Cheruvallil-Contractor, 2015). It is these young people who are directing and shaping numerous initiatives in many areas of life aimed at expressing their everyday lived experiences. The 2014 'poppy hijāb' campaign is an example of the bridges that these youth are building between their religion and their nation (Scott-Baumann and Cheruvallil-Contractor, 2015). They are also consumers who have the buying power and tastes to have an impact on sales, marketing and branding strategies of large multinational companies. Now that some families are in their third or fourth generation, perhaps the time has come for you, as teachers, to examine the contention that Islam in Britain is a 'migrant' religion.

Others have argued that the Muslim communities in Britain are uniquely positioned to participate in international debates around the meaning and significance of Islam in the contemporary world (Peicker and Akbarzadeh, 2014). As a relatively youthful population with access to media technologies and many freedoms, they are contesting ideologies both from within their own communities and those related to materialism, secularisation and the hegemony of the powerful (Scourfield et al., 2013). There is a wider scope for them to exercise individual choice regarding religious matters. Since Islam is not part of the dominant social norms of society, religious education and nurture is not taken for granted. Hence, the need for religious activism. Nevertheless, they are part of global networks which comprise missionary organisations, religious entrepreneurs, and various religious and political movements. Thus they have access to a wide range of resources from which to choose the place of Islam in the West (Scourfield et al., 2013).

Muslims in Europe

In the European context, the history of Islam goes far beyond the recent economic migration and their exotic presentations influenced by travelogues and historical points of interest. Islam was known by the people of Britain from the seventh century because of the Muslim incursion into Europe, with Arabs coming as close to England as Poitiers in France in 732 (Ansari, 2018). There is sporadic evidence of Muslim visits to England during this period. Al-Idrīsī (1100–1166CE), the North African Arab scholar patronised by the Sicilian kings, travelled to the west of England (Ansari, 2018: 29). In addition to this, Aslan (2012) notes that Muslims are seen through the stereotypical perspective of being the unskilled labour force without education levels residing in impoverished conditions. However, reflecting on the situation of Austria, Aslan (2012) suggests that such an image in the daily encounter with Muslims, who number twenty million across Europe, obscures the history of Islam in Skopje, a city older than Istanbul, and that the Islamic theological faculty in Sarajevo has educated Imāms since the sixteenth century. Moreover, in the University of Vienna, Islamic law and Oriental languages have been taught since the eighteenth century and there was a permanent office for a Muftī in Vienna. Practically, the history of Muslims in Spain offers you many opportunities for classroom work in various subjects.

Unsurprisingly, therefore, the exclusivist and exceptionalist claim regarding Europe is also being revised. Muslims in Britain are asking how to define Europe and the 'West' and simultaneously what Islam is. Khan (2017), in documenting Western Muslim biographies, questions why Christianity, despite being born in the Middle East, has always been considered to be a 'Western' faith and why Islam is deemed to be an alien intrusion into the Western hemisphere. As such, Khan (2017) argues that Islam is as much a 'Western' faith and culture as Christianity, and therefore any attempt to project Islam as an alien and foreign intrusion into the western hemisphere is historically, culturally and geographically questionable as well as factually incorrect. Similarly, the history of Muslims in the British Isles is often ostensibly seen through the lens of migration. However, Matar (1998) has shown that these relationships and interactions have been much earlier and more complex. Between 1158 and

1685, Islam, he concludes, left its mark in Britain in a way that was unparalleled by other non-Christian civilisations which Britons encountered. It has been noted that Muslims have always participated in the governance of their places of residence; Muslims serve in parliaments, the military, government agencies, police, and play a role in local and national agencies. Some in the West ask whether Muslims can be loyal citizens of the West. In turn some Muslims ask whether the West will truly accept their loyal citizenship or whether they will remain under suspicion even in their country of birth (Esposito and Delong-Bas, 2018). To this end, *The Muslim Museum Initiative* is an organisation which aims, using a timeline, to explore the history and heritage of Muslims in Britain, which you might find useful.

Voice of a Muslim

As a British Muslim, I am concerned to see a phase in society where crime, especially hate crime and Islamophobia has become normalised. Schools can be the best place to start educating about how to confront and tackle Islamophobia. As hate crimes and populist groups in Europe rise, the need to develop better training for teachers and parents is really significant. Schools can act as that safe place where people can discuss and debate issues without the fear of prejudice. If we can educate young people about the need for tolerance and humanity we are more likely to live in a society where prejudice and bigotry are challenged. (Sarfarāz, Pakistani, community activist, male)

Muslims among Muslims

In countries where Muslims are in the majority, the extent to which Sharīʿah is implemented varies. There are countries where the system is merely secular, while others apply Sharīʿah as their legal code or as a hybrid system which blends European colonial legal structures with parts of Sharīʿah. Thus, some Muslims in Britain will have been exposed to and experienced Sharīʿah as a system of governance in varied ways. This may also influence their relationship and understanding of it.

However, the discourse of Muslims in Europe is in part couched in a language which makes use of terms which induce fear. These include 'extremist Islam', 'Islamism', 'political Islam', 'fundamentalism', 'revivalism' and 'radicalisation of

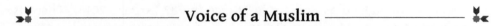

European Muslims'. Their usage leads to an oversimplification (Peter, 2014: xv). Nevertheless, they are still applied in categorising various groups of Muslims. In addition, these groups are generally understood through the lens with which they are classified today, i.e., radical. However, these terms are frequently criticised due to their vagueness. Thus, it is necessary to speak of them as specific groups rather than political or radical Islam (Peter, 2014: 5). Also, these groups should not be read as offshoots of groups in Muslim countries, otherwise this ignores the specific European context under which they function and of their lives in Europe (Peter, 2014).

Scholars have attempted to map the various groups within Muslim communities and to establish links between European Muslim actors on the one hand and the respective Islamic movements in other parts of the world (Peter, 2014: 84). In some cases, these links are uncontroversial such as sections of Hizb ut-Tahrir who consider themselves part of a global movement with a message intended to transcend any geographical divisions and create a global khilāfah. However, for others, ascertaining exactly what connects them to Islamic movements in Asia and Africa and in what ways they converge or diverge is challenging. Nevertheless, there is considerable diversity within them. Some groups acknowledge their historical links but do not indicate any institutional affiliation and are independent in their activities. However, they are deeply embedded in Europe and have clear links abroad. Importantly, experts note that it is not always possible to ascribe a uniform outlook to members as these groups espouse different programmes and ideas as well as a lack of clarity on how a group 'belongs' to a given Islamic movement (Peter, 2014: 84). There are polemics of various kinds which these groups target at each other; sometimes they spill over into taking control of a mosque (Nielsen and Otterbeck, 2016: 148).

These groups are highly diverse with respect to their histories, their aims and the contexts in which they are rooted as shown in Table 12.1. Nevertheless, what they do have in common in the West is their perception of being religious in ways which are both abnormal and unacceptable (Peter, 2014: 3). It is this perception, argues Peter (2014), which is the common element in the broad variety of names given to them. Some of these groups are also conceived as being exceptional and reactionary as they emerged out of the crisis following colonialism and modernisation. In other words, they are thought to be temporal. Such a reductive perception comforts not only geopolitical interests in the West but also the possibility of maintaining the belief that the process of secularisation held typical for Europe has universal value and defines the basic route to follow for the rest of the world (Peter, 2014). It is important to recognise that not all belong to those listed in Table 12.1, for instance the Gülen movement is also popular among some Turkish communities (Alam, 2019).

Table 12.1 Muslim movements

Wahhābī	• Founded by Muḥammad ibn 'Abd al-Wahhāb (1703–1792CE) in Saudi Arabia • Decline of Muslims due to not practising Islam of the Prophet and his Companions • Solution was to return to pristine Islam identical to the early generation (Alkhateeb, 2017)
Muslim Brotherhood (*Jamā'at al-Ikwān al-Muslimūn*)	• Inception by Ḥasan Al-Bannā' (1906–1949CE) in Egypt • Emerged from social, political, economic and cultural changes, and anti-colonial struggles • Jamāl Uddin Afghānī (1838–1897CE) and Muḥammad 'Abduh (1849–1906CE) preferred a revolutionary approach and a more gradual and 'rationalist' model of re-reading sources • Muḥammad 'Abduh and Rashīd Riḍā (1865–1935CE) witnessing state secularism, ablution of Khilāfah (Caliphate), and division of the Ottoman Empire defended the return to the 'times of the pious predecessors' (*al-salaf al-sāliḥ*) to renew the interpretation of religion and awaken society • Did not call themselves Salafis and were critical of *taqlīd* and scornful of Sufism (Brown, 2017) • A movement to 'advise' government authorities on how to govern in an 'Islamic' way and not to establish an 'Islamic state' (Rodrigo, 2014)
Deobandī movement	• In 1866, scholars established a *Dār ul 'ulum* in a town called Deoband, India • Developed into Deobandī 'thought' • Characterised by 'puritanical' tendencies of folk Islam • Insists on learning Qur'ān, ḥadīth and Sharī'ah and on individual spiritual discipline, learned through individual instructions from authorised Sufi shaykhs (Nielsen and Otterbeck, 2016)
Tablīghī Jamā'at (Society for Propagation)	• Founded by Mawlānā Ilyās (1885–1944) in India • Apolitical and missionary movement within Islam • Focusses on personal piety • Emphasises change in thoughts and actions • Rooted in the Deobandī movement

Barelwī/Sunnī	• Mawlānā Ahmad Raza Khan (1856–1921CE) considered the founder • Keeps Prophet Muḥammad (ﷺ) central (Sanyal, 2005) • Rituals are mediated through intercession of spiritual leaders and popular festivals of their birth (***urs***) • Asserts the popular features of Sufi and folk traditions • Self-identify as the *Ahl al-Sunnah wal-Jamā'at* (Sunnī)
Ahl al-Ḥadīth ('People of the Prophetic Traditions')	• Reformist movement emerged in India in the late nineteenth century • Distinguished by their stance on theology, jurisprudence and ritual • Stresses the Qur'ān and authentic Sunnah; emphasises following of early people of ḥadīth or pious predecessors (*salaf*) • Rejects institutional forms of Sufi orders • Adheres to independent reasoning (*ijtihād*) rather than *taqlīd* (following) • Rejects visitations to graves of 'saints' • Sufism is restricted to individuals (Nielsen and Otterbeck, 2016)
The Jamā'at-i-Islamī	• Founded by Sayyid Abul A'la Mawdūdī (1903–1979CE) • First to develop the self-contained modern theory of an Islamic state • Trained in secular and religious institutions, influenced by the British interference with the Ottoman empire and the failed campaign of the Indian independence movement • Western political conceptions of secularism and nationalism were incompatible with Islam • In UK, significantly transformed (McLoughlin, 2014) • Thoroughly engaged with Western philosophical thought and used it as a prism to perceive the Qur'ān and Sunnah (Hartung, 2014)

(Continued)

Table 12.1 (Continued)

Salafiyya ('pious predecessors')	• Self-identify themselves as the 'saved' group • Complete repudiation of idolatry in all its forms • Criticises modern political leaders for substituting God's commands for man-made laws, Sufis, Shī'as and the classical Muslim law schools (Brown, 2017) • Consider Qur'ān and authenticated ḥadīth sufficient • Presented as methodology (Salafī), political ideology (Wahhābī) and creed (Atharī)
Hizb ut-Tahrīr (Party of Liberation)	• Converted Islam into a revolutionary, self-sufficient, rational ideology and its totalising politicisation of religion • Raison d'être is the reunification of all the Muslim lands and reconstruction of a modern Khilāfah • Refuses to recognise the legitimacy of current Muslim governments (Hamid, 2014; 2016)
The Aḥmadiyya/Qadiani Community	• Mirza Gulam Aḥmad (1835–1908CE) of Qadiyan, India, Pakistan claimed to be a prophet hence out of Sunnī • HQ in Rabwah, Pakistan, then in the UK • Seen as the promised messiah (Jesus ['Isā]), claimed to be Al-Mahdi and the last avatar of Vishnu • Declared out of the fold of Islam • Two groups; Qadianis and the Lahori Party • Observes conventional Sunnī expressions, involved in social projects (Glassé, 2013; Nielsen and Otterbeck, 2016)

The Prevent strategy

Since the 1990s, counter-terrorism has become a big business and self-perpetuating industry whose effects on society have been questioned in terms of its cohesion and happiness (Fergusson, 2017: 2). To assess the 'Islamist' threat, Fergusson (2017: 3) travelled the country talking to Muslims in mosques, shops, schools, homes, community centres, and on streets. In his encounters with Muslims of different characteristics, including a month of fasting, he found some of the following which are supplemented with research:

- A community resentful at the collective blame apportioned to them for the proportionately tiny number of violent extremists among them.
- The mood in many cities is tinged by fear, paranoia, anger, confusion and under assault from many directions, including from the government itself.
- The government wants British Muslims to integrate better but its policies are in danger of producing the opposite effect and creating a wedge between Muslims and the rest.
- The Prevent and Counter-terrorism and Security Act of 2015 is having a negative impact on society.
- Case studies presented to the Independent Reviewer of Terrorism Legislation showed that Prevent has led to young children being viewed through the lens of security and has led to the self-censorship of young children in schools.
- Some British Muslims support a range of counter-measures, including government intervention, and reject the assertion that the Prevent agenda is an anti-Muslim initiative.
- Academic research found that Prevent does not make society safer, but sows fear, suspicion and mistrust, curtails engagement in political debates and results in self-censoring by some Muslims (Versi, 2015; Frampton et al., 2016; Fergusson, 2017; Ghani and Nagdee, 2019; Saeed, 2019).

In regard to the contemporary issue of terrorism, the Muslim leadership, especially Imāms, are invariably embroiled in the security framework and expected to act as counter-radicalisation forces. Certainly, Imāms do condemn violent extremism and exhort people to live in harmony. However, to lay the onus on them is to misplace the sophisticated nature of radicalisation (Peter and Ortega, 2014). Some youth, rather than being lectured on extremism, would prefer them to focus on making Islam relevant and meaningful to life in Britain. Some expect their Imāms to be social media savvy not just for charismatic personalities but, importantly, to speak up against establishmentarianism, injustice, war, corruption, the double standards of 'Western' powers and exploitation which is what is absent from many mosque platforms. It is this that many yearn for from their leadership – to be true to the principles they stand for.

Muslims are no longer the insignificant religious minority which they once were in the UK. Notwithstanding the fact that there is much misinformation about Muslims in Britain, this makes their future and that of Britain intertwined. For most Muslims it is not paradoxical to hold both national and religious identities. The vast majority of them feel loyal to Britain and, far from being 'secret enemies of the state', feel it is a good place to live and practise their faith freely. Some insist Britain is a great country and feel proud to be British (Frampton et al., 2016). However, for some, patriotism exceeds sentiments attached to the nation and its symbols, and is about community values (Fergusson, 2017).

You have learnt about some of the values which underpin Muslim life not only in Britain but everywhere, and may have reflected on how similar they may be with the 'old-fashioned' Britain such as the significance placed on family, respect for authority, sense of community, generosity and hard work. For example, in Ramaḍān 2016, the Charity Commission reported that they raised around £100 million, the equivalent of £38 a second (Fergusson, 2017).

As teachers, it is crucial to be aware of some of the challenges Muslims are facing. Their involvement in crime, gangs, drug use and trafficking is of serious concern. Some mosques have initiatives to tackle these societal problems but many are beyond the reach of these, mainly young people. Moreover, it is reported that there are more than 12,500 British Muslims in prisons which is almost 15 per cent of all prisoners and three times the proportion of Muslims in the country as a whole (Fergusson, 2017). Over the years, there has been a noticeable increase in seminars and publications on the art and science of good parenting to assist Muslims to respond to such challenges. For example, some local institutes and mosques have participated in partnerships with other civic and faith organisations in anti-gun campaigns. It would be wrong to indicate, however, that mosques are only places of worship and religious education. Increasingly they are becoming sites of diverse activities. Thus it is now commonplace to find Muslim Scout Groups hosted in a mosque, regular social activities for men and women, classes in English for adults or school tuition for younger children. Larger mosques may even host a gym, restaurant and other facilities on site along with the prayer hall. Some mosques provide services to the wider public also, and not just the immediate Muslim community, through employment workshops or food banks for the poor (as you read in Chapter 9).

It is also clear that the often depicted religious character and general social conservatism of British Muslim communities should not detract from the essentially secular character of the lifestyle of some Muslims. In terms of their everyday concerns and priorities, British Muslims answer no differently from their non-Muslim neighbours. When asked what the most important issues facing Britain today are, the most likely answer was NHS/hospitals/healthcare (36 per cent), unemployment (32 per cent) and immigration (30 per cent). Contrary to what is often asserted on both sides of the political spectrum, the priorities and everyday concerns of the overwhelming majority of Muslims are inherently secular (Frampton et al., 2016).

Case study 12.1 Belonging

Ṭāhir had recently arrived in the Foundation Stage in a school which could be described as 'monocultural', where there were very few pupils from black and minority ethnic groups. His parents were both professional and had moved from a larger city to a smaller town. The parents confirmed that Ṭāhir was their only child who was happy and had confidently gone to school. At home he enjoyed playing with toys, constructing things and liked to be read to. However, Ṭāhir would come to school each morning clutching a crunched head covering (*topi/qalansuwa*) in his hand. Both the class teacher and the teaching assistant (TA) noticed that he was apparently feeling uneasy and seemed to take comfort in holding onto his cap. The reservation became more evident immediately after his parents left him. Both adults decided to support and settle him as quickly as possible. Mark, the TA, spoke with his parents to find out more about Ṭāhir so that he could prepare and plan resources and activities for the full participation of Ṭāhir. When the father came to collect Ṭāhir, the classroom teacher shared the plan. As part of a series of strategies, on the first day the TA provided in a corner an investigative area with different kinds of artefacts, images, books and everyday material reflecting his religious and cultural background. During child-led play, as the class teacher was working with a group, Ṭāhir was seen by both adults drifting towards the corner. He was exploring the resources there and appeared to be relaxed. Suddenly, he put on his hat on and walked to a table and joined in with a group. He knew he belonged to the classroom. Thereafter, the TA and the teacher reflected on their successful practice.

This case study leads you to reflect on:

- the ways in which the staff created an enabling environment for Ṭāhir
- how an effective child-centred surrounding was created
- the nature of the changes made by the staff and the extent to which the resources focussed on the experiences rather than the product
- the values demonstrated by all adults.

Summary

This chapter has demonstrated to you the long history of Muslim settlements in the British Isles and Europe. Their increase in recent years is attributed to communal and socio-political factors. A high percentage of contemporary Muslims were born in the UK and live happily amongst secular western contexts; some are observant of their faith requirements whilst others can be described as being nominal.

In addition to their diverse ethnicities, languages, length of stay, varying levels of religious practice, there exists considerable variation within Islam. There are groups and sub-groups, many of which due to brevity could not be included. Some of these groupings are based on matters of religion and expression of faith, theological and philosophical, and socio-political ideologies and methodologies. Several have been discussed which are distinct to the South Asian diaspora as a reflection of their historical and demographic representation of Islam in the UK. There are groupings among the Shīʿa as well. Out of this colourful matrix, there are some who are distancing themselves from the ethno-cultural orientations of the previous generation and religio-political perspectives and creating a version which they term British Islam.

Reflection tasks

- Consider the historical relationship of Muslims and the British Isles.
- Examine the relevance of highlighting different perspectives among Muslims.
- Discuss the factors which lead to the development of some revival movements.
- Analyse the concerns raised about the Prevent Agenda.
- Evaluate the future of Muslims in Europe.
- Describe the future of Islam and Muslims in the UK.

Further reading

Ansari, H. (2018) *The Infidel Within: Muslims in Britain Since 1800*, revised and updated edn. London: Hurst & Co Publishers, Ltd.

This book uses archival research and first-hand experience of Muslims in Britain. It covers settlement, identity, women, families, education, mobilisation of Muslims in political, religious, economic life and their relationship with modernity, secularism and democracy.

Bowen, J.R. (2016) *On British Islam Religion, Law, and Everyday Practice in Sharī'a Councils.* New Woodstock: Princeton University Press.

This is an historical and ethnographic examination of Islamic institutions focussing on Sharī'ah councils, and their interpretation and application of Islamic law. It shows these councils as a unique experiment in meeting Muslims' needs in a secular context.

GLOSSARY

Abyssinia – Ethiopia; ancient Christians of the Monophysite church (Arabic: *Ḥabashah*)

Adab – politeness, courtesy, morals, also literature (pl. *Ādāb*)

Ahādīth – lit. report, narrative, speech; technically traditions relating to the sayings, actions, approval of the Prophet (ﷺ) as conveyed by the Companions (sing. *ḥadīth*)

Aḥkām – rules (sing. *ḥukm*)

Ahl al-Sunnah wal-Jamā'at – people of the community and the Sunnah who accept the legitimacy of the first four *khulafā'* (sing. *khalīfah*) and their successors; their law-making process is guided by the community and legal experts; refers to Sunnī community

Ākhirah – lit. the final or second; Afterlife, Hereafter, Life after death

Aḳhlāq – character, conduct, ethics, morals (sing. *ḳhulq*)

'Ālam al-arwāh – world of souls

Al-Ashhur al-Ḥurum – sacred months; four months wherein war was prohibited; sacred for the gravity of committing a sin; sacred due to the position Allah awarded them

al-Baqī' – the cemetery of Madīnah near the mosque of the Prophet (ﷺ); also Jannatul Baqī' (Garden of Heaven) where some wives, relatives and many Companions are buried

Al-Firdaws – name of the highest level of paradise; Firdawsī (940–1020 CE) was a famous poet and composer of Shahnamah

Al-Ḥudaybīyyah – a plain approximately 12 km south of Makkah; a famous battle

Al-lawḥ al-maḥfūẓ – lit. a slate or board; it is the Preserved Tablet on which Allah has recorded everything that is to happen and the Qur'ān as well (85:22)

Al-Nabī al-Ummī – lit. unlettered prophet, an epithet of the Prophet (ﷺ)

Al-Qurṭubī – from Córdoba, the theologian Imām Abu ʻAbdullah Muḥammad ibn Aḥmad ibn Abū Bakr (1214–1273CE)

Al-salaf al-ṣāliḥ – the first three generations of Muslims to which all Muslims look upon as a model; often exclusive claims are made by those following the Salafī movement

Amulet – usually calligraphic verse of the Qur'ān sealed in cloth, jewellery or leather worn around the neck or elsewhere to ward off evil or *jinn*; in West Africa gri-gri; in North Africa hijāb/hamā'il; and among South Asians ta'wīz

ʻAqīqah – slaughtering an animal for the newborn; includes a series of birth rituals – *tahnīk* (rubbing lips or gums), *ḥalaq* (shaving), *tasmiyah* (naming), *khitān* (circumcision)

A-q-l – mind, reason, intellect

Aṣḥāb al-kahf – lit. companions of the cave; 'Christians' slept for years avoiding cruelty; 'Seven Sleepers'; Qur'ān is unconcerned with identifying who and how many they were (18:10-31)

Aṣḥāb al-Ṣuffāh – lit. people of the bench; poor Muslims who were found around a bench/veranda of the Prophet's (ﷺ) mosque who were sustained by him whilst he simultaneously lived in poverty

ʻAwrah – that part of the body which is not permissible to expose

Barakah – blessing of Allah; sensation felt at sacred places; spiritual power effulging from holy people or objects (pl. barakāt)

Bid'ah – innovation; addition to religion; deviating from the Islamic tradition

Chishtiyyah – A Sufi *ṭarīqah* linked to Khwaja Mu'inuddin Chishti (1138–1236CE)

Companion – (Ar. *Saḥābī*), one who had been in the company of the Prophet (ﷺ) as a Muslim

Dajjāl – the great imposter to appear at the end of time leading evil forces

Dār – lit. house; usually used with educational institutes or medical centres

Dars – lesson; could be Islamic sermon

Dars-i-Niẓāmi – the syllabus taught in some Dārul ʻUlūm especially among South Asians; also the Niẓāmī curriculum/method of education

Dārul ʻUlūm – lit. House of Knowledge; generally educational institutes of higher learning in Islam where students study Islamic sciences (see madrasah below)

D-b-r – to reflect (4: 82)

Dhū al-Qarnayn – lit. 'two horned'; to some Alexander the Great; traveller to East and West (18:83)

Dīnār – a monetary unit of the time which is still used in some countries today

Duā' – supplication to Allah; petitioning; prayer

Duā's (Child's Gift) – a book for children consisting of supplication for various occasions and actions, a primer used in some maktabs

Eschatology – branch of theology that is concerned with death, the Afterlife, and the end of the world, Hell, Heaven

Faqīh – erudite scholar, jurist (pl. fuqahā')

Faqīr – from (Ar.) '*faqr*' meaning poverty; ascetic adopting poverty, worship, minimises possessions; seeker on the spiritual path in need of God

F-h-m – to understand (21:79)

Fidyah – lit. redemption; expiation of shortcomings by means of fasting, sacrifice, feeding the poor, of giving oneself

Fiqh – lit. comprehension; the science of jurisprudence

Fiṭrah – natural disposition; primordial nature; harmony between God, humans and creation

F-k-r – to ponder (2:219; 30:84)

F-q-h – to comprehend, to learn (4:78; 18:93)

Fuqahā' – one who comprehends; a jurist; a scholar of Islamic law; expert in jurisprudence (sing. Faqih); ; (f. faqihah)

Ghayb – the unseen

Ghazawāt – lit. a raid; battle and war; also for *jihād*; ghāzi – a warrior; (sing. ghazwah)

Ghusl – a full bath or shower whereby water reaches all parts of the body, mouth and nostrils

Hābil – a son of Adam, the one killed by Qābil; Abel

Ḥadath – impurities; major removed by ghusl and minor removed by wuḍū'; affect the execution of several acts of worship

Hadī – sacrifice of animal offered by the Qārin and Mutamatti' (types of Ḥajj) pilgrim, distinct from 'Udhiyya

Ḥadīth – lit. news, story; the saying, action and approval of Muḥammad (ﷺ) (pl. ahādīth)

Hagar – mother of Ismā'īl, wife of Abraham

Ḥāji – the title given to a male who has performed the pilgrimage (Ḥajj)

Ḥajjah – the title given to a woman who has performed the pilgrimage (Ḥajj)

Ḥākim – a ruler, governor, judge

Ḥalāl – lit. released; opposite of *ḥarām*; a term denoting that a certain act is permissible and approved for Muslim usage, not only in terms of diet

Ḥalaqah – lit. ring; study circle consisting of a teacher and students

Ḥarām – lit. forbidden; opposite of *ḥalāl*; a term denoting that a certain act is forbidden and disapproved for usage, not only in terms of diet

Ḥarīm – lit. restricted space; in some Muslims' homes the area dedicated for women, the origin of the English ḥarem; ḥaram

Ḥawāriyyūn –lit. faithful friend; disciples of Jesus; features four times (sing. ḥawārī) in the Qur'ān

Ḥawza – title of theological seminary among Shī'a; also al-Ḥawza al-'Ilmīyya; an institute educating religious students in Qur'ānic sciences, theology, jurisprudence and other sciences

Ḥenna – a paste made from plant leaves used for decorating parts of the body; a dye

Ḥijāb – lit. partition; a curtain (33:53); metaphysically that which separates humans from Allah; female covering, also *purdah, burqa, telekung, thawb, ḥaiak, chador*

Ḥijāz – a region; the area from the Red Sea coast of Arabia and to the north to Syria, the western region of Saudi Arabia which separates the east, south and other west regions; Hejāz

Hijrī – name of the calendar Islamic, from Hijrat (migration of the Messenger (ﷺ))

Ḥisāb – accountability; reckoning, accounting

Ibn – son of; *bint* daughter of

'Īd – celebration, happy occasion; Eīd alternative spelling to 'Īd

'Īd al-`Adhā – it is independent of the day of 'Arafat (pilgrimage), marked by those not on Ḥajj, commemorates Prophet Ibrāhīm's willingness to sacrifice his son, lasts between 2–4 days

'Īd al-Fiṭr – the annual Muslim Feast of the Fast-Breaking marked on the first of Shawwāl showing the end of Ramaḍān; also Ramazān Bayrāmı in Turkish, 'Lebaran in Indonesia'

Iḥsān – to be in a constant state of awareness of God; excellence; to do good

Ijmā' – consensus; a principle of Islamic jurisprudence; the agreement of jurists which becomes a legitimate basis as a source of law

'Ilm – knowledge of Islam; science (pl. 'ulūm)

Imām – lit. leader; for Sunnis usually the ritual prayer leader; in Shī'ism divinely chosen leaders as successors of the prophet; honorific title Imām Razī; leaders of a school of thought like Imām Abū Ḥanīfah and ḥadīth Imām al-Bukhārī

'Irfān – recognition; gnosis; the means to realising the Divine; philosophical school like *ishrāq*; a name

Jamā'at – congregation, organisation, participating in an outing in Tablīghī Jamā'at

Jāmi' – large mosque, school, university; gatherer; one of the names of God

J-h-l – to be ignorant (6:111; 12:89)

Jihād – root is *juhd* meaning to exert oneself, to struggle and be willing to fight for God and good against evil, to strive for self-purification, armed defence of the faith

Ka'bah – the cuboid structure in the middle of Makkah built by Ibrāhīm and Isma'īl

Kāhin – soothsayer, wizard; priest; believed to possess supernatural powers (f. *kāhinah*)

Karbala' – the plain in modern day 'Irāq where Al-Ḥusaīn the son of 'Alī was martyred

Kātib – writer

Khalīfah – (caliph) a deputy; refers to the successor to Prophet Muḥammad (ﷺ) as leaders of the Sunnī community; a leader

Khānqāhs – Sufi lodge, convent; place for devotional gathering with other facilities

Khaybar – an oasis which had a fortress situated about 90m from Madīnah, where the Battle of Khaybar was fought in 7AH/629CE

Khiḍr – lit. the green one; the person mentioned in (18:60–82) whose company Mūsā sought and who was taught a certain knowledge (18:65)

Khimār – face/head female covering in its divergent forms (pl. khumur)

Khuṭbah – a sermon – an address delivered before prayer on Friday and at a wedding ceremony, and after prayers on ʿĪds – acts as a reminder and counsel delivered by a *khatīb* (speaker) or Imām

Kufr – unbelief, rejection, ingratitude, conceal

La yafqahūn – those who do not understand (9:87; 9:127)

La yaʻqilūn – those who do not reason (2:171; 59:14)

La-yubsirūn – those who do not see (2:17; 7:198)

Laylat al-Barā'ah – Night of forgiveness, night preceding the 15th; or Laylat Nisf min Shaʻbān night of the middle of Shaʻbān, also Shab-i-Barāt

Laylat al-Isrā' wa al-Miʻrāj – lit. Night of Ascent; before migration, the journey undertaken by Prophet Muḥammad (ﷺ) from earth to heaven

Laylat al-Qadr – lit. night of destiny or power; the night of revelation of Qur'ān, odd night of last ten days in Ramaḍān, usually taken as 27th; destinies set in this night

Madhhab – lit. 'way'; one of the recognised schools of law (pl. madhāhib); religion; maslak

Madīnah – City of the Prophet (Madīnat an Nabī) in modern-day Saudi Arabia; death and burial place of Muḥammad (ﷺ)

Madrasah – lit. place of lessons; a college wherein Islamic law, jurisprudence, Qur'ān, ḥadīth are taught at higher level, also a secondary school; a maktab

Maḥārim –lit. the impediments; those with whom marriage is impermissible (sing. maḥram)

Mahdī – lit. guided one; a future figure in Islam who will appear at the end of the world to establish justice; for Twelver Shīʻites the Twelfth Imām who entered into occultation

Majlis – lit. a place of sitting; gathering of various kinds – government council, education circle, session, lecture

Ma'jūj – Magog; violent people who will feature towards the end of time

Makkah – city in modern-day Saudi Arabia; birthplace of Muḥammad (ﷺ)

Manzil – a stage, home; also a stage in the spiritual journey; a section of the Qur'ān where one pauses (pl. *manāzil*)

Maqāṣid –aim, purpose, objective (sing. *maqsad*)

Ma'rifah – lit. knowledge; gnosis esoteric knowledge; Persian: Ma'rifat

Mawlid – lit. birthday; mawlid un-Nabi is the day for commemorating the birth of Muḥammad (ﷺ)

Mehndi – elaborate designs made with henna paste applied on hands, hair, face, fingernails, and feet usually by brides but also on festive days

Mīqāt – lit. fixed time or place; at considerable distances away from Makkah are entry boundaries called *Mīqāt* (pl. *mawāqīt*) wherefrom pilgrims adorn the *Iḥrām*, for example Yalamlam to the southeast and Juhfah to the northwest

Mīzān – balance; equilibrium in the cosmos and universe; eschatological justice, measuring instrument in the Hereafter (pl. mawāzīn)

Mu'adhdhin – the one who calls the *Adhān* summoning Muslims to daily prayer

Mudarris – one who teaches; a lecturer, especially a teacher of law or one of their ancillary subjects

Muftī – a Muslim jurist qualified to issue a published legal ruling (fatwā) or decision on doctrine or fiqh

Muḥaddith – specialist knowing ḥadīths, their chain of transmissions, names of narrators, and the various wordings; f. muḥadditha

Muḥammad ﷺ – the 'Praised one'; also Aḥmad the 'most laudable'; both derived from the verb *ḥamada* to praise, glorify

Mujtahid – a scholar who is well versed to engage in *ijtihād* (an independent intellectual effort) to clarify a question or point of law

Muqarnas – honeycomb ornamented vaulting in Muslim architecture; features in domes, niches, archways; symbolises complexity of creation

Murīd – lit. seeker; in Sufism one intending spiritual purity or gnosis; *dervish, faqīr; sālik*

Muṣḥaf – the name given to the complete physical object of the Qur'ān

Muslimah – female Muslim (pl. Muslimāt)

Naqshbandiyyah – A Sufi *ṭarīqah* linked to Shaykh Bahā al-Dīn al-Bukhārī Naqshband (1318–1389)

Naṣīḥa – counsel, advice, positive recommendation

Niqāb – face veil

Niṣāb – the basic allowance before Zakāh becomes liable

Nudba – lit. weeping; duā' nudba, a supplication of help and lamentation held by Shī'a on Friday and 'Id days

Nūr – lit. light

Pir – a spiritual guide, master, mentor; *murshid; shaykh*; Sidi

Polyandry – marriage of a woman to more than one man, prohibited in Islam

Polygyny – marriage of a man to more than one wife, permissible in Islam

Provisions for Seekers – a short compilation of aḥadīth taught in many maktabs and madrasahs. It facilitates Arabic grammatical rearing of Arabic learners and reflects the eloquent and comprehensive nature of the Prophet's (ﷺ) speech

Qābil – a son of Ādam, the killer of Hābil; Cain

Qādiriyyah – A Sufi ṭarīqah linked to Shaykh 'Abd al-Qādir al-Gilānī (1077–1166CE)

Qalam – pen, pencil (68:1)

Qiblah –the direction facing the Ka'bah in Makkah; initially Jerusalem was the Qiblah

Qirtās – parchment (6:7)

Qurrā'– specialist reciters of the Qur'ān (sing. Qāri)

Rak'ah – unit of Muslim prayer with repeated recitals, words, postures and movements (pl. rak'āt)

Rawdah – lit. garden; a specific area of the Prophet's mosque between the minbar and burial chamber of Muḥammad (ﷺ) regarded as a garden of Paradise

Ribāt – frontier fortress or a Sufi retreat, hospice

Risālah – Prophethood; message; the mission of a messenger; a treatise

Rūḥ – spirit, soul (pl. arwāh)

Rukū' – lit. bending; a sub-division of a section or the Qur'ān

Ṣadaqat al-fiṭr – lit. cleansing after fasting; commonly *fitrah or fitrana*, or *Zakāt al-fiṭr*; the cost of a meal or grains given by each person in a household to the needy at the end of Ramaḍān

Ṣaḥābī – a companion of Prophet Muḥammad (ﷺ) (pl. Ṣaḥābah; f. Ṣaḥābiyyah)

Sakīnah – lit. calm, peace; root is *sakana* 'to dwell', 'to be still'; peace of God on hearts (48:4)

Ṣalāt – usually daily obligatory and other prayers; also salutations upon Muḥammad (ﷺ) (pl. *ṣalawāt*). Constrast this with prayer as in Duā' above

Ṣalāt al-Istikhārah – a two-unit optional prayer offered at the time of making decisions followed by a personal supplication seeking goodness in the matter

Sālik – lit. traveller; a member of Sufi ṭarīqah; in general everyone is a traveller in this world; also a seeker of knowledge (pl. sālikūn)

Shafā'ah – intercession of which there will be many, the most significant of which will be of Muḥammad (ﷺ)

Shahādah – from the verb *sha-hi-da* to witness; confession or profession on faith: I bear witness that there is no god but Allah and I bear witness that Muḥammad is His servant and messenger

Sharī'ah – lit. the path; derived by Muslims from the Qur'ān, Ḥadīth, consensus and analogy

Shaykh – lit. 'old man'; spiritual mentor, teacher, leader of tribe, any figure with religious authority (pl. shuyūkh, f. shaykha)

Shī'a – lit. party, faction; one from the party of 'Alī; also Shī'ite and Shī'i

Silsilah – lit. chain; interlink, the connection between mentors and tutees in various disciplines mainly in Sufism and ḥadīth

Sīrah – biography; literary genre, narrative histories of Muḥammad's (ﷺ) life

Suhrawardiyyah – A Sufi ṭarīqah linked to Shaykh Shihāb al-Dīn al-Suhrawardī (1154–1191CE)

Sulūk – lit. journeying; spiritual journey of the outer path (sharī'ah) and the inner path (*ṭarīqah/haqiqah*) of Islam

Sunnah – the trodden path; sayings and example of Prophet Muḥammad (ﷺ) which was passed down from the first generation onward to set the norms for the community; source of law

Sūrah – a chapter of the Qur'ān (pl. Suwar)

Tabi'ūn – followers; the generation following the Companions of the Prophet (sing. *tābi'*)

Tablīgh – lit. to convey; mission to convey Islam; compatible with da'wah i.e. inviting to faith. The Tablīghī Jamā'at derives its name from this

Ta'dib – moral training, education and disciplining; from *adab* the root meaning is 'good manners'; Islamic etiquette, manners, respect

Tadrīs – from the verb darrasa 'to teach' (and see above mudarris)

Tahajjud – voluntary prayer (Ṣalāh) offered after 'Ishā prayers; observing vigil at night

Tajwīd – lit. beautify; the system for the correct pronunciation and rendition of the Qur'ān

Takbīr – from the verb *kabbara* 'to magnify'; gives the verbal noun *takbīr* meaning to announce the greatness; the phrase Allahu Akbar (God is Greater) is called *Takbīr* and features in Adhān, Ṣalāh and pious proclamations; *Akbar* is superlative thus Allah is Greatest or nothing is Greater

Takbīr al-Tashrīq – to declare greatness of God in a raised voice by saying: Allah is the Greatest. Allah is the Greatest. There is no deity worthy of worship but Him. Allah is the Greatest. Allah is the Greatest. And for Allah is all praises; a verbal act performed during specific days in the month of Dhul-Ḥijjah

Talāq – the pronouncement of divorce or repudiation by husband

Talāq al-bid'ah – issuance of three pronouncements of divorce in one sentence or in one pure period (*ṭuhr*)

Talāq al-sunna – or *Talāq al- ḥasan* is the issuance of a divorce after consummation using three pronouncements given in three pure states in which intercourse has not taken place

Ta'līm – imparting and receiving knowledge, teaching (see 'ilm above)

Ta'līm (Faḍāil e A'mal) – a manual on the merits of actions used mainly by Tablīghī Jamā'at

Tarbiyyah – lit. to grow, increase, development, nurture; upbringing of children

Tartīl – recite as per rules of *tajwīd*; reciting in a measured way (73:4)

Taslīm – declaring the greeting Al-salāmu 'alaykum (peace be upon you) or at end of Ṣalāh

Ṭawāf – walking round the Ka'bah seven times

Ta'wil – returning to first primary meaning; spiritual hermeneutics, allegorical interpretation

Turba – mausoleum, tomb, funerary complex

Turbah – soil; a clay tablet upon which forehead is prostrated in prayer symbolising the earth, necessary among most Shī'a, sacred soil of Karbalā' preferred otherwise from anywhere; mohr

'Uḍḥiyyah – animal sacrifice required annually of all who meet its conditions (Qurbāni); distinct from Hadī

'Ulamā' – religious scholars, learned person; Imāms, teachers, judge; also Mawlānā (sing. 'Ālim)

'Urf – lit. something recognisable; local custom, tradition, or laws which may exist alongside Islamic law

Urs – marriage, union of a saint with God, also commemorating the death date of a Sufi/Pir

Uṣūl al-fiqh – lit. roots of jurisprudence; foundations of Muslim law

Uṣūlliyyūn – experts in the sources and foundation of Sharī'ah; major school of Shī'i theology

Wahhābī – a follower of the movement initiated by Muḥammad ibn 'Abd al-Wahhāb

Wakīl – an agent, representative of bride; attorney

Walī – lit. friend; guardian; Friend of God, saint; ruler (pl. `Awliyā')

Wird – devotions; set of practice in a particular Sufi order including supplication, recitation of Qur'ān, acts of worship, *dhikr* performed on a regular basis

Yā'jūj and Mā'jūj – a people who will appear towards the end of time and create havoc; Gog and Magog

Yaqīn – certitude

Yathrib – the original name of Madīnah

Zanjīr – the act of striking the chest or back with chains or knives in Shī'a remembering the suffering of Al-Ḥusaīn, self-flagellation

Zāwiya – a term for madrasah in the Maghrib; mosque; Sufi lodge

Zinā – illegal sexual intercourse, both adultery and fornication; a grave sin

REFERENCES

Al-'Abidīn, I.Z. (1988) *The Psalms of Islam* [Al-Ṣaḥīfat Al-Kāmilat Al-Sajjādiyya] (W.C. Chittick, Trans.) London: The Muhammadi Trust.

Abū Dāwūd, S.A. (1996) *Sunan Abū Dāwūd* (A. Ḥasan, Trans.). Lahore: Sh. Muḥammad Ashraf.

Abu Ghuddah, A. (2017) *Prophet Muhammad the Teacher*. Claritas Books: Swansea.

Abd Al-Ati, H. (1995) *The Family Structure in Islam*. Indianapolis: American Trust Publications.

Abdulla, R.S. and Keshavjee, M.M. (2018) *Understanding Sharia: Islamic Law in a Globalised World*. London: I.B. Tauris.

Adh-Dhahabī, S. (2012) *The Major Sins* (A. Bewley, Trans.). London: Dar Al Taqwa.

Aḥmad, A. (2012) *Musnad Imām Aḥmad ibn Hanbal*, (Nasiruddin Al-Khattab, Trans.). Riyadh: Darussalam.

Ahmed, F. and Lawson, I. (2016) 'Teaching Islam: Are there pedagogical limits to critical inquiry?', in N.A. Memon and M. Zaman (eds), *Philosophies of Islamic Education*. London: Routledge, pp. 236–250.

Alam, A. (2019) *For the Sake of Allah: The Origin, Development and Discourse of the Gulen Movement*. New Jersey: Blue Dome Press.

Alavi, S.M.Z. (1988) *Muslim Educational Thought in the Middle Ages*. New Delhi: Atlantic Publisher & Distributors.

Aleem, S. (2011) *Prophet Muhammad(s) and His Family: A Sociological Perspective*, revised edn. Bloomington: AuthorHouse.

Alkhateeb, F. (2017) *Lost Islamic History*. London: Hurst & Co. Publishers, Ltd.

Altalib, H., AbuSulayman, A. and Altalib, O. (2013) *Parent-Child Relations: A Guide to Raising Children*. London: The International Institute of Islamic Thought.

Amir-Moezzi, M.A and Jambet, C. (2018) *What is Shi'i Islam?* London: Routledge.

Ansari, H. (2018) *'The Infidel Within': Muslims in Britain Since 1800*, 2nd edn. London: C. Hurst Publishers.

Ansari, M.F. (1994) *The Quranic Foundation and Structure of Muslim Society*. Karachi: Darul Ishaat.

Armstrong, A. (2007) *Muhammad: A Prophet of Our Time*. New York: HarperCollins.

Ashour, M. (1989) *The Jinn in the Qur'an and the Sunnah*. London: Dar Al-Taqwa.

Aslan, E. (2012) 'Foreword', in E. Aslan and Z. Windisch (eds), *The Training of Imams and Teachers for Islamic Education in Europe*. Frankfurt an Main: Peter Lang.

Al-Azami, M. (1996) *On Schacht's Origins of Muhammadan Jurisprudence*. Cambridge: Cambridge Islamic Texts Society.

Azami, M.M. (2012) *Studies in Hadith Methodology and Literature*. Illinois: American Trust Publications.

Al-Azem, T. (2016) 'The transmission of Adab: Educational ideals and their institutional manifestations', in N.A. Memon and M. Zaman (eds), *Philosophies of Islamic Education*. London: Routledge, pp. 112–126.

Azimabadi, B. (1993) *300 Authenticated Miracles of Muḥammad*. Delhi: Adam Publishers.

Baldock, J. (2004) *The Essence of Sufism*. Toronto: Arcturus Publishing.

Bano, M. (2017) *Female Islamic Education Movements: The Re-democratisation of Islamic Knowledge*. Cambridge: Cambridge University Press.

Bayram, A. (2013) *Shi'ism in the Middle East*. Raleigh: Lulu Publishers.

Boyle, H.N. (2004) *Quranic Schools: Agents of Preservation and Change*. London: RoutledgeFarmer.

Breuilly, E., O'Brian, J. and Palmer, M. (2007) *Religions of the World*, 3rd edn. Gisborne: Alto Books.

Brice, K. (2010) *A Minority within a Minority: A report on Converts to Islam in the United Kingdom*. London: Faith Matters.

Brown, D.W. (2017) *A New Introduction to Islam*, 2nd edn. Oxford: Blackwell Publishers.

Brown, J.A.C. (2018) *Hadith: Muhammad's Legacy in the Medieval and Modern World*, revised edn. London: Oneworld Publications.

Buck, C. (2009) 'Discovering', in A. Rippin (ed.), *The Blackwell Companion to the Qur'an*. Oxford: Wiley-Blackwell, pp. 18–35.

Al-Bukhārī, M.I. (1986) *Ṣaḥīḥ Al-Bukhārī* (M.M. Khan, Trans.). Lahore: Kazi Publications.

Burge, S. (2012) *Angels in Islam: Jalal al-Din al-Suyūti's al-Habā'ik fi akhbār al-malā'ik* [Culture and Civilisation in the Middle East]. London: Routledge.

Buturovic, A. (2010) 'Death', in J. Elias (ed.), *Key Themes for the Study of Islam*. Oxford: Oneworld, pp. 123–140.

Campanini, M. (2016) *The Qur'an: The Basics*, 2nd edn. London: Routledge.

Chittick, W.C. (2012) *In Search of the Lost Heart*. Albany: State University of New York Press.

Cole, J. (2018) *Muhammad: Prophet of Peace Amid the Clash of Empires*. New York: Nation Books.

Coles, M.I. (2008) *Every Muslim Matters: Practical Guidance for Schools and Children's Services*. Stoke on Trent: Trentham Books.

Crotty, R. and Lovat, T. (2016) *Islam: Its Beginning and History, its Theology and its Importance Today*. Adelaide: ATF Theology.

Daftary, F. (2013) *A History of Shi'i Islam*. London: I.B. Tauris.

Daryabadī, A.M. (1991) *Tafir-ul-Qur'an* [Translation and Commentary on the Holy Qur'an]. Karachi: Darul Ishaat.

Delong-Bas, N.J. (2018) *Islam: A Living Faith*. Minnesota: Anselm Academic.

Von Denffer, A. (2011) *'Ulūm al Qur'ān: An Introduction to the Sciences of the Qur'ān*, 2nd revised edn. Markfield: The Islamic Foundation.

Din, S. (2017) *Muslim Mothers and their Children's Schooling*. London: UCL Institute of Education Press.

Ebrahim, H. (2017) *Early Childhood Education for Muslim Children: Rationales and Practices from South Africa*. London: Routledge.

Esposito, J.L. (2016) *Islam: The Straight Path*, 5th edn. New York: Oxford University Press.

Esposito, J.L. and DeLong-Bas, N.J. (2018) *Shariah: What Everyone Needs to Know®*. New York: Oxford University Press.

Fergusson, J. (2017) *Al-Britannia: A Journey through Muslim Britain*. London: Transworld Publishers.

Frampton, M., Goodhart, D. and Mahmood, K. (2016) *Unsettled Belonging: A Survey of Britain's Muslim Communities*. London: Policy Exchange.

Furber, M. (2016) *Ibn Rajab's Refutation of Those Who Do Not Follow the Four Schools*. Kuala Lumpur: Islamosaic Publishing.

Gabriel, T. (2018) 'Family and society', in C. Partridge (ed.), *A Brief Introduction to the World Religion*, revised by T. Dowley. Fortress Press Minneapolis, pp. 81–84.

Gade, A.M. (2009) 'Recitation', in A. Rippin (ed.), *The Blackwell Companion to the Qur'an*. Oxford: Wiley-Blackwell, pp. 481–493.

Gaibie, S. (2017) *Narratives of the Great Seven Readers*. Cape Town: al-Tanzil Institute of Quranic Sciences.

Geaves, R. (2017) *Islam in Victorian Britain: The Life and Times of Abdullah Quilliam*, reprint edn. Markfield: Kube Publishing Ltd.

Gent, B. (2018) *Muslim Supplementary Classes and Their Place Within the Wider Learning Community*. Manchester: Beacon Books.

Ghani, H. and Nagdee, I. (2019) 'Islamophobia in UK universities', in I. Zempi and I. Awan (eds), *The Routledge International Handbook of Islamophobia*. London: Routledge, pp. 188–197.

Al-Ghazālī, A.H. (1989) *The Remembrance of Death and the Afterlife*. Cambridge: Islamic Text Society.

Al-Ghazālī, A.H. (2009) *'Ihyā Ulum-id-Din* [Revival of Religious Learnings] (F. Karim, Trans.) Karachi: Darul Ishaat.

Gilliat-Ray, S. (2010) *Muslims in Britain: An Introduction*. Cambridge: Cambridge University Press.

Glassé, C. (2013) *The New Encyclopedia of Islam*, 4th edn. Lanham: Rowman & Littlefield Publishers.

Guillaume, A. (2007) *The Life of Muhammad: A Translation of Isḥāq's Sīrat rasūl Allāh*. Oxford: Oxford University Press

Gülen, F. (2006) *The Messenger of God: An Analysis of the Prophet's Life*. New Jersey: The Light.

Günther, S. (2016) 'Your educational achievements shall not stop your efforts to seek beyond: Principles of teaching and learning in classical Arabic writings', in N.A. Memon and M. Zaman (eds), *Philosophies of Islamic Education*. London: Routledge, pp. 72–93.

Gwynne, P. (2018) *World Religion in Practice: A Comparative Introduction*, 2nd edn. Chichester: John Wiley & Sons.

Haider, N. (2011) *The Origins of the Shī'a: Identity, Ritual and Sacred Space in Eighth-Century Kufah*. Cambridge: Cambridge University Press.

Haleem, M.A.S. Abdel (2015) *The Qur'an*. Oxford: Oxford University Press.

Hamid, S. (2014) 'Hizb ut-Tahrir in the United Kingdom', in F. Peter and R. Ortega (eds), *Islamic Movements of Europe: Public Religion and Islamophobia in the Modern World*. London: I.B. Tauris.

Hamid, S. (2016) *Sufis, Salafists and Islamists: The Contested Ground of British Islamic Activism*. London: I.B. Tauris.
Hamidullah, M. (1939) 'Education system at the Time of the Prophet', *Islamic Culture, 12*: 48–49.
Hardaker, G. and Sabki, A.A. (2019) *Pedagogy in Islamic Education*. Bingley: Emerald Publishing.
Hartung, J. (2014) 'The Jama'at-I Islami', in F. Peter and R. Ortega (eds), *Islamic Movements of Europe: Public Religion and Islamophobia in the Modern World*. London: I.B. Tauris.
Hasan, A. (2007) *The Principles of Islamic Jurisprudence*. Delhi: Adam Publishers.
Al-Hassan, A.Y. (2001) 'Factors behind the rise of Islamic science', in A.Y. Al-Hassan, M. Maqbul and A.Z. Iskandar (eds), *The Different Aspects of Islamic Culture, Volume Four: Science and Technology in Islam*. Beirut: UNESCO Publishing, pp. 55–86.
Hathout, H. (2008) *Reading the Muslim Mind*. USA: American Trust Publications.
Hawkins, B.K. (2004) *Introduction to Asian Religions*. London: PearsonLongman.
Hawramani, I. (2018) *Baby Names for Muslims*. Independently published.
Hewer, C. (2006) *Understanding Islam*. London: SCM Press.
Hibbard, S.W. (2013) 'Islam and the State', in A.B. McCloud, S.W. Hibbard and L. Saud (eds), *An Introduction to Islam in the 21st Century*. Oxford: Blackwell Publishers, pp. 111–133.
Hujwīrī, 'A.U. (2014) *The Kashf al-Mahjub* [The Revelation of the Veiled] (R.A. Nicholson, Trans.). Warminster: Gibb Memorial Trust.
Hussain, A.M. (2013) *A Social History of Education in the Muslim World*. London: Ta-Ha Publishers.
Hussain, A.M. (2016) *The Muslim Creed: A Contemporary Theological Study*. Cambridge: The Islamic Texts Society.
Ibn Jamā'ah, B. (1991) *Al-Tazkirat Al-Sāmi' wal-Mutakallim fi Ādāb al-'Ālim wal Muta'allim* [The Memoir of the Listener and the Speaker in the Training of the Teacher and Student] (N.M. Ghifari, Trans.). New Delhi: Adam Publishers.
Ibn Kathīr, I. (2000) *Tafsīr Ibn Kathīr* [Commentary of Ibn Kathīr]. Riyadh: Dar-ul-Salam.
Ibn Kathīr, I. (2011) *Stories of the Prophet*, 2nd edn (H. Maqbool, Trans.). Riyadh: International Islamic Publishing House.
Ibn Khaldun, A. (1989) *The Muqaddimah: An Introduction to History* (N.J. Dawood, ed.). Chichester: Princeton University Press.
Ibn Mājah, M.Y., Al-Qazwīnī (1993) *Sunan Ibn Mājah* (M.T. Ansari, Trans.). Lahore: Kazi Publications.
Imani, K.F. (1998) *A Bundle of Flowers from the Garden of Traditions of the Prophet & Ahlul-Bayt (a.s.)*. Isfahan: Scientific and Religious Research Center.
Al-Jawziyyah, I.Q. (2008) *Tuḥfat al-Mawdūd bi Aḥkām al-Mawlūd* [A Gift to the Loved One Regarding the Rulings of the Child]. Riyadh: Dar Ibn al-Qayyum.
Jazīrī, A. (2009) *Al-Fiqh 'ala madhāhib al-arba'a* [Islamic Jurisprudence According to the Four Sunnī Schools] (N. Roberts, Trans.). Louisville: Fons Vitae.
Kaltner, J. and Mirza, Y. (2018) *The Bible and the Qur'an: Biblical Figures in the Islamic Tradition*. London: Bloomsbury Publishing.
Kermani, N. (2018) *God is Beautiful: The Aesthetic Experience of the Quran* (T. Crawford, Trans.). Cambridge: Polity Press.

Kerr, D. (2018a) 'The unity and variety of Islam', in C. Partridge (ed.), *A Brief Introduction to Islam* (revised edn by T. Dowley). Minneapolis: Fortress Press, pp. 61–64.
Kerr, D. (2018b) 'Worship and festivals', in C. Partridge (ed.), *A Brief Introduction to Islam* (revised edn by T. Dowley). Minneapolis: Fortress Press, pp. 75–80.
Khan, M.M. (1994) *Summarised Ṣaḥiḥ Al-Bukhārī*. Riyadh: Maktaba Dar-ul-Salam.
Khan, M.M. (2010) *The Muslim 100: The Lives, Thoughts and Achievements of the Most Influential Muslims in History*. Markfield: Kube Publishers.
Khan, M.M. (2017) *Great Muslims of the West: Makers of Western Islam*. Markfield: Kube Publication.
Khan, S.A. (2013) 'Islam in South Asia', in A.B. McCloud, S.W. Hibbard and L. Saud (eds), *An Introduction to Islam in the 21st Century*. Oxford: Blackwell Publishers, pp. 203–216.
Kheri, A.A. (2008) *A Comprehensive Guide Book of Islam*. Delhi: Adam Publishers.
Krayem, G. (2016) 'Balancing freedom of speech and the rights of Muslim minority groups in the Australian context', in E. Kolig (ed.), *Freedom of Speech and Islam*. London: Routledge, pp. 45–62.
Lamrabet, A. (2018) *Women and Men in the Qur'an* (M. Saleem-Murdock, Trans.). Basingstoke: PalgraveMacmillan.
Lange, C. (2016) *Paradise and Hell in Islamic Traditions*. New York: Cambridge University Press.
La'Porte, V. (2001) 'Islam', in I.S. Markham and T. Ruparell (eds), *Encountering Religions*. Oxford: Blackwell Publishers, pp. 337–371.
Largen, K.J. (2013) *Finding God Among Our Neighbours: An Interfaith Systematic Theology*. Minneapolis: Fortress Press.
Leaman, O. (2016) *The Qur'ān: A Philosophical Guide*. London: Bloomsbury.
Lings, M. (2006) *Muhammad: His Life Based on the Earliest Sources*, 5th revised edn. Rochester: Inner Traditions.
Lowry, J. (2010) 'Institution', in J.J. Elias (ed.), *Key Themes for the Study of Islam*. Oxford: Oneworld, pp. 200–219.
Lumbard, J. (2015) 'The Quranic view of sacred history and other religions', in S.H. Nasr (ed.), *The Study Quran: A New Translation and Commentary*. New York: HarperOne, pp. 1765–1784.
Makki, A. (2010) *Mawqif A'immat al-Harakat al-Salafiyyah min al-Taṣawwuf wa al-Sufiyyah* [Sufism and the Imams of the Salafi Movement]. Cairo: Dar al-Salaam.
Mālik, M.A. (2000) *Muwatta' Imām Mālik* (F. Matraji, Trans.). Karachi: Darul Ishā'at.
Mandaville, P. (2007) 'Islamic knowledge in Britain: Approaches to religious knowledge in a pluralistic society', in R.W. Hefner and M.Q. Zaman (eds), *Schooling Islam: The Culture and Modern Politics of Muslim Education*. Oxford: Princeton University Press, pp. 224–241.
Mansoorpuri, M.S.S (2002) *Muhammad: Mercy for the Worlds*. Karachi: Darul-Ishaat.
Maqsood, R.W. (2005) *Thinking about Marriage*. London: The Muslim Women's Institute.
Maqsood, R.W. (2010) *Islam: An Introduction*. Reading: Hodder Education.
Matar, N. (1998) *Islam in Britain 1558–1685*. Cambridge: Cambridge University Press.
Mattson, I. (2013) *The Story of the Qur'an: Its History and Place in Muslim Life*. Chichester: Wiley-Blackwell.

Mawdūdī, S.A.A. (2016) *Let us be Muslims* (revised edn; K. Murad, ed.). Leicester: The Islamic Foundation.
McLoughlin, S. (2014) 'The Islamic Foundation in the United Kingdom', in F. Peter and R. Ortega (eds), *Islamic Movements of Europe: Public Religion and Islamophobia in the Modern World*. London: I.B. Tauris.
Momen, M. (1985) *An Introduction to Shi'i Islam*. London: Yale University Press.
Momen, M. (2016) *Shi'i Islam: A Beginner's Guide*. London: Oneworld.
Morgan, M.H. (2007) *Lost History: The Enduring Legacy of Muslim Scientists, Thinkers, and Artists*. Washington: National Geographic.
El-Moslimany, A. (2018) *Teaching Children: A Moral, Spiritual, and Holistic Approach to Educational Development*. Surrey: The International Institute of Islamic Thought.
Mubarakpuri, S. (2002) *History of Makkah* (N. al-Khattab, Trans.). Riyadh: Darusalaam.
Al-Muḥaqqiq, M. (2001) 'The classification of the sciences', in A.Y. Al-Hassan, M. Maqbul and A.Z. Iskandar (eds), *The Different Aspects of Islamic Culture; Volume Four: Science and Technology in Islam*. Beirut: UNESCO Publishing, pp. 111–131.
Muir, W. (1923) *The Life of Mohammad*. Edinburgh: John Grant.
Muslim, H. Al-Qushayrī (1971) *Ṣaḥīḥ Muslim* (A.H. Ṣiddiqi, Trans.). Cairo: Dar Al-Manar; Lahore: Kazi Publications.
Nadwi, A.H.A. (2011) *The Four Pillars of Islam*. Malaysia: Islamic Book Trust.
Nadwi, A.H.A. (2015) *Saviours of Islamic Spirit* (A.Y. Mangera, Trans.). London: White Thread Press.
Nadwī, A.H.A (2017) *A Guidebook For Muslims* (3rd edn; M. Ahmad, Trans.). Lucknow: Academy of Islamic Research and Publications.
Al-Nasā'ī, A.S. (1994) *Sunan al-Nasā'ī* (M.I. Siddiqi, Trans.). Lahore: Kazi Publications.
Nasr, S.H. (1987) *Science and Civilization in Islam*, 2nd edn. Cambridge: The Islamic Text Society.
Nasr, S.H. (1993) *A Young Muslim's Guide to the Modern World*. Cambridge: Islamic Texts Society.
Nasr, S.H. (2012) *Islam in the Modern World*. New York: HarperCollins.
Nickel, G. and Rippin, A. (2008) 'The Qur'ān', in A. Rippin (ed.), *The Islamic World*. London: Routledge, pp. 145–156.
Nielsen, J. and Otterbeck, J. (2016) *Muslims in Western Europe*, 4th edn. Edinburgh: Edinburgh University Press.
Noibi, D. and Haleem, H. (1999) 'Islam', in C. Richards (ed.), *The Illustrated Encyclopaedia of World Religions*. Shaftsbury: Element, pp. 150–177.
Nomānī, M.M. (1971) *The Qur'ān and You*. Karachi: Haji Arfeen Academy.
Nomānī, M.M (1978) *The Quran and You*, 2nd edn. Lucknow: Academy of Islamic Research and Publications.
Nomānī, M.M. (1982) *Islamic Faith and Practice*. Karachi: Haji Arfeen Academy.
Nu'mānī, S. (2004) *Imam Abu Hanifah*. Multan: Idara Taleefat-e-Ashrafiyya.
Nyazee, I. (2006) *The Guidance* [Al-Hidāyah by B. Al-Marghinani]. Bristol: Amal Press.
Pānipatī, T. (1991) *Tafsīr Mazharī*. Karachi: Darul Ishaat.
Peter, F. (2014) 'Introduction', in F. Peter and R. Ortega (eds), *Movements of Europe: Public Religion and Islamophobia in the Modern World*. London: I.B. Tauris.
Peter, F. and Ortega, R. (eds), *Movements of Europe: Public Religion and Islamophobia in the Modern World*. London: I.B. Tauris.

Peuker, M. and Akbarzadeh, S. (2014) *Muslim Active Citizenship in the West*. London: Routledge.
Al-Qurṭubī, T. (2003) *Tasfīr Al-Qurṭubī Classical Commentary of the Holy Qur'an* (A. Bewley, Trans.). London: Dar Al-Taqwa.
Ramadan, T. (2017) *Introduction to Islam*. Oxford: Oxford University Press.
Raudvere, C. (2015) *Islam: An Introduction*. London: I.B. Tauris.
Rāzī, F. (2000) *Al-Tafsīr Al-Kabīr wa Mafātīh al-Ghayb* [The Great Exegesis and Keys to the Unseen]. Beirut: Dārul Fikr.
Revell, L. (2012) *Islam and Education: The Manipulation and Misrepresentation of a Religion*. London: Institute of Education Press.
Riddell, P. (2018) 'Sacred writings', in C. Partridge (ed.), *A Brief Introduction to Islam* (revised by T. Dowley). Minneapolis: Fortress Press, pp. 69–74.
Ridgeon, L. (2009) 'Islam', in L. Ridgeon (ed.,) *Major World Religions: From their Origins to the Present*. London: RoutledgeCurzon. pp. 230–288.
Rippin, A. (2006) 'God', in A. Rippin (ed.), *The Blackwell Companion to the Qur'ān*. Oxford: Blackwell Publishing, pp. 223–233.
Rippin, A. and Bernheimer, T. (2019) *Muslims: Their Religious Beliefs and Practices*. Oxfordshire: Routledge.
Rodrigo, R.O. (2014) 'The Muslim Brotherhood: Creation, evolution and goals', in F. Peter and R. Ortega (eds), *Movements of Europe: Public Religion and Islamophobia in the Modern World*. London: I.B. Tauris.
Saeed, T. (2019) 'Islamophobia and the Muslim student: Disciplining the intellect', in I. Zempi and I. Awan (eds), *The Routledge International Handbook of Islamophobia*. London: Routledge, pp. 175–187.
Salahi, A. (2002) *Muhammad: Man and Prophet*. Markfield: The Islamic Foundation.
Saleh, W. (2017) 'Quranic commentaries', in S.H. Nasr (ed.), *The Study Quran: A New Translation and Commentary*. New York: HarperOne, pp. 1645–1658.
Sanyal, N. (2005) *Ahmad Riza Khan Barelwi: In the Path of the Prophet*. Oxford: Oneworld Publications.
Saritoprak, Z. (2018) *Islamic Spirituality: Theology and Practice for the Modern World*. London: Bloomsbury.
Saud, L. (2013a) 'Islamic beliefs: The development of Islamic ideas', in A.B. McCloud, S.W. Hibbard and L. Saud (eds), *An Introduction to Islam in the 21st Century*. Oxford: Blackwell Publishers, pp. 51–80.
Saud, L. (2013b) 'Religious structures: Tawhīd', in A.B. McCloud, S.W. Hibbard and L. Saud (eds), *An Introduction to Islam in the 21st Century*. Oxford: Blackwell Publishers, pp. 31–50.
Saud, L. (2013c) 'Islamic political theology', in A.B. McCloud, S.W. Hibbard and L. Saud (eds), *An Introduction to Islam in the 21st Century*. Oxford: Blackwell Publishers. pp. 81–108.
Sayeed, A. (2013) *Women and the Transmission of Religious Knowledge in Islam*. Cambridge: Cambridge University Press.
Schimmel, A. (1997) *Islamic Names*. Edinburgh: Edinburgh University Press.
Scott-Baumann, A. and Cheruvallil-Contractor, S. (2015) *Islamic Education in Britain: New Pluralist Paradigms*. London: Bloomsbury.

Scourfield, J., Gilliat-Ray, S., Khan, A. and Otri, A. (2013) *Muslim Childhood: Religious Nurture in a European Context*. Oxford: Oxford University Press.
Seddon, M. (2014) *The Last of the Lascars: Yemeni Muslims in Britain 1836–2012*. Markfield: Kube Publishing.
Shafī', M. (1995) *Ma'āriful Qur'ān*. Karachi: Maktab-e-Darul 'Uloom.
Shurunbulali, H. (2007) *Nūr al-Idāh* [The Light of Clarification] (W. Charkawi, Trans.). USA: Ligare Book Printers.
Ṣiddiqi, A.Ḥ. and Ṣiddiqi, M.S. (1987) *The Islamic Concept of Religion and its Revival*, 2nd edn. Lahore: Kazi Publication.
Siddiqui, A.R. (2018) *Shariah: A Divine Code Of Life*. Markfield: The Islamic Foundation.
Siddiqi, M.I. (1994) *Great Scholar of Islam in Sunan Al-Nasā'ī*. Lahore: Kazi Publications.
Siddiqi, M.I. (2010) *The Family Laws of Islam*, revised edn. New Delhi: Adam Publishers.
Sikand, Y. (2005) *Bastions of the Believers*. New Delhi: Penguin Books.
Silverstein, A.J. (2010) *Islamic History: A Very Short Introduction*. Oxford: Oxford University Press.
Smart, N. (1992) *The World's Religion*. Cambridge: Cambridge University Press.
Smith, J.I. and Haddad, Y.Y. (2002) *The Islamic Understanding of Death and Resurrection*. Oxford: Oxford University Press.
Sonn, T. (2009) 'Introducing', in A. Rippin (ed.), *The Blackwell Companion to the Qur'an*. Oxford: Wiley-Blackwell, pp. 3–17.
Sonn, T. (2016) *Islam: History, Religion and Politics*, 3rd edn. Chichester: Wiley Blackwell.
Steigerwald, D. (2009)' Twelver Shī' Ta'wīl', in A. Rippin (ed.), *The Blackwell Companion to the Qur'an*. Oxford: Wiley-Blackwell, pp. 371–385.
Stewart, D. (2010) 'Prophecy', in J. Elias (ed.), *Key Themes for the Study of Islam*. Oxford: Oneworld, pp. 281–303.
Suyūtī, J. (2007) *Tafsīr al-Jalālayn* [Commentary of Jalālayn] (F. Hamza, Trans.). Amman: Royal Aal al-Bayt Institute for Islamic Thought.
Sway, M.A. (2017) *A Treasury of Al-Ghazālī: A Companion for the Untethered Soul*. Markfield: Kube Publishing.
Al-Ṭabarī, M.J. (1989) *Jāmi' al-bayān 'an ta'wīl āy al-Qur'ān* [The commentary on the Qur'ān] (J. Cooper, Intro. and notes). Oxford: Oxford University Press.
Tabrīzī, M. (2012) *Mishkāt al-Masābīh* [A Niche for Lamps]. Karachi: Makataba al-Bushra.
Tan, C. (ed.) (2014) *Reforms in Islamic Education: International Perspectives*. London: Bloomsbury.
Al-Tirmidhī, M.'I. (2007) *Jāmi' At-Tirmidhī* (Abu Khaliyl, Trans.). Riyadh: Maktaba Dar-ul-Salam.
Trevathan, A. (2016) 'Spirituality in Muslim education', in N.A. Memon and M. Zaman (eds), *Philosophies of Islamic Education*. London: Routledge, pp. 57–71.
'Umaruddin, M. (1996) *The Ethical Philosophy of Al-Ghazzali*. Delhi: Adam Publishers.
Usmani, M.T. (2000) *An Approach to the Qur'ānic Sciences*. Karachi: Darul Ishaat.
Usmani, M.T. (1990) *The Authority of the Sunnah*. Karachi: Idaratul Quran.
Usmani, M.T. (2001) *The Legal Status of Following a Madhab*, 2nd edn. Karachi: Zamzam Publishers.
Versi, M. (2015) *Meeting between David Anderson QC and the MCB*. London: Muslim Council of Britain. Available at: www.mcb.org.uk/wp-content/uploads/2015/10/20150803-Case-studies-about-Prevent.pdf (accessed 17 May 2019).

Waghid, Y. (2011) *Conceptions of Islamic Education: Pedagogical Framings*. New York: Peter Lang.
Walī Allah, S. (2017) *Ḥujjat Allāh Al-Bālihgha* [The Conclusive Argument from God] (M.K. Hermansen, Trans.). Beirut: Dar Ibn Katheer.
Wallace-Murphy, T. (2006) *What Islam Did for Us*. London: Watkins Publishing.
Wan Daud, W.M. (1989) *The Concept of Knowledge in Islam and its Implication for Education in a Developing World*. London: Mansell Publication.
Wills, G. (2017) *What the Qur'an Meant and why it Matters*. New York: Viking.
Al-Yahsubī, 'I. (2011) *Muhammad Messenger of Allah* [Ash-Shifa'] (A.A. Bewley, Trans.). Granada: Madinah Press.
Yusuf, H. (2017) 'Death, dying, and the afterlife in the Quran', in S.H. Nasr (ed.), *The Study Quran: A New Translation and Commentary*. New York. HarperOne, pp. 1819–1855.
Al-Zarnūjī, B. (2001) *Ta'līm al-Muta'alim Tariq al-Ta'allum* [Instruction of the Student: The Method of Learning], revised 2nd edn (G.E. Von Grunebaum and T.M. Abel, Trans.). Chicago: The Starlatch Press.
Al Zeera, Z. (2001) *Wholeness and Holiness in Education: An Islamic Perspective*. Surrey: The International Institute of Islamic Thought.
Zebiri, K. (2008) *British Muslim Converts: Choosing Alternative Lives*. Oxford: Oneworld.

INDEX

Page numbers in *italics* refer to figures; page numbers in **bold** refer to tables.